DISCARDED

Shelton State L...
Shelton State Coll...

P9-BZX-316

DATE DUE

OCT 1 4 2013	
	PRINTED IN U.S.A.

Praise for *The War for Wealth*

"*The War for Wealth* is a lucid and compelling reality check that alerts America to the need for creative leadership on issues that could prove as dangerous to global stability as terrorism in the not-too-distant future, including the unintended consequences of globalization."

—Dr. Henry A. Kissinger,
former United States
Secretary of State

"Globalization may be a watchword of our era, but it is also a cliché that cries out for redefinition and fresh analysis. Gabor Steingart provides precisely that in this timely, provocative, and challenging contribution to the debate over the world of today—and tomorrow."

—Strobe Talbott, president of the
Brookings Institution;
author of The Great Experiment

"Gabor Steingart shows here that he has a subtle and rare comprehension of how the old categories for approaching the global economy are entirely inadequate for the challenge ahead. Read this, and understand."

—Jonathan Alter,
Newsweek *columnist*

"Gabor Steingart, one of Europe's leading economics journalists, has written the essential book rethinking globalization. Steingart challenges the naive, flat-earth mentality of the U.S. economics establishment, and calls upon the United States to revise its ideology and diplomacy for the benefit of a balanced form of capitalism, Western democratic values, and America's own survival as a successful economy and society. If you read one book on globalization this year, make it Steingart's *The War for Wealth*."

—*Robert Kuttner, coeditor of* The American Prospect;
cofounder of the Economic Policy Institute;
author of The Squandering of America

"Gabor Steingart has done us a great service. He is not satisfied with the doomsday scenarios which are so popular these days among the opponents of globalization. He describes, he analyzes, and he suggests solutions. A must-read for those trying to make sense out of the new economic order. Steingart's vision of a new transatlantic United States of the West is creative and convincing."

—*John Kornblum,*
former United States
Ambassador to Germany

"New thoughts for a new Western policy, an excellent book for change."

—*Wolfgang Nowak, managing director*
of the Alfred-Herrhausen-Society

"In *The War for Wealth*, Steingart has written an accessible, important, and disturbing analysis of global economic trends that will have profound implications for the United States. He challenges conventional terms of debate between free traders and protectionists by asking how and whether a dynamic market economy and our welfare states can compete and thrive as hundreds of millions of low-wage workers in China, India, Russia, and beyond enter the global labor market."

—*Jeffrey Herf, professor,*
Department of History,
University of Maryland

The
WAR
for
WEALTH

DISCARDED
Shelton State Libraries
Shelton State Community College

Shelton State Libraries
Shelton State Community College

The WAR *for* WEALTH

THE TRUE STORY OF GLOBALIZATION, OR WHY THE FLAT WORLD IS BROKEN

GABOR STEINGART

Shelton State Libraries
Shelton State Community College

New York   Chicago   San Francisco   Lisbon   London
Madrid   Mexico City   Milan   New Delhi   San Juan
Seoul   Singapore   Sydney   Toronto

The **McGraw·Hill** Companies

Copyright © 2008 by Gabor Steingart. All rights reserved. Printed in the United States of America. Except as permitted under the United States Copyright Act of 1976, no part of this publication may be reproduced or distributed in any form or by any means, or stored in a data base or retrieval system, without the prior written permission of the publisher.

1 2 3 4 5 6 7 8 9 0   DOC/DOC   0 1 4 3 2 1 0 9 8

ISBN 978-0-07-154596-9
MHID   0-07-154596-4

McGraw-Hill books are available at special quantity discounts to use as premiums and sales promotions, or for use in corporate training programs. To contact a representative please visit the Contact Us pages at www.mhprofessional.com.

Previous edition, *Weltkrieg um Wohlstand*, published in Germany. Copyright © Piper Verlag GmbH, Muenchen 2006.

This book is printed on acid-free paper.

CONTENTS

Shelton State Libraries
Shelton State Community College

INTRODUCTION

Have you ever been to Kabul, the capital of Afghanistan? You can count yourself lucky if you haven't. There isn't a sadder city in the world.

Most of all, it's because of the children. Kabul is a city of ruins—and a city of children. The little ones are everywhere, running through the old part of town in their colorful clothing, their eyes as big as their expectations.

Some time after the ouster of the Taliban, I traveled with a group of politicians and military officials to Kabul, where we visited the city's only girls' school, which had finally opened—with Western assistance—after years of the Taliban's oppression of women.

There were no desks or benches. The girls sat on the floor surrounding their female teachers, reading out loud and giggling. Many of the children were not much older than my own two daughters. Their eyes sparkled. They listened to the teachers' every word. If the spark of freedom truly exists, it was there in the eyes of those children. Perhaps they were still too young to have even heard the word *freedom* yet, and certainly no one had told them about the great country of the United States of America and of its constitution that guarantees the pursuit of happiness. But even without knowing these things, these girls, or so I believed at the time, were finally experiencing both freedom and happiness. We were surrounded by unbridled optimism and the hope for a different, better, and truly human life. I was convinced that for the girls of Kabul, the West's involvement in Afghanistan, both militarily and humanitarian, had been worthwhile.

But I was naïve. We returned home to news reports that the girls' school had been destroyed during the night by unknown attackers. Fearing for the students' lives, the administration closed the school. I remembered what a local army general had told me, and what I had refused to believe at the time: that the Taliban had returned.

Today I see Kabul as a place of shattered hopes. My experiences there—and today's reality—have forced me to confront a question of fundamental importance: is it even possible to bring a medieval society into the modern age with money, determination, and military might? Can we build nations the way we build aircraft and houses?

Have you ever been to Shanghai? You can count yourself lucky if you haven't, because you can feel the desire to outrival the greatest Western cities. And if you have, you might have been shocked by the city that is taking shape in southern China—it looks like the next New York, the next Wall Street, and you immediately get the feeling that you are in the middle of the beating heart of a new global power.

The rooftop terrace at M on the Bund, one of Shanghai's finest restaurants, offers an excellent view of the financial district, including the futuristic Shanghai Stock Exchange building, which looks like a recently landed spaceship. The diners on the restaurant's terrace are rich and self-confident, and the prices on the menu (which don't seem to trouble any of the guests) can easily hold their own with anything New York or Washington, D.C., has to offer. Downtown Shanghai, with its traffic jams, its constant buzz of commerce, and its colorful entertainment districts, says more about today's China than the Chinese Communist Party could ever express. And the message it conveys is simple: We have arrived!

I wrote this book because I believe that we spend too much time scratching our heads about places like Kabul and Baghdad and paying too little attention to Shanghai. We get ourselves into heated debates over Islam and the problems of the Sunnis and the

Shiites, and yet the greatest danger terrorism poses could very well be that it distracts our attention. It prevents us from recognizing our true rivals. The United States and the remaining Western world waste far too much energy and attention on pursuing and trying to understand a group of Stone Age warriors that barely outnumbers a division of the U.S. Army.

Don't get me wrong. The risk of terrorism is very real, and we must protect ourselves. But our fears have been spun out of proportion. The Taliban consists of military dwarves and political pygmies. A country like Iran, with a gross domestic product the size of Connecticut's and a military budget only as big as Sweden's, doesn't deserve the attention of the entire American public and its government.

Nowadays, world history isn't being written in Afghanistan, Baghdad, or Tehran, but in Shanghai. The fateful word confronting our generation is not *terror*, but *globalization*. It is the rise of India and China, not the goings on in the mountains of Pakistan, that will leave their imprint on this era. The war for wealth, a bitter struggle for a share of affluence, and the related struggle over political and cultural dominance in the world, are the real conflicts of our day. The war on terror is overblown, the man in the White House has set the wrong priorities, and the public—deliberately or not—is being kept in the dark over the true extent of the global shift of power and wealth.

In this book, I hope to tell the true story of globalization, in an understandable way but without mincing words, and with respect for the new powers but free of naïveté. It differs greatly from the official story we are fed. Why? Because the true tale of globalization is anything but a win-win situation.

A metamorphosis of virtually unprecedented proportions is taking place outside our direct field of vision. China and India, with populations of more than a billion people each, two countries we considered part of the Third World only yesterday, are suddenly surging ahead. We are all contemporary witnesses of, and participants in, an eruption of vitality that is unique in world history. The era of Western dominance, those two centuries in which first the Europeans and then the Americans overshadowed the rest of the world with their economic might, is coming to an end. After two world wars, the center of the world has shifted from Europe to America, and now it is shifting once again, this time toward Asia. A new topography of power is taking shape. What began with the rise of Japan, and continued with the success stories of the Asian Tigers—Singapore, Hong Kong, Taiwan, and South Korea—is now coming full circle. By 2025, China and India will likely dominate the world market with their purchasing power.

Meanwhile, the West is turning into a miniaturized version of itself. Its population is both shrinking and aging, its inventive spirit is diminishing, and its relative share of the economic pie is getting smaller. Europe's share of the global market, three times the size of China's and India's combined before World War I, will shrink to only 15 percent of the economic power of these two countries within the next two decades. The United States, still the world's dominant economic power today, will also have fallen behind China and India by then.

Globalization has shifted the economic emphasis away from the West. Asia's emerging economies have managed to significantly expand their productive cores—the sphere in which capital and labor come together to generate the wealth of a nation—in the last two decades. Meanwhile, the productive core of the West is shrinking. The U.S. share of global exports, for example, has been cut in half since 1960.

But China is not America's biggest problem. America's problem is America itself or, to be more precise, its broad lack of understanding and awareness of the world's rising powers. It's business as usual in the United States, even as the foundation on which the country has based its economic strategy has changed fundamentally. Anyone who hopes to change the world for his own benefit must see and recognize the magnitude of the challenge.

What many in the West fail to realize is that what is happening in the Far East is not an extension of the present but the beginning of a new present. The rules of the world economy are being rewritten, but not by the West. The flat world once dominated by the West, the world in which the United States, Canada, and Europe held sway over world markets with their companies, their currencies, and their rules and regulations, is broken. The new world is not flat. It is a structure with many sharp edges and deep chasms. Unless Western politicians recognize the need for decisive and concerted action, these chasms will eventually swallow up many in the West, first ordinary workers and later portions of the middle class.

Anarchy prevails on the global labor market today. A brutal and primitive form of capitalism, with its starvation wages and its lack of workers' rights and protections for the environment, is now in competition with a more sophisticated capitalism, which seeks to protect both the environment and its workers. We may consider ourselves modern and enlightened, and yet we are on the losing end of this struggle. The world is out of kilter, and it is fast becoming an unpleasant place in which to live. But most of all it challenges us to take political action.

For the Asians, taking control of the low-wage labor market was only the beginning. Their attack on the middle class and modern, high-tech jobs is still in its infancy, as Asian nations invest more and more of their revenues in research and education. Their goal is dominance, not being part of a silent partnership. They want to lead instead of follow.

The truth is that the winners and losers in the war for wealth have already switched roles. Asia's new strength leads to the weakening of the West. Its rise is the West's descent. As Asia booms, Europe faces mass unemployment and growing national debt. In the United States, the balance of trade deficit, consumer debt, and risks to the stability of the dollar are all growing. The American economy is now on shaky ground. The country will not be able to afford this form of the present for much longer. U.S. society, built from the ashes of the Civil War and committed to the values of freedom, equality, and equal opportunity, now faces a series of challenges of historic dimensions.

The new world is by no means more peaceful than the old. Today's victories are being won on the economic battlefield—only to be transported to the political and military sphere. Intoxicated by their meteoric rise of the past decades, the leaders of China and India recently declared that their goal is to "establish a new world order." Asia's arms buildup has already taken on enormous proportions, as nuclear weapons become the status symbol of the continent's nouveau riche.

Despite international commerce and intensive trade relations, the risk of armed conflict has not declined by any means. Asia's rise to power is accompanied by feverish anxiety on the continent. The Asians' newly acquired economic might has both boosted their self-confidence and created growing mutual distrust. Economic inequality—within and between nations—generates a potentially explosive situation.

This book examines the forces that are driving these global changes. Where does the immense energy behind globalization come from? How is the sheer magnitude of these processes changing and reshaping life in the United States? Who are globalization's winners and losers? What will happen to the wealth we enjoy today? What can we do to stop these processes? Finally, how can America respond strategically if it hopes to preserve the power and prosperity of its citizens under changed conditions?

Good policies begin with the ability to recognize reality. The goal of this book is to help make this recognition possible.

Shelton State Libraries
Shelton State Community College

CHAPTER 1

RETHINKING GLOBALIZATION

A QUESTION OF SURVIVAL

Henry Paulson, Naomi Klein, and the Great Self-Deception

When Henry M. Paulson, the former CEO of Wall Street firm Goldman Sachs, walked into my office one day, it was obvious that he was itching for a fight. He had gone jogging that morning. Now it was time to exercise his brain.

Paulson was in a good mood. He had come to argue with me about globalization, he said, as he sat down in the middle of my dark green leather couch. He said that a colleague had told him that I was writing a book critical about the new global economy and its consequences for Americans.

I had a pretty good idea of what I was in for: a self-confident declaration of his belief in free trade and the market economy, and of his unshakeable faith in the greatness of the United States, from now until eternity. But someone like Hank Paulson wasn't about to end his sermon with "amen." He prefers "you get it?"

He began by saying that "globalization has been a positive force. It lifts hundreds of millions of people out of poverty, and it benefits this country and every country that has opened itself up to competition."

I expressed a few of my doubts. Is today's America truly well prepared for its new rivals from Asia? Are Americans taking China seriously enough as a strategic adversary? How do the global economy's rules change under the influence of guided economies like India's, China's, and Singapore's? The U.S. manufacturing economy had once propelled workers into the middle class, so what will replace this engine of job creation? Will the outsourcing of manufacturing jobs be followed by a second wave in the service economy? What does a widening gap between winners and losers mean for a Western democracy? My doubts bounced off Paulson like a ball bouncing off a wall.

What about the bloated U.S. government budget deficit? We need more growth, he answered.

What can we learn from the United States' huge trade deficit with other countries? He replied, "Problems with the balance of trade will eventually resolve themselves on their own."

When I remarked that the strength of the dollar depends on the goodwill of China's Communist Party leaders, Paulson said, "I'm not the least bit concerned about the dollar crashing."

In response to my contention that globalization is dividing America into winners and losers, Paulson said, "In global competition, there is no freedom to win anything unless there is the freedom to lose something." The idea that America itself could be among the losers didn't occur to him.

A few months later, in June 2006, U.S. president George W. Bush named Henry Merritt Paulson Jr. the seventy-fourth treasury secretary of the United States of America.

✦ ✦ ✦

Naomi Klein, the well-known antiglobalization activist, is as charming as she is combative. She rebels against everything that is sacred to Hank Paulson. Last summer I visited Klein in her native Toronto to learn more about her worldview. In her books *No Logo* and *The Shock Doctrine* she accuses the U.S. government of favoring corporate America and oppressing the American people.

"The shock therapists take advantage of every major shock— the attack on the World Trade Center, Hurricane Katrina, and the Indian Ocean tsunami, to push their neoconservative model," says Klein. Her eyes sparkle when she talks about the United States, the home of the men she despises: George W. Bush, Milton Friedman, and the executives at Halliburton. As far as she is concerned, the United States is big, powerful, and malicious.

Klein is especially offended by U.S. capitalism. She believes that it is "on the rise," that its aim is global dominance, and that critical voices like hers no longer count. What reforms would be needed? I ask her. "Reform is an empty word for me," she says. And what does she expect from the Democratic Party and their candidates? "Nothing," she says, "really nothing."

The political contrast between Klein and Paulson couldn't be more dramatic, or at least it would seem that way. He worships entrepreneurs, of whom she isn't particularly fond. He loves profit, which she hates. He sees social differences as God-given, while she sees them as blasphemy. For Paulson, the United States today is a fortress of good. Klein sees it as a bastion of malice. He welcomes today's globalization as vociferously as Klein rejects it. She sees shadow where he sees light.

As we gaze at the Toronto skyline from Klein's hotel room, I think of Paulson. There are more similarities between the two of them than Klein would like to admit. In truth, both see the world from the same point of view, but the difference is that they're looking at it through different glasses: his are rose-colored and hers, dark brown.

The proponents and opponents of globalization see themselves as adversaries, but the truth is that they stand before us, hand in hand, their backs turned on today's new challenges. Both want to revert to the cat-and-mouse game of the 1980s and 1990s, which pitted capital against labor, corporations against oppressed workers, conservatives against leftists, the sons and daughters of the middle classes against one another, and the West against itself.

Both barely acknowledge the fact that big things are happening beyond their field of view. And both accept it as a matter of course that the United States, as the world's sole remaining superpower, will endure as the center of a world dominated by the West. The only difference between Paulson and Klein is that he welcomes the United States' dominance while she rejects it. He says "thank God" while she groans loudly and says "oh, my Lord."

But their worldviews are not, as they both believe, parallel galaxies. In fact, combine the two and you have today's prevailing Western sense of identity, one in which the economic dominance, military might, and cultural hegemony of the United States of America constitutes the center of all thought. Those in Paulson's camp worship this center, while those in Klein's curse it. And yet both sides—the Establishment and the anti-Establishment—live on the same moon.

The New Galaxy

We were born into a world that will soon cease to exist in its current form. Far away from our cities and villages, a rare metamorphosis is taking place. The old world, dominated by the West, is disappearing in the fog of history, while the new one is only beginning to take shape. We live in an age of transition. The U.S. and Western European share of the world's population, about 20 percent in the days of former U.S. president John F. Kennedy, has declined to 12 percent today and will drop even further, to only 9 percent, by the middle of the century. The new arrivals are as numerous as they are industrious. Billions of people, yesterday's third world populations, are gaining new strength. We are witnessing a remarkable outbreak of economic vitality, as former German chancellor Helmut Schmidt recently remarked. We are facing "a new paradigm," presidential candidate Hillary Clinton recognized.

The days of Western dominance are coming to an end. After the two world wars, the hub of the world migrated from Europe to America, and now it is shifting toward Asia. A new topography of power is taking shape. What is happening in Asia is indeed not a continuation of our present, but the beginning of a new one.

What began with the rise of Japan and continued with the growth of the Asian Tigers—Singapore, Hong Kong, Taiwan, and South Korea—is now being completed by the Chinese and the Indians. Their successes of the last 10 years are the most impressive development in global economic history. It took the British just under 60 years, and the United States and Japan about 40 years, to double their respective per capita gross domestic product (GDP). It took China all of 12 years. By 2035, China and India together will likely dominate the world market with their purchasing power. And the United States, still the dominant player on the world market today, will have fallen behind.

The economic machine of the West will remain strong in the future, but it will no longer be the world's strongest. Life goes on in New York, Washington, Chicago, Miami, Los Angeles, Seattle, and Boston, but a new advanced civilization is developing in faraway Asia, and its self-confidence could quickly turn into a sense of superiority. We will soon see ourselves sharing our prosperity with others or even losing parts of it.

Until now, the West has merely shrugged its shoulders as it acknowledged the meteoric rise of the Asian countries and their culture of a controlled market economy. Westerners find it difficult to understand what is happening there. None of our prominent thinkers, from Karl Marx to Adam Smith to Milton Friedman, has prepared us for this type of system. The Asian economic model calls into question everything we have generally believed was necessary for a society to function—free markets, private enterprise, the rule of law and democracy.

Depending on their mentality, Western leaders are either amazed or fearful. But they remain unresponsive. It's as if they were all standing in the control room at the Kennedy Space Center, staring helplessly at the rows of computer screens. They witness the decline in the West's relative strength, recognize the tremendous growth of the emerging economies, perceive how the rules of engagement are changing in the world's markets, see the new galaxies approaching, and sense that the day is coming closer when this rising economic energy will transform itself into political strength. And yet they fail to follow up their perceptions with any action that is even remotely adequate.

The terrorist threat at home, a Middle Eastern war being waged on several fronts, and a population jolted out of complacency by climate change appear to be too much for Western leaders to handle. These leaders are being stressed and overstretched. The control room is filled with a tense silence.

As a result, the U.S. president does his best to instill a sense of false security in the population. The Bush administration inserted the following statement in its 2002 assessment of National Security Strategy of the United States of America: "The great struggles of the twentieth century between liberty and totalitarianism ended with a decisive victory for the forces of freedom—and a single sustainable model for the success of nations: freedom, democracy, and free enterprise."

In truth, it was not the Star Wars program and the combative rhetoric of former president Ronald Reagan ("Tear down this wall, Mr. Gorbachev") that ended the cold war, despite what many historians today would have us believe. "Marxism-Leninism as an economic system met its Waterloo," a triumphant Francis Fukuyama, the neoconservative guru of his day, wrote at the time. But the end of the Soviet Union was brought about by exhaustion, a defeat without enemy action. The communists destroyed themselves because they were unable to organize their economy. It was suicide, not murder. The Red empire died in its own bed, not on the battlefield.

Everything that had sustained the Soviet system gradually melted away over decades: the productive core of its industry, their standard of living, the quality of the Red Army's weapons, and the contentment of the Soviet people. In the end, hope had even evaporated within the military and the intelligence services, leaving it up to Mikhail Gorbachev to preside over the demise of the Soviet Union, essentially playing the role of its bankruptcy administrator.

The cold war was only a small piece of a much bigger picture. The truly epochal changes occurred well outside the bounds of the ideological battlefield that once pitted capitalism against communism, West against East. The decline of Soviet communism coincided with the rise of Asia, not of the United States. The new emerging nations had grown tremendously in many respects—in terms of population, economic power, self-confidence, and military strength. The time of the cold war was in truth a time in which the greatest economic miracle in world history took place— and went virtually unnoticed. To this day, cold war triumphalism prevents many from understanding what really happened during that era. If it were rewritten today, the National Security Doctrine would read something like this:

> *The great struggles of the twentieth century between liberty and totalitarianism ended with a surprise winner. In Asia, a group of nations formed, in the slipstream of the East-West confrontation, in which dictatorship, planned economy and market economy came together to form a new, previously unknown system. Free societies stand before new, possibly even greater challenges today, because— unlike the extinct Soviet Union—their new strategic rival has well-functioning and fast-growing economic machinery.*

The "America, Don't Move" Party

Many roads lead to the demise of a nation. Self-deception is one of them. The belief in the immortality of the present and the comfortable feeling of being one of history's victors is in fact a sign of an apocalyptic mood. It is a form of optimism that acts like a neurotoxin that clouds consciousness, artificially brightens the mood, and only recognizes a challenge in merely schematic form, if at all.

No one has analyzed the reasons for the rise and fall of nations more precisely than the Harvard historian David Landes, who has spent much of his academic life studying wealth and poverty in the world's nations. One of his conclusions is that the rise and fall of nations is not determined by climate and natural resources, military might, financial muscle, technical expertise, or even inherent biological traits. Culture is the decisive factor, he says—culture in the sense of moral values and behaviors.

A population's sheer willpower to achieve great things and to defend its achievements is also an important factor. Part of defending those achievements is the ability to question them. Landes leaves us with a bitter insight: those who hope to be the winners of the future must be able to divorce themselves from their past. Winning the future is simply a constant process of reevaluation, regrouping, and letting go.

For most people, this process is a painful one, which is why it so often fails. Throughout history, the failures of great societies have always begun as failures from within. The advanced civilization of the Incas disappeared without a trace, the realm of the Russian czars proved to be incapable of surviving, the Prussians were officially finished by the Allies in 1945, and the once-impressive realms of the Romans, Spaniards, and British all ended as "failing empires." Their rulers didn't lack the ability to exercise occasional self-criticism, but they did lack the strength to establish a culture of change.

It's paradoxical that establishing something in order to change the status quo can in fact preserve the status quo. But the basic concept is simple: a nation must subject itself to change before change subjugates the nation. This is the eternal law of the rise and fall of nations, which no one has ever been able to prove wrong. The "open society" of which philosopher Karl Popper spoke must first be an "open-minded society" if it hopes to avoid drowning in the maelstrom of change.

British economist John Maynard Keynes knew this when he famously said, "If things change, I change my opinion." But Keynes's axiom is widely ignored today. Instead, what we see now is that things have changed, but we have not.

"I do not think much of a man who is not wiser today than he was yesterday," Abraham Lincoln once said. But many people seek

self-affirmation, not new knowledge. They were smarter yesterday than they are today, or at least that's what they believe. As a
result, they are loath to see yesterday's knowledge disturbed or
even invalidated by new ways of looking at things.

An entire society that loves its status quo so much that it sees
its own change as an underhanded attack on its way of life will not
be able to hold on to its spot in the ranking of nations. Those who
are capable of change continue on while those who stand still lose
political power and economic prosperity—and their cultural influence wanes.

It is difficult to say whether the United States has already
started down this path, but it is clear that a dangerous situation has developed. Lasting industrial decline, growing balance-of-trade deficits, and acting as the world's largest debtor
present tremendous challenges for any nation, even in normal
times. But in light of a rival that has no debt, and in fact has
surpluses, with industry that is flourishing and rushing from
one export success to the next, the challenge quickly becomes
a threat. Even more dangerous than the situation is the mood.
In the West, a culture of ignorance and avoidance has developed, resulting in a failure of leaders to accurately assess the
situation.

The opponents and proponents of today's globalization are
united in being mistaken. Without knowing it or wanting it, they
are part of a single party one could call "America, Don't Move."
This party appears on no ballot, never holds party conventions,
and has never organized a fund-raiser. It doesn't send any of its
luminaries to appear on *Meet the Press* or post promotional videos
on YouTube, nor does it hire pollsters to investigate the opinions
of farmers, housewives, and minorities.

And yet the party's influence on the political mood is enormous.
Henry Paulson and Naomi Klein are in good company. Liberal
college professors and stern central bankers, senior economists
and leftist students, corporate CEOs, and presidential candidates
of every stripe are part of this movement, which wants everything
to remain the same but is unwilling to pay the price to achieve

that goal. In doing so the movement ignores a cardinal rule: change is needed to preserve the status quo.

The most prominent characteristic of the "No Movers" is the pose with arms locked stubbornly across the chest. These people reject change in thought because it comes with the risk that new thought could mean the need for new action. As a result, an entire nation is eating away at the intellectual capital of years gone by.

Given the stability of its values and the stubbornness of its supporters, the "America, Don't Move" Party will likely survive the next election unharmed. This movement is influential because it is invisible. It is aggressive because it is apathetic. It is dominant, partly as a result of the incredible lethargy of its supporters. And for all those who support a pragmatic agenda of change, both inside and outside political parties, it poses an asymmetrical threat.

Sensing decline, the members of this party cling to the doctrines of the past, which only increases the risk of decline. To explain this clouded and distorted view of reality, we must examine the seven fallacies of the globalization debate.

The Seven Fallacies of the Globalization Debate

Fallacy No. 1: The natural progression for a developed economy is to move from an industry-based to a service-based economy. Seen in this light, the disappearance of industrial jobs is even a good sign because it clears the way for the new economy. Happy farewell to the blue-collar worker! This is what we have learned. We have been told that this is merely a repetition of the change from an agriculture-based economy to the age of industrialization.

But history doesn't like repeating itself. What we see outside may be not the end of the industrial age, but merely a shift of industrial work to Asia. All over the world there are more people doing industrial jobs than ever before. Today there are 600 million blue-collar workers worldwide. Even in India, most of the new jobs are in the industrial sector. Only 1.3 million of the nearly 500 million workers in the Indian workforce are working in the software industry. All the rest are employed in agriculture, trade, and regular industry.

Only the Western countries are losing these jobs. Germany has lost 29 percent and France 17 percent of jobs in these sectors since 1991. In the United States, the economy has lost more than a quarter of its industrial jobs since the late 1970s.

Many economists continue to defend the old theory that the Indians and the Chinese are merely going through the same industrial age Western societies have already put behind them. But this way of thinking fails to adequately explain today's development in India and China, because they are building their industrial and service sectors at the same time. Clearly, we are experiencing, not a postindustrial age worldwide, but a series of simultaneous developments for which we have not been prepared. It is as if the Middle Ages and the modern age were happening at the same time.

So far, we have been placated with the claim that the promised world of a service economy is the successor of the industrial society. But the balance of trade shows a different truth. Western industrial exports have been replaced with a great emptiness. The impressive export successes of the past are nothing but empty gaps today.

Perhaps the service sector economy is simply a part of the industrial society: service jobs are at the end of the production chain, not an independent unit. For example, the pilot flies an airplane, one of the most advanced industrial products. The waiter serves meals made by the food industry. The investment banker is selling pieces of a real automotive plant or pharmaceutical production facility, even if what he really sells are artificial products like high-yield or junk bonds. At the end of the chain we find all the jobs with which we are all too familiar: researchers, blue-collar workers, marketing specialists, back-office people, and sales forces.

Let's put this in terms of the family: the service jobs are in all likelihood not the sons and daughters of the industrial father but simply his brothers and sisters. This sounds banal, but it has serious consequences for our political behavior. If the service and industrial sectors are parts of one and the same family, we cannot separate ourselves from one without destroying the family as a whole. To put it more provocatively, if we allow manufacturing jobs to be offshored without blinking, service jobs will soon follow suit. Families want to stay together, not be torn apart. But that's exactly what is happening, and corporate outsourcing experts even have a term for the phenomenon: "network outsourcing."

Fallacy No. 2: Economics and morals have nothing in common. This statement is often what we are told, but it is a fallacy. Every product is made up of only three things: First, there are raw materials such as oil, plastics, steel, rubber, glass, paper, and wood. Second, there is knowledge, the know-how to build a sports car, a computer, or a mobile phone from all this plastic, steel, rubber, and glass. Third, there is the set of conditions that enable a company to bring together the raw materials and knowledge. These production conditions—that is, laws, regulations, and a country's unwritten traditions—make up the real difference.

The Asian and Western countries buy resources from the same dealers, at similar prices. The know-how mostly comes from the Western countries, whether legally or illegally. The key difference, though, is the values of each country.

The third component consists of more than just a worker's salary. It includes not only Western values such as the worker's benefits, coffee breaks, separate bathrooms for men and women, holiday pay, sick pay, overtime pay, a Christmas bonus, unemployment insurance, and pension benefits, but also the health and safety regulations that protect the workers. Western values also include the protection of the environment, clean air, clean water, and proper housing, as well as the way children are treated: as children, not as working slaves. Children are sent to school, not down a coal mine. These values, which are documented thousands of times over in collective wage agreements, company agreements, laws, company regulations, and, to some extent, international treaties, are what make the difference in today's world economy.

The Chinese have no significant natural resources today. They haven't invented anything meaningful since gunpowder and paper money long ago. Their rise is not technology driven. They owe their rise to clever politicians, an astonishing feat of strength by ordinary people, and a generous underbidding of Western standards. It would be nice if this were polemics, but it is nothing but the truth. The Chinese ignore Western intellectual property rights and they forbid independent trade unions. Their biggest advantage at present is an endless supply of very cheap labor and a political system that undermines Western regulations. They pay only low costs for environmental protection, they pay nearly nothing for a pension system, and they have very poor standards of health and safety in the workplace. They are willing to do everything for less. So, economics and morals are strongly connected, but in a different way than many of us thought.

Today we can buy a washing machine made by Whirlpool, General Electric, or Miele that includes a piece of the welfare state. Or we can buy a Chinese brand that comes directly from the Yangtze Delta and has no built-in social welfare costs. If we order a car that comes with the whole social package, it will be made by Ford in Detroit and cost an additional $1,600. It would be cheaper to buy a car from the Hyundai dealer next door. In doing so we reduce our cost of buying a car, but that lower price comes at the cost of our own well-being. We pay less, but we lose more. The real cost of buying a cheaper, Asian-made car is more than just the sticker price. We pay less in the shop, but the economy as a whole suffers, and in the end even the individual pays an additional price.

We paid less for the car, but the tax bill goes up. In fact, for years the American form of increasing taxes has been to eliminate services. The bill for an import boom that is not offset by an export boom comes in two parts, only on of which is paid at the cash register. There is a relationship between the rising import penetration and the increasing national deficit, as well as between Middle America's love of cheap foreign products and the collapse of the bridge over the Mississippi in Minneapolis. While the consumers create wealth abroad, the government budgets at home are written mostly in red ink.

Fallacy No. 3: The new world is flat. It is, according to award-winning journalist Thomas Friedman. But that statement, too, is untrue. Before today's globalization began, the Western way of doing business defined the playing field. Wall Street was setting the standard in the financial market, and there were strong similarities between European and U.S. labor markets. Nearly 500 million employees in the West, including the United States, Canada, and Europe, were working under comparable conditions. Their world was indeed flat. The experts called it a "level playing field." They competed on price and performance, but governments and corporations were not embroiled in a political contest to undermine each other's values. Their competition was tough, but fair.

Those were glorious days for the ordinary American workers. Their well-being and that of their companies were interconnected. If executives at Ford in Detroit drank champagne, the average American's eyes were sparkling with joy.

The rest of the world was disconnected from the West. Africa was far away; the Soviet Union and its satellites were cruising in another solar system, and much of Asia seemed to be living in the Middle Ages. People there were poor, sick, and unable to take part in the world economy. India was a planned economy in the Soviet style, and China was one of the poorest regimes the world had ever seen. Mao Zedong killed nearly 50 million people with a policy he called the Great Leap Forward.

Then the unbelievable happened: Mao died and his successors started to reform the country in a very radical way. When the Soviet Union crashed, India followed. Since that time we have seen turmoil in the world labor market. The West's workforce of 500 million suddenly saw itself confronted with an army of 1.2 billion potential employees in the emerging markets. These new workers were willing to work under conditions not much more advanced than those of the mid–nineteenth century. The level playing field had become fragmented. For ordinary people in the West, the world had become anything but flat.

The highly developed capitalism of the West now had to compete with a system that favored the crude customs of Manchester capitalism. Nowadays, Western capitalists can hardly believe their eyes when they see what's going on in Asia. In many places in the East, social welfare is virtually nonexistent, the environment is being sold for a pittance, and people often have fewer rights than the ordinary American house pet. This set of circumstances is as taxing on Asian workers as it is on the West.

Under the current conditions free trade often means unfair practices and translates into pressure for those who cannot compete. The ordinary workers in the West are suffering, and their industrial jobs are the first to slip away. Even the West's more skilled workers should not feel too secure about their jobs. The contest to undermine economic adversaries on the basis of values has barely gotten underway. It's cheaper to produce drugs in countries where there are no ethics commissions to regulate pharmaceutical research. The foreign financial industry also tries to benefit from less regulation. And the software industry is already salivating over the millions of well-trained Asians with few political rights.

Most people think Asia is exporting only products, but in fact these countries are also exporting their labor and environmental practices. This is the dark side of free trade. It would be a mistake to demonize free markets. But it would be just as wrong to put them on a pedestal. America must search for a third way between die-hard free traders and unreconstructed protectionists. Trade is a question of interest and not a matter of belief. A nation's trade does not necessarily need to be ideologically clean, at least not primarily, but it must be useful. Trade issues are no less political than questions of environmental protection, national security, and demilitarization.

Fallacy No. 4: The tide of globalization automatically lifts all boats. Many authorities have told this to us, and claim that we don't have to worry. This statement may be true in the long run, but for now it seems to be a fairy tale. It doesn't reflect today's reality. Globalization nowadays is an extremely divisive force for the American population. The latest available data from the U.S. Census Bureau published in August 2007 sent a very clear message: this is the first boom period in American history where the upper classes go up while significant parts of the middle class go downhill.

Although median household income, adjusted for inflation, has not reached the prerecession high of 1999, income inequality is at an all-time high. According to the U.S. Census Bureau, the share of income going to the 5 percent of households with the highest income has never been greater. They earned more than 50 percent of the national pretax income in 2006. This should come as no surprise: many businesspeople love today's globalization more than their own spouses. What they have told us about great opportunities and win-win situations is true, but it's true mostly for them. They are now living in the "shining city on a hill," to which Ronald Reagan once hoped to lead the entire nation.

But a large segment of the population has become bogged down along the way. For many Americans, their country has become a shady place down in the valley. About 16 percent of the U.S. population, or 47 million people, lack health insurance. Nine million people have been added to the ranks of the uninsured during the past seven years. It is important to know that about two-thirds of those Americans who became uninsured last year were members of middle class households with pretax incomes of $75,000 or more.

This phenomenon is all the more surprising when we consider that the United States in mid-2007 was in the fifth year of an economic boom, which raises some important questions: what has really happened in this country? Where do these new uninsured people come from? Why have their lives developed in this adverse direction? The answer is disturbing: they are mostly members of the middle class working for international companies. Their corporate leaders have cut back employer-provided coverage over the last decade—to improve the competitiveness of the company. This is precisely the paradox of globalization: while the competitiveness of American companies is on the rise, the standard of living of the average family is shrinking. Truth number one: globalization connects people. Truth number two: on the same day, and in the same country, it divides society. Economic growth and social decline are no longer mutually exclusive.

Fallacy No. 5: Globalization is a great work of peace. Many people believe this. Nations that are economically intertwined do not shoot at one another. That's the great hope. But the new world is by no means more peaceful than the old. Today's victories are won on the field of business, and from there they are passed on to politicians and military leaders. Giddy with their almost magical successes of the last few decades, the prime ministers of China and India recently declared that their goal is to bring about "a new world order." Asian countries have already embarked on a massive military buildup, one in which the nuclear warhead is seen as a status symbol of the newly affluent.

Despite the international flow of goods and intensive interdependence in commerce, the risk of armed conflicts has certainly not diminished. The rise of Asia is accompanied by intense nervousness on the continent itself. Asia's newly acquired economic strength has boosted the Asians' self-confidence and intensified their mutual distrust. Economic imbalance—both within and between nations—has incredibly explosive potential. Asia is experiencing the rebirth of nationalism all across the continent.

Much of the new wealth is flowing into the coffers of the arms industry. Never before has so much money been spent in Asia on new weapons systems, including nuclear warheads. The growth rates and the tensions are high. Those who wish to defuse that potential may have to do precisely the opposite of what the current U.S. government, the World Bank, and the U.S. Federal Reserve System are trying to do, which is to constantly increase growth rates. Their agenda means one thing: speed, speed, speed. To bring about change, economists must borrow an expression from environmentalists: sustainable development.

Fallacy No. 6: The nation can no longer do anything for the people in its care. Both the left and the right continually emphasize the powerlessness of the national state in the current age. A growing number of people believe that globalization has weakened the power of governments, because this is what politicians are constantly telling them.

Western democracies invest a great deal of effort in protecting their democratic ideals. Governments pay thousands of intelligence agents to protect the open society from its enemies. They have even created a plethora of laws with the sole intent of making life difficult for troublemakers. There is no lawless hinterland for the declared enemies of the open society. In fact, this is where openness has its limits. We limit it to protect it, and the result is a well-fortified democracy.

Less consideration is paid to the economic system. Western democracies may have rituals that require politicians to champion a "market economy" that is responsible for those left behind and for the environment. Even neoconservatives describe themselves as "compassionate conservatives." But none of them are backing up their avowed beliefs with firm action. To this date, there is no established framework for globalization, nor is anyone searching for it. In fact, it would appear that the economic system of the West is being given up without a fight. Ironically, the biggest enemy of the market economy is the complacency of its friends and the ignorance of its beneficiaries.

A misunderstanding—one that is apparently difficult to dispel—is held up as an excuse for this failure to take action: globalization, it is claimed, is a force of nature, a powerful law of historic progression, and a global inevitability that only the residents of remote rainforests and totalitarian regimes like North Korea's can escape. It is, as contemporaries explain, the rhythm of the times, and those seeking to elude it will suffer the penalty of their own decline. We are led to believe that globalization will steamroll anyone who attempts to stand in its way.

The powerlessness of national institutions is held up as proof of the omnipotence of globalization. Isn't it true that trade unions, environmental agencies, political parties, and government officials sometimes seem small and naked as they stand before the public?

Of course, the national organizations that represent its citizens' interests, from unions to political parties, are justified in complaining that their relative significance is waning in the age of the global economy. But this loss of significance is not some document issued by a global spirit. If domestic companies had remained within their national borders, no one would have been able to stop their loss of significance. They too faced a choice between decline and expansion.

What we are experiencing today is an economy that is expanding worldwide, and those who are complaining the loudest are the ones who have remained within the space once considered their sovereign territory. Economic policy stands at the threshold of a new and unfamiliar world, but it lacks the confidence to cross that threshold. Instead of joining the chorus of complainers, anyone making economic policy should follow in the footsteps of corporations, not just physically but intellectually.

The interests of the employed are no less global than those of capital. Nowadays they must be represented both inside and outside the sovereign state, and representing those interests internationally requires far greater skill than in the past. Those who hope to influence the price of labor as a commodity and the conditions under which it competes must expand their range of activity and adjust their methods to conform to new possibilities. In other words, they must transform themselves from trade politicians into globalization politicians, from observers into activists.

The state should keep its hands out of the flow of trade. Whenever it intervenes, it does nothing but harm. This has been the position in the United States until now. Anyone with a reasonable understanding of the statesmanship of today must admit that one cannot dismiss this concern out of hand. History has shown that the state often fails to live up to high expectations. It is not altogether comforting to imagine the state as a custodian of international trade.

And yet it is a necessary concept. The concern about the state's role in trade is based on a fallacy that cannot be disregarded, even though those who voice their concerns the loudest are precisely the ones who seek to downplay it. The state may be exercising restraint in the United States, but it does not do so in India, Singapore, Japan, Korea, and Malaysia, and certainly not in China. In fact, the state plays a dominant role in those countries—the ones currently reporting the most mind-boggling successes. It is the greatest promoter and protector of their export industries, and it organizes and guarantees the conditions that result in the underbidding of Western countries.

The rise of China is principally the achievement of politicians, not market forces. The country's leadership has committed itself to a guided market economy, and Western heads of state are nothing short of astonished to witness the sheer enthusiasm and boldness with which the Chinese government plays a highly risky game with many unknowns. Unlike the Soviets, who lackadaisically managed the deficiencies of their country, the Chinese planning commissioners are planning an ascent to the stars. They are organizing an economy that has virtually no natural resources and little experience with free markets, has no freely convertible currency, and must rely on a labor force that is essentially made up of farmers and peasants. The invisible hand of the market, of which Adam Smith spoke, is guided and directed by the iron fist of the state. We should look to the Far East with goodwill and respect, but we should also jettison our naïveté.

The Chinese example is not worth emulating, but it does stimulate thought. A new debate over society's understanding of government seems long overdue in the United States. This does not mean that the country should reinstate Big Government, but perhaps what's in order is some form of Smart Government that goes well beyond the confines of the state serving as a custodian.

Fallacy No. 7: Globalization is a hot issue. Too hot to handle for a single person? Is the individual almost powerless to do anything to change his or her situation? Has the citizen never been more insignificant, because the present has made him or her a political dwarf? In her book *A Year Without "Made in China,"* author Sara Bongiorni aptly describes the basic sentiments of an average American family: a fluctuation between resignation and sentimentality. It starts with shopping, she writes: "When I see the words 'Made in China,' part of me says, good for China, while another part feels sentimental about something I have lost, but I am not sure what exactly."

Is the budding resignation justified? I don't think so. But are antiglobalization protests the alternative? Hardly. Being against globalization is like being against a cold. These protests are posturing, not politics. We are not born to tolerate history, even to tolerate it angrily. In a democracy, we are called upon to shape history: realistically and optimistically, bravely and cleverly. We are at least consumers and citizens, employees and investors, we have purchasing power, the power of taxpayers and political power. The thing we have to learn now is to use these assets properly under the new conditions. The challenge is to figure out how to ensure that globalization serves the people. The United States faces a great but truly historic debate over how citizens and their state can regain their lost sovereignty, and how they can design the ground rules so that globalization makes the world a better and not just a faster place. This is nothing less than democratization of globalization, a framework or order for the worldwide economy that takes away its archaic and authoritarian characteristics. Beginning to read this book could be the first step away from the current gloomy mood.

The desire for endless growth and the fear of decline are not new phenomena. People throughout history have tried to interpret the signs on the horizon, draw their conclusions, and avoid the seemingly unavoidable. The world is a fair place in at least one respect: there is no guarantee of success, nor is failure predetermined. History, going forward, is open-ended.

This is why it is worthwhile to step back a few decades to approach the great pendulum of the present from a somewhat removed vantage point. Many things become more apparent from a safe distance. History, says philosopher Karl Jaspers, illuminates the present.

Chapter 2

EUROPE OVER ALL

THE DRESS REHEARSAL
FOR GLOBALIZATION

The Imperialists Are Coming

Anyone who compares the powerful of the nineteenth century with those at the beginning of the twenty-first century realizes one thing: life was a great deal more difficult in the days of Napoleon, Queen Victoria, and Kaiser Wilhelm II than under the leadership of Gordon Brown or George W. Bush. The rulers were crude and undemocratic, and they had little regard for anyone whose ethnic roots or skin color differed from their own. They raised no objections when hundreds of thousands had to die so that their interests could be protected. In the days of Napoleon and Victoria, actions that today would draw the attention of the secretary general of the United Nations and inevitably end in a war crimes tribunal guaranteed nothing more damning than a gilded entry in the history books. Indeed, a proudly displayed lack of regard for fellow human beings was the badge of an entire epoch.

But the powerful of yesterday had a leg up on today's leaders in one respect: they were more honest. They relied on their ambassadors and foreign ministers to engage in the high art of secret diplomacy, while the despots themselves took a more direct approach when dealing with one another. They all, friend and foe alike, knew exactly where they stood. With a bit of imagination, one can practically hear the powerful men of past centuries translating their wishes into words in their rasping voices, united across national boundaries by one character trait: ruthlessness. Napoleon was exceedingly straightforward when he made his position clear to Austrian prisoners of war: "I want ships, colonies, and trade." Faraway continents were discussed like bargains to be snapped up before a neighbor could get there first.

"The absorption of the greater portion of the world under our rule simply means the end of all wars," said the English colonial politician (and owner of many diamond mines) Cecil Rhodes, who would go down in African history as the most ruthless of colonizers. His battle cry has stood the test of time: "Expansion is everything." Even the Americans had their say. The United States, said then president Theodore Roosevelt, ought to "speak softly and carry a big stick."

Nowadays public life is a cleverly illuminated masquerade. The players on the global political stage do their best to smooth out the sharper edges of their actions. Meanwhile, the truth becomes so veiled as to be almost unrecognizable. When governments talk about international partnership, what they really mean is dominance. The captains of industry speak of competition, and yet their deepest desire is to establish monopolies. Everyone—from corporate bosses to politicians—is selling us globalization these days, painting it as some monumental effort to achieve world peace because, after all, a person who engages in trade with someone else isn't likely to be at one's throat at the same time.

But this approach isn't as logical as it sounds. From its inception, globalization has produced the kinds of imbalances and tensions that once before spelled the collapse of the world's architecture.

Nor is the current state of globalization as stable as it seems. Anyone who takes a closer look at the individual components of the world economy can sense the tension and feel the underlying rumblings, and can gain a sense of what could still be coming our way. A look into our past helps us to understand the present. Current and future generations can count their blessings that an appreciation for the truth was more common in the days when the dress rehearsal for globalization was on the agenda.

Democracy had been invented but not implemented. Freedom of the press was a wish, but it was not yet a reality in most places, so the despots had neither the people nor the media czars to fear. They said what was on their minds, which all too often translated into very little. All those "public relations" experts had not been born yet. There were no spin doctors, and no one knew what an opinion poll was. This absence of things that we take for granted today allows us to obtain a genuine, unbiased impression, through the centuries, of the days when global trade began to expand.

What remain as the central issues today were in their infancy in the nineteenth century: the rise and fall of economies, the thirst for raw materials and expansionism, and workers' rights versus business profits. But the dominant question for countries has been the same for ages: servitude or world dominance?

When the first factories opened their doors and, a short time later, the first steam-powered warships left their berths, a type of person debuted who we might consider a repulsive individual today. He called himself an imperialist, which sounded as inconsiderate as it was meant to be. Art and culture were his window dressing, but the use of force, domestically and abroad, was his true passion. The world, for the imperialist, was one big adventure playground.

England's Queen Victoria dispatched the Royal Navy to the four corners of the earth to conquer territory many times larger than her own realm. Spain's rulers waged four overseas wars in the second half of the nineteenth century alone, although, to the royal family's vexation, Spain lost each war. In his 16 years at the French helm, Napoleon hardly managed to endure a single year without being at war. The freedom call of the French bourgeoisie—Liberté, Egalité, Fraternité—was translated into something entirely different in practice: Infantry, Cavalry, Artillery.

In the end, colonial fever infected all social classes in the European nations. The powerful of the day were interested, not in being bystanders to history, but in actively shaping history.

For those whose primary goal was conquest, other peoples were worth very little. German philosopher Johann Gottfried Herder, who is mentioned in today's literature as a man of enlightenment, compared the Chinese to a "church mouse in hibernation," who were not to be trusted in the least. "The human race in this region," Herder wrote, "will never become like the Romans or the Greek. The Chinese are and will remain a people nature has provided with narrow eyes, short noses, a flat forehead, little beard growth, long ears and protruding stomachs. Their institutions have already achieved everything they are capable of achieving."

No one in Europe contradicted these notions, an omission the Chinese still hold against the Europeans to this day. In fact, slandering the Chinese was all the rage in Europe. The French philosopher and foreign minister Alexis de Tocqueville was completely serious when he claimed: "The Chinese have lost the power to change."

Such rude generalizations were generally taken as a verbal green light for the men in uniform, who used them as justification to act with even greater brutality. The Europe of the day was a collection of countries in which committing murder overseas had become second nature. Waltzes were played at royal houses, while marching music was the preferred style abroad. British author Edward Morgan Forster had a character in one of his novels express the sentiment many Britons in the colonies had already expressed or had at least thought: "We are not here to behave well." For most people, the right of the strong was justification enough to embark on armed conflicts with other peoples. The baptismal font of an entire generation was filled with blood.

The Human Being as Raw Material:
The Birth of Industrial Capitalism

Before the imperialists could set out to conquer the world, certain technical conditions had to be established. There could be no mass production without factories, no world trade without steamships, no tanks without steel mills, and no gas grenades without a chemical industry. In other words, a true globalization of the economy and of war was inconceivable without industrialization.

It was only through a large number of groundbreaking inventions toward the middle of the nineteenth century that it became possible to establish worldwide capitalism. "The world had torn itself free like a ship from its moorings," says Harvard professor David Landes, in describing the events of the time. But it was by no means the entire world that had done so. In fact, it was only the Western portion, which made up about one-seventh of global population at the time.

A breathtaking upward progression began, carrying first Europe and then the United States to the stars. The Indians and the Chinese, who until the year 1500 had enjoyed close to the same per capita income as Western Europeans, were the greatest losers in the race toward affluence. Knowledge exploded, but not in their countries. The economy blossomed, but far from their latitudes.

At the beginning of the Industrial Revolution, per capita income in Western Europe was about twice as high as it was in China. By the end of the era of communist dictator Mao Zedong, about 150 years later, the ratio of Western European to Chinese per capita income had jumped to about 14 to 1. At the beginning of the eighteenth century, that is, before the age of the steam engine began, Indian economic output was about half that of Great Britain. But by the beginning of the twentieth century, the average Briton was producing seven times as much as the average Indian, partly because artificially generated energy helped him perform his work more efficiently.

This jump in productivity was unprecedented. Thanks to new technologies, the West, beginning with Europe and followed by the United States, had detached itself from the rest of the world. Humanity was divided into the technological have-nots and the owners of the new miracle machines. For the span of 100 years, it seemed that the two worlds had moved apart irreversibly, that is, until the have-nots began their own breathtaking race to catch up with the West. But why did the world economy's big bang happen in the first place? Why did it happen when it did? And why only in the West?

Based on everything historians have learned on these issues, by far the most important driving force behind the sudden development of the Western inventive spirit was chance. One coincidence combined with a second coincidence, setting a chain reaction of coincidences into motion, which has changed life on earth to this day. Much of what the experts portray as certainty in this regard is conceived backward. To this day, no one can clearly answer the truly decisive questions: Why at this particular time? Why in Europe first? Why did everything happen with this unbelievable momentum that changed world history and continues to do so today?

Many in the West believe that it was primarily Protestant Christianity, together with its work ethic, that made people into inventors. Others claim that it was the moderate climate that gave European inventors a leg up over their counterparts in sub-Saharan Africa or Central Asia. But why should the English drizzle or Germany's April rains be better suited to reflection than the sun over Marrakech or humid summers in Shanghai? Others insist it was the topography that made the difference. In the British Isles and in Alpine valleys, protected by bodies of water or mountain chains, people were able to think more freely, because their societies were more fragmented than in large, centrally controlled realms like Russia or China. But don't the circumstances of living on an island or in a mountain village promote a way of life we would normally equate with provincialism?

According to a third group of scholars, it was the beneficial effects of the Enlightenment and the related state-supported efforts of universities and scientific colleges that gave the West its initial boost. But if that was the case, why was it Richard Arkwright, a hairdresser and wigmaker, who perfected the spinning machine? Why did a certain Edmund Cartwright, who normally made a living as a pastor and author, earn a place in the history books as the designer of the first steam-powered loom? And why does the world have Massachusetts artist Samuel Morse, who painted many landscapes and a portrait of U.S. president James Monroe, to thank for inventing the first functioning electromagnetic telegraph?

We should be especially suspicious of those who believe to have discovered some sort of law of history. According to the laws of nature, they say, early capitalism produced all the inventions it required for its own development. It made sense, so it happened. The output of textile workers could not be increased any further with physical strength alone, so the "Spinning Jenny" came on the scene. The stagecoach and sailing ship could no longer handle the volume of mass-produced goods that had to be delivered to customers, which meant the time had come for ocean steamers and locomotives. And how else could people talk to one another across America's vast expanses, if not through the telegraph line?

But since when has reason prevailed in the history of humankind? If history were a force blessed with reason, why do we look back on a relentless train of tragic mistakes and faulty decisions with far-reaching consequences? It was a supreme act of irrationality when the fifteenth-century Chinese emperors burned their commercial fleet, thereby imposing isolation on their realm for hundreds of years. Wouldn't it have made more sense if those assembled in Berlin's Sportpalast on a February evening in 1943 had responded with a resounding "no" to their hysterical speaker's question: "Do you want total war?"

All of the conditions cited above that made the Industrial Revolution possible are reasons, but not one of them is *the* reason. The Industrial Revolution is a string of coincidences, and even the breathtaking accumulation of these coincidences could be nothing but coincidental. It was not Hegel's concept of "world spirit" nor was it God or high politics that brought the Industrial Revolution to Europe and the United States. Indeed, it was what one would generally refer to as a stroke of good fortune.

But that happens to be the luck of the draw. The development that brought with it a high degree of rationality came about in the most irrational of ways. Something mysterious had happened to the inhabitants of the West. The greatest of all changes took place within an individual's innermost self.

The New Way of Looking at Things: Discoverers Become Inventors

At some point in the eighteenth century, there was a sudden surge in interest in the sciences. More and more young people wanted to become mathematicians, while fewer and fewer were drawn by theology. Affluent citizens set up laboratories at home, and the pioneers of the new age met in venerable clubs like the Royal Society in London and the Académie des Sciences in Paris. The members of the Lunar Society preferred to meet on nights when there was a full moon, hoping that this would give them the greatest possible inspiration.

The new way of thinking of those who belonged to these clubs was surprising. The scientist, who until then had prided himself in being somewhat removed from ordinary life, began to see himself no longer as merely an observer of reality but also as someone who takes part in changing reality. The spectator became an actor, and the scientific discoverer also began to see himself as a conqueror. Instead of simply admiring the world from behind a microscope or a telescope, the scientist decided to become a creator of reality, because the reality he was experiencing seemed inadequate. In this sense, scientists were being somewhat accommodating to ordinary people. In return, the people took a big step in the direction of science.

Mechanic schools and tinkerers' clubs began springing up all over Europe. The practical inventor stepped onto the world stage. He observed birds in flight and wanted to fly. He observed fish and dreamed of underwater boats. He sensed the power of water and heat and went about finding ways to harness it. Many members of the business community were eager to try out thousands of minor production improvements in actual practice. The act of inventing offered them an attractive way to get rich. The number of patent applications rose sharply, especially in England. Whereas barely 300 patent applications were filed in 1770, that number had increased to 1,124 in 1810 and, within another 20 years, to 2,452 inventions registered with the state. Science had abandoned its niche and had made itself available to the world as a productive force. The real novelty of the age was not the one-time invention, but the invention of inventing.

The object of interest had also changed. Whereas curious souls in the preceding centuries had focused their attention on the discovery of mysterious animals, plants, and people overseas, the new thirst for knowledge was centered on the laws of science, mathematics, and astronomy. Following the journeys to faraway places in the previous epoch, individuals were now embarking on inward voyages of discovery. This development helped shape the nineteenth century into a time of bold thoughts and unprecedented innovations. The technical innovations made many things possible for the first time (for example, driving an automobile), while making other things (such as textile production) tremendously more efficient. Most of all, they extended life expectancy, partly as a result of significant improvements in hygiene. By the end of the nineteenth century the average Briton was living 12 years longer than in the early 1800s.

Almost everything that continues to drive the world economy to this day was devised in the countries we now refer to as "the West." An Italian invented the electric battery in 1800, and a Frenchman invented the sewing machine. The English launched the first large ship made of iron in 1838, and photography was developed in the late 1820s. And one invention would establish the conditions that made the next invention necessary. It would have been impossible to dream up the locomotive without New York native George Westinghouse's compressed air brake, for the rolling monstrosity could not have been brought to a standstill quickly enough. And even the powerful new locomotives would not have made it across the Alps without the new Swedish miracle substance, dynamite, which was needed to build the first railway tunnels.

Sparks and flashes of inventiveness were everywhere, almost as if the West were connected to a burning fuse. But the great breakthrough in production technology was introduced by Henry Ford, who went down in history as the inventor of assembly-line production. But Ford didn't so much invent as borrow the concept of the assembly line in 1913. A visit to a slaughterhouse opened his eyes. He watched as the carcasses, attached to hooks, traveled through the buildings, where each step of the process was performed by a different group of butchers. Ford transferred the idea to automobile production. He began with the chassis. The various technicians would then install the engine and the transmission before the cables were laid, the windows installed, and finally the doors mounted. Ford built a four-story production hall, in which the various parts passed from the top floor to the ground floor, finally leaving the building as a mass-produced automobile.

Ford's contemporaries were overwhelmed by what was happening before their eyes. The economist Friedrich List wrote an homage to the generation of inventors, the words of which still ring true today: "They have enabled man to pull the treasures of the earth from the deepest chasms, into which he could not penetrate before, to battle the power of the wind and the waves, to travel from one place to the next with the speed of a bird; they have increased the wealth, pleasures and populations of the nations, and the charitable effects of their work will continue to grow from generation to generation."

The Factory Worker: Foot Soldier of the Industrial Age

The presidents, emperors, ministers, and high-ranking officials of the Western world soon realized that the new technologies would have a greater impact on the fortunes of their nations than any spoils of war. While the inventors wanted fame and the business-people wanted to increase their profits, the statespeople, not unlike their counterparts today, were interested in nothing less than expanding their power.

Only those with the technological wherewithal could send their merchant fleets to faraway lands with any expectation of success. And if the profits of such trade, denominated in talers, pounds, or dollars, were occasionally a long time in coming, at least the gain in status that came with being the owner of the latest in technology could be acquired more quickly.

The road to industrial capitalism was irreversible. Machines were turning their wheels throughout the West. They needed coal, iron ore, and water to operate; they were loaded with grain, cotton, tobacco and wood; and at the end of the process they spat out guns, soap, matches, textiles, cigarettes, and all manner of foodstuffs. Productivity records were set that were unprecedented and would never be duplicated. Fifteen of the cigarette rolling machines invented in 1881 could satisfy the entire annual demand for cigarettes in the United States. Until the early nineteenth century, when farmers and craftsmen pursued their arduous but not uncomfortable daily chores, productivity was growing at an annual rate of only about 0.15 percent. By the end of the century it had quadrupled. Iron production doubled in Europe between 1870 and 1890 alone, while steel production grew tenfold between 1880 and 1900.

Just about everything changed in this new age, including what people talked about, and the way they thought, saw, felt, and lived. The Industrial Revolution was probably the greatest revolution of all time. No continent or country could remain isolated from it for long, and no person, party, or state has been able to permanently change its outcome. According to the *Communist Manifesto*, first published in 1848, "All that is solid melts into air, all that is holy is profaned"—an indication of the awe-inspiring power of the Industrial Revolution.

But there was also great dismay over the impetuous power of a change that had produced two outcomes—seemingly limitless wealth and, close by its side, factory workers without rights who lived in bitter poverty. In his novel *Hard Times* Charles Dickens offered a vivid description of the conditions of the day: "It was a town of machinery and tall chimneys, out of which interminable serpents of smoke trailed themselves forever and ever, and never got uncoiled. It had a black canal in it, and a river that ran purple with ill-smelling dye, and vast piles of building full of windows where there was a rattling and a trembling all day long, and where the piston of the steam-engine worked monotonously up and down like the head of an elephant in a state of melancholy madness."

And yet the new cathedrals of capitalism exerted a magical pull on the masses from the countryside. There was no longer any turning back. While populations grew in villages, the advent of modern farming methods meant that fewer and fewer people were needed to farm the land. The future belonged to the cities, and within only a few decades agriculture's share of employment melted away. By 1870, 40 percent of Britons were already employed in industry.

The United States followed suit, but with some delay. More than half of the population still worked in agriculture in 1870, and only one in four Americans lived in a city with a population of at least 2,500 inhabitants. But within the next 40 years, the share of industrial workers increased to two-thirds of the total working population.

Initially, these industrial advances did not improve the social situation. As a result, trade unions and workers' parties, which were prepared to fight for the rights of their members, arose in France, England, and Germany. The imperialists in all countries were outraged. In 1905, Germany's Kaiser Wilhelm II felt that brewing domestic unrest posed a threat to his ambitious foreign policy plans. Angry "that, because of our social democrats, we cannot take a single man out of the country without exposing ourselves to external danger," he proposed solving both problems with force: "First shoot, behead and neutralize the socialists, by bloodbath if possible, and then [wage] war abroad, but not first and not hastily."

Faster, Higher, Deeper:
Capitalism in Crisis

As the nineteenth century progressed, tensions began to notably rise within the new industrial societies. Chimneys were belching smoke, human beings and machines were working in time, and the new factories were spitting out massive quantities of goods for which domestic markets were too small.

And yet the new factories kept producing like mad. The first signs began to emerge that this dress rehearsal for globalization was not destined to end well. The new system was—and to this day remains—excessive and unstable. In real life, it did not automatically arrive at the equilibrium theoreticians had hoped it would. From the beginning of the 1870s until the mid-1890s, wholesale prices in Great Britain declined by 45 percent. For the first time, the workforce was confronted with two phenomena with which we are all too familiar today: while some could expect to see their wages cut, others could look forward to unemployment.

It was the age of the bosses in industrial capitalism. Withheld wages, corporal punishment, and arbitrary firings were the order of the day. The workday lasted up to 18 hours, and only the bare outlines of what we refer to today as a social welfare state existed. Conditions were so bad that, in 1891, Pope Leo XIII had to remind the new masters of the world that they could "not treat their workers like slaves." But many ignored his admonition and did so nonetheless. The conditions were comparable to those in China and India today, where millions of simple factory workers, with no one representing their interests, are forced to work until they drop. The ruthless methods of the new system were already evident at its inception.

Industrial capitalism also appeared to possess a true system error. The growing supply of goods produced by the industrial megamachine was offset by the population's stagnating purchasing power. In other words, workers were producing more food and clothing than they could afford to buy.

There were two ways to deal with the flood of goods. The first option, never seriously considered, was to curtail industrial production. Industrial capitalism thrives on everyone's inherent yearning for more. The desire for more profit, more wages, and more affluence has remained its driving force to this day.

Because the first option was not viable, the second option came into the picture and became increasingly popular: export. By trading with others abroad, domestic producers can unload the products for which there are no buyers at home. Even if the domestic market is saturated, foreign markets can certainly be capable of absorbing more goods. Products that may seem unmarketable in one country can even develop into big sellers in another. This is especially the case when the other country is far away and a businessperson can employ different methods—and sometimes more brutal ones—to capture the market.

In the 1800s, overproduction in the economy, with all its disastrous consequences—declining wages and unemployment—led to growing tensions in the societies in question. This in turn produced unrest, especially among workers. To avoid civil war, Cecil Rhodes told the leaders of the day, they had to become imperialists. The imperialist, for his part, was busy pushing forward into foreign lands. His lust for natural resources—rubber, zinc, petroleum, coffee, tea, gold, and diamonds—was insatiable, as was his need for foreign workers, and he was determined to gain control over both. Why go to the trouble of exporting, he reasoned, when he could gain access to everything at once—goods, laws, and a police force, all bundled together in a single, convenient package? And if he was already selling goods to foreign markets, it certainly seemed more advantageous to own those markets. This was the way the imperialist thought.

At first, no one noticed the brewing disaster. To contemporaries, it seemed wholly inconceivable that 15 million Europeans could soon be lying dead on their battlefields. The assumption of power in the colonies not only comforted the souls of Europeans, it also helped fill their treasuries. Without much cost or effort, they had divided up a quarter of the globe among themselves.

Prosperity was on the rise, and world trade had reached its pinnacle, at least for the time being. A strong Europe had reached the zenith of its power and standing in the world. The dress rehearsal for globalization appeared to have been an out-and-out success. Europe found itself in a splendid and exalted position in the world.

Megalomania Takes Hold in Great Britain

The original imperialists knew no shame. They arrived on the scene as occupiers and administrators of protectorates, as promoters of their domestic economies, and as coolly calculating destroyers of anything that stood in their way. They paid little heed to cultural traditions and human life. The imperialist was an attacker out of conviction, and as such was someone who regarded pity as an expression of weak resolve. "Capitalism carries within itself war as clouds carry rain," said French socialist Jean Jaurès.

Indeed, the word *war* was on everyone's mind in those days: price war, trade war, economic war, colonial war—all conflicts that would inevitably lead to global war. Depending on the West's particular interests, the inhabitants of foreign continents could be anything from willing laborers to cannon fodder to consumers. Their land and forests served as free depositories of natural resources.

At the time, the powerful believed that seizing land as expeditiously as possible was the best way to secure and expand the influence and prosperity of their own nations. It was a truly impetuous form of world trade, and the injuries and humiliation that were inflicted as a result have survived to this day in the collective memories of entire peoples. From its inception, world trade was anything but the peaceful system of exchanging goods and services it is widely portrayed as today. Instead, it was based on an archaic system of displacement and destruction—openly admitted then and painstakingly concealed today. From the very beginning, England, a trading nation even before the start of industrialization, served as a model for other nations. The British destroyed the commercial fleets and production sites of other peoples in order to intervene in their economic cycles, a strategy at which they were highly successful at first. They murdered for a small measure of additional prosperity, and they hoped that the end result of their efforts would be visible profits in their coffers. Britain's trading and war fleets, which sailed in concert and were the world's largest at the time, served as the most important instrument in the country's efforts to promote exports.

Only when other trading nations developed powerful navies did open battles at sea fall out of fashion. From then on England sought peaceful resolutions to its conflicts with other developing industrialized nations, which were also not especially squeamish in their choices of weapons. The world's less-developed regions, on the other hand, continued to be attacked, conquered, and assimilated into the British Empire as either markets for or sources of its goods and raw materials. On the eve of World War I, the British Empire controlled about 20 percent of both the earth's habitable area and its population. Statistically speaking, this meant that every English man controlled eight other people, and that Britain controlled nearly 39 square miles of foreign territory for each square mile of its own soil. France, the second-largest colonial power of the day, could hardly compete. It controlled only about the same number of people it could claim as its own population, and about 18 times its own territory.

China: A World Empire in the Stranglehold of the West

The China of the nineteenth century was easy prey. The country was large but weak. It was rich in tradition but lacking in military technology. The Chinese emperor, Qianlong, had turned his back to the West, which turned out to be the gravest of his many mistakes. In the fall of 1793, Qianlong missed his last opportunity to come to terms peacefully with England, one of the global powers of the day. In return, the West attacked him, and his country was literally plundered alive, a piece of history most Westerners have forgotten. But it was a history the Chinese were far less willing to forget.

It began innocently enough. In September 1793 a delegation of the British crown traveled to the emperor's summer residence in Beijing, bringing along a host of attractive gifts: a German-made planetarium, a telescope, air pumps, window glass, and iron and steel products from Birmingham and Sheffield. The British wanted to trade with the Chinese, and their gifts were meant to give the man in Beijing a sampling of the sorts of novelties trade would bring. But the emperor disdainfully rejected the calling card of the modern age. "I set no value on objects strange or ingenious, and have no use for your country's manufactures," Qianlong wrote in a letter to the British king. In a completely faulty assessment of his position of power, he also wrote a sentence that the British translators, mindful of the king's frame of mind, never even translated: "We, Emperor by the grace of heaven, instruct the King of England to acknowledge our instruction."

England, faced with an unwilling China, decided to try force instead of persuasion. Using their commercial fleet, the industrious British began trading with Chinese black market merchants. Unimaginable amounts of opium—2,500 tons per season at the peak of the trade—produced in India made their way to China, and soon the Chinese people were practically anesthetized. The drug displaced the state and damaged the country's economy. Drug addicts could be seen everywhere in China's cities. Experts estimate that close to a quarter of the Chinese people were addicted to opium at the time. The British had marched in without even setting foot in the country.

When the Chinese emperor ordered his men to confiscate crates filled with drugs, war with the invisible invaders was inevitable. The British had only been waiting for an opportunity to make a move. Only then did the Chinese imperial army receive its first taste of the deadly collection of modernity produced by England's weapons factories. First came the cannons, followed by the guns. In August 1842, under the Treaty of Nanjing, China was forcibly brought into the world market.

In the coastal cities of Guangzhou, Shanghai, Xiamen, Fuzhou, and Ningbo, the British opened trade offices that, as extraterritorial regions, were not subject to Chinese law. The victors took the island of Hong Kong as their trophy. The monopoly previously enjoyed by Chinese trading companies was lifted and the opium trade was de facto legalized. In the wake of winning the war, the British continued to impose a system of "unequal contracts." Under these trade agreements, they sat on both sides on the table, eliminating tariffs and granting themselves the most favorable trading conditions. It was no surprise that Britain's war spoils served as a stimulant to the remaining colonial powers. The Europeans, nowadays the peaceful trading partners of the Chinese who like to remind Beijing of the need to respect human rights, were once far less interested in the rights of what was then a population of 400 million.

The Russians occupied Guandong, the French annexed Tonkin, and the Japanese seized the island of Formosa and pushed Korea, a Chinese vassal state until then, to become independent. The Bay of Jiaozhou, together with the port city of Qingdao, went to the German Reich, Port Arthur to the Russians, Weihaiwai to England, and the region of Guangzhou initially to the French. The struggle for control became especially heated in the port city of Shanghai, where the French and the British were once again at odds over which of the two powers was to have the say in the city.

While hardly anyone in the West remembers any of this, every Chinese student learns about these events at a young age. The West, as much as it accuses China of human rights abuses today, has committed all of the same abuses against the Chinese in the past. The country was debased, humiliated, and kept poor. For 70 years the West used one of the world's oldest civilized nations— the country where gunpowder, smallpox vaccination, paper, porcelain, silk, and the compass were invented—as a self-service shop. The standard of living in Asia, with the exception of Japan, did not improve between the beginning of the nineteenth century and the middle of the twentieth. For 150 years the continent literally stood still.

Once-proud China had become little more than a facsimile of a sovereign state. Its chants, characters, and police force were preserved, but the government in Peking was no longer in charge of its own realm. The Western poltergeist had taken over. China, which on the eve of World War I was home to a quarter of the world's population and, with its 440 million inhabitants, contained more than one and a half times as many people as Western Europe, had become a colony of the West.

Who Goes, Who Comes? A First Assessment of Globalization

The Europeans, who wanted more wealth and power, ended up getting nothing but war and destruction. From an economic standpoint, worldwide colonialism turned out to be an enormous miscalculation. Those societies in which the modern age had begun found themselves transported into a decades-long state of excitement and growth. In the end they discharged their fears of decline and dreams of hegemony in two horrendous wars.

At the start of the twentieth century, in the space of only four decades, Europe twice disappeared under mountains of rubble and corpses. The continent that had impressed the world with its inventiveness and then intimidated and dominated it in almost every respect was going up in flames. In Berlin, little was left standing at the end of 1945 but the Kaiser Wilhelm Memorial Church. Everything around it had collapsed. Even when the financial district in the City of London was rebuilt, the world financial center remained headquartered in New York, where, seeking safety, it had moved during the war.

The two great military conflicts of the twentieth century did not emerge out of thin air. Indeed, they were preceded by a global economic war that had lasted decades. The concept of a peaceful exchange of goods only existed in the pages of classic economic texts. The British produced cloth, the Portuguese made wine, and the exchange of cloth for wine would be beneficial to both—in the words of British national economist David Ricardo. It could have happened that way, but it didn't. While Karl Marx underestimated the cleverness of capitalism, Ricardo gave it too much credit.

The system that makes it possible to transform money into more money requires a well-oiled political control system. If that system is either absent or deficient, the monetary cycle and, in fact, any reasonable economy, breaks down. The intricate system of world trade overheats and explodes when questions of power push everything else aside. It is at that point that the various militaries take over, leaving businesspeople with little more than the role of financial backers of a battle of nations.

If there is one overriding mistake that was made during the history of Europe, it is that the Industrial Revolution was not followed by a revolution of political thought. The inventors and tinkerers had sped up the economic world, but the governments remained stationary. With democracy only a fledging movement, the politically powerful were able to continue playing their game, pitting nations against nations and armies against armies. The United States looked on from a distance, concerned and fearful, but also increasingly cognizant of its own budding opportunity.

There were many things that kept Europeans from peacefully coexisting. No one was adept at seeking compromise, the will to settle conflicts amicably was absent, and, most of all, there were no institutions that could have conveyed a sense of equanimity. There was no European Union or United Nations, no monetary association to speak of, nor did the idea of an International Monetary Fund (IMF) or World Bank even exist. Instead there was much whispering and rumbling, in a time when the churches had already lost their formative power and a feverish nationalism was taking shape as an ersatz religion. The pressure was rising, but there were no relief valves.

The conflicts of interests between countries had become more acute over the decades. From the beginning, rising prosperity had a twin that accompanied it every step of the way: fear. Wherever life was improving, there was constant fear that everything could be over in an instant. To this day, the craving for wealth and the fear of losing it are the two most important driving forces in modern history.

The countries of Europe had fundamentally miscalculated. The colonial policies they had pursued so fervently failed to produce lasting prosperity. The British Empire seemed exhausted. England's rapid rise from an island nation to a global power had stretched its political and economic forces beyond their capacity. The nationalist leaders of Germany rallied the people behind their cause. "We must colonize, whether we want to or not," German chancellor Prince Bernhard von Bülow told his fellow Germans. France, the second-largest colonial power, was still on the losing end of nations before the war broke out—it was unable to transform its additional land conquests into economic strength, and its relative significance shrank. Italy lagged behind, as it remained an agrarian state in which industrial production was secondary. And Russia had missed the boat altogether when it came to globalization.

After the turn of the century, the Western states were almost twice as prosperous as their Eastern neighbors. The people of the East had invented little, and even their few inventions attracted scant attention. The largely agricultural societies of Eastern Europe were certainly aware that great things were happening in the West, but they were not eager to emulate their fellow Europeans. They were spectators of and not participants in world history.

Western Europeans were able to study the contradictions of globalization early on at their own doorsteps. The nations of the world had moved closer together and had become more deeply divided at the same time. The Russians, losers in the push for modernization, would soon develop their own alternative to the West's methods—communism and its system of planned economies. Economic division had preceded political and military alienation. The later division of the continent had its roots in this economic continental drift, long before Lenin and Stalin mounted the political stage.

The False Start: Why the Dress Rehearsal for Globalization Was Doomed to Fail

The intensifying global economic war spelled decline for some, especially the British. Early on, Adam Smith noted the high costs of securing the colonies. "Our statesmen should finally realize the golden dream they and the people have dreamed, or they should awake from it," the economist called out to his nation. Smith argued that if the provinces of the British realm could not be made to contribute to the support of the Empire, Britain ought to separate itself from them. Great Britain, he said, would be well advised to revise its views and plans to reflect the actual mediocrity of its situation.

But the British crown refused to hear or see reality. It suffered from a raging colonial fever, even though its campaigns of conquest were increasingly turning into losing propositions. The victories England celebrated over other peoples were camouflaged defeats because they were accompanied by an erosion of economic power. What the British had in fact conquered, in many instances, were huge deserts, high mountain chains, impenetrable jungles, and, not to be forgotten, the millions of people across continents who could agree on one thing: that they would provide their foreign rulers with only the barest minimum of what they demanded.

For many members of the British elite, there were good reasons to prolong the colonial system. The military class lived well. The colonial masters basked in their self-importance. The shipping companies were holding their own. But this was no way to create value. Britain's departure from the world stage seems almost willful in retrospect, with each workday bringing the country a small step closer to its own pretense. Britain had frittered away its vigilance-based economy with its constant efforts to control, spy on, and conquer its colonial subjects. As a result, it lacked the necessary reserves to expand its prosperity.

Those who wanted to could already see what was happening: operating this model of globalization—the subjugation of peoples and continents for the sole purpose of exploiting them—was not profitable. The initial investment in the conquest was too high, as was the cost of subsequently securing that conquest. The productivity of the entire territory declined because the new acquisitions were motivated to do everything but work.

In the end, the British were no longer conquerors, but merely defenders. The 350 million people in the colonies were simply unwilling to subordinate themselves to 40 million Britons. There was unrest throughout the vast empire, including revolts in India. Almost every incremental gain in prestige, most of all the naming of Queen Victoria as the Empress of India, was soon paid for with a loss of stability. By the end of the 1850s, the British had to recapture one-third of their Indian territory. As rich as the British Empire was, it was beset by conflict. In London there was pompous talk of "permanent interests." But what exactly justified these interests? Who benefited from the constant fighting? So much could have been created with all this money and energy, perhaps even a more stable global power.

Meanwhile, the inventive spirit to which England owed its magical rise to prominence was increasingly going to waste. The actual core energy of capitalism, that sphere of the economy in which the groundbreaking ideas arise that are later responsible for technological advances, experienced a palpable loss of intensity. Soon everyone was depending on others. Britons at home looked to the colonies, while those in the colonies took their cue from the people back home in Britain. The Empire, with its mandated territories, protectorates, dominions, strategic bases, and settled territories, was the surest way to achieve minimal returns at an immeasurable cost. The five-year war of independence with what would become the United States cost England today's equivalent of almost 234 million pounds and ended in 1783 with the loss of its most profitable colony. The British were humiliated, but America was finally free. The United States would soon be strong enough even to outpace the motherland economically.

The British were not the least bit interested in analyzing the reasons for their failure. For them there was no pausing or even the briefest reflection. Eager to put the disgrace of American inde-

pendence behind them as quickly as possible, England's politicians, military leaders, and royal family rushed out to establish a
"Second Empire."

While expanding its territory, the global power continued to
hemorrhage ideas. The 1851 World's Fair marked both the high
point and turning point of the British Empire. The English exhi-
bitions managed to win virtually every prize at London's Crystal
Palace, a number that had declined to only 10 percent by the time
of the 1867 World's Fair in Paris. No longer did an intense fire burn
in the country's productive core as it had in earlier decades. There
was little left but inactivity in the places where bold ideas would
normally trigger the great surges of productivity in any economy.
Through the filter of history, it is easy to recognize the symptoms
of decline we continue to witness in other nations today. If the
innermost part of the productive core melts, the outer zones quickly
cool off and a shrinking process begins to take place along the edges,
rapidly transforming a once-impressive economy into a basket case.

By 1913, the British were responsible for only 14 percent of
global economic output. They had become a society in decline
that no longer had anything to serve up against the United States,
the rising economic power of the day. Indeed, the rise of the
United States and the decline of the British Empire went hand in
hand. Great Britain was no longer the worldwide "économie dom-
inante" that French economist François Perroux believed had
always existed. The United States was gradually becoming the
new "master of the universe."

The great war of nations had another consequence. At the end
of World War I, the United States was in a better position than
when the war began. In 1913, the United States was producing
about one-third of the world's industrial products. Only five years
later, after the war had turned Europe into a zone of devastation,
U.S. production had increased to more than 50 percent of the
world's industrial products. By the end of World War II, Europe
had departed from the grand world stage.

In the cold light of day, imperialism was the precursor to the
free fall of open economic systems, which resulted in a large part

of Africa, half of Europe, and large portions of Asia becoming socialist. Although old Europe could have assumed a leading global position economically at the time, it would have been impossible politically. Europe was made up of Germans, French, Britons, Dutch, and Spaniards, but what it was lacking was Europeans. The age of the steam engine had replaced the era of the stagecoach, but countries had not changed to the same extent. They had remained stagecoach nations.

As the history of Europe throughout the nineteenth and in the first half of the twentieth century shows, economic globalization alone is no guarantee of peace. Put in overly simplified terms, one could portray Europe's rise as the work of tinkerers, technicians, and politicians. But the military and politicians are to blame for its decline. The Western European empires collapsed, prosperity shrank, France and Great Britain left the global stage, and the German national state lost first its self-respect and then, for several decades, its sovereignty. The dress rehearsal for globalization had been a fundamental failure for Europeans. A former colony, of all things, would now experience its great debut—the United States of America.

CHAPTER 3

THE AMERICAN CENTURY

A FINAL APPRAISAL

The Reluctant Nation

Judging by the circumstances of the day, it would have been difficult to envision a superpower ever taking shape in North America. The motley crew that stepped off the *Mayflower* in November 1620, onto the shores of what was then a British crown colony, was not exactly of nation-building stock. Like the ensuing wave of new arrivals that would come to America on board Atlantic freighters, the first European settlers were religious fanatics, dreamers, and adventurers from England and many other European countries. A disproportionately large share of these early settlers would have been described at home as eccentrics and troublemakers, or perhaps more charitably as idealists. More stranded than landed, they were not missed at home.

They had come for the promise of free land, gold, and great fortune—the same things all people seek who leave their country with little more than the clothes on their backs and the possessions in their suitcases. They are the same things that drive Mexicans,

Russians, Serbs, Croats, Ethiopians, and Afghans today to leave behind their friends and families to give their lives new meaning in the West, or perhaps only in the nearest major city. This similarity between emigrants today and the settlers of the New World makes the differences all the more glaring. They were cosseted by fate like no other generation of settlers before or after. Their needs were so readily and abundantly met that it seems only too understandable that some still consider themselves to be a chosen people today.

The settlers had landed on one of the largest, most fertile, and climatically pleasant spots on earth, a place that offered an abundance of gold and oil to boot. Under these circumstances, it was impossible not to be industrious. When the time came, they pushed forward with industrialization at a breathtaking speed that soon left old Europe speechless.

They drove telegraph masts into the ground, laid railroad track, and invented mass production of the automobile. They used their natural and created wealth as a basis to establish not only what British historian Paul Kennedy calls a "Great Power," but in fact the greatest empire since the fall of the Roman Empire. To this day, the dollar dominates global economic activity and the American financial system sets the world standard. Like the proconsuls of the Roman Empire, the U.S. military now has its five regional commanders distributed around the globe, controlling operations in Europe, Latin America, the Middle East, the Pacific Region, and North America. Approximately 320,000 American troops are now stationed outside the United States—about the same number of people who lived in the North American colonies around 1700. They direct both humanitarian and combat missions and help with the rebuilding of failed states. And they wage war, with great matter-of-factness, against anyone who interferes with their security interests.

What is most surprising and astonishing about all this is that the United States was able to develop into a superpower in the first place. The road to global prominence and prosperity was not predestined by any means, despite persistent claims to the contrary. At first, the paths pointed in many directions, one being the brink of disaster. In fact, the conditions for a strong, unified, and enduring nation were less favorable in America than elsewhere. The first settlers had no concept of the essence of this new nation, not even as a vision.

The first settlers had left their native countries behind because they were convinced that their all-encompassing conflict with church and crown and all of Europe's other petrified institutions was too arduous and unpromising, not because they had an interest in pursuing careers at the center of a global empire.

Indeed, the arduous nature of life in the new colonies also left little room for reflection. Before the settlers lay a fertile strip of coastline, and beyond it a vast realm that could only be crossed by horse and covered wagon, at least initially. They had neither an army nor a constitution. The struggle to survive left no room for intellectual flights of fancy. Everywhere the newcomers looked, they encountered a hostile native population as it crisscrossed the land in search of food. The Native Americans' will to survive was diametrically opposed to the new arrivals' desire to claim the land for themselves. As is so often the case, the establishment of a new culture began with the destruction of an existing one.

In time, and through the War for Independence, a state had arisen as an act of self-defense and self-assertion, but it was one that had no aspirations to be a state. The settlers had unintentionally created symbols of nationhood to which they were in fact fundamentally opposed. Soon they were indulging in the sort of flag worship they had once scorned in England. They spent their time debating civil rights and liberties and discussing constitutional goals, pursuits they had shunned in the past. They became united despite a complete absence of any such intention. "If we don't stand together we will all hang alone," Benjamin Franklin is said to have told his fellow Americans.

At first the "United States of America" was not much more than a misnomer. About the only thing that united the 13 colonies was their helplessness. The war had merely concealed, not healed, the country's inner disunity. A state without a national concept, without a national people, and without a generally accepted right of taxation had been created. It was little more than a shell, lacking an innermost center of power and control.

State in an Acid Bath:
A World Power Takes Shape

Two hundred and forty years after the arrival of the first settlers, the country still lacked the three fundamental requirements it needed to become a global power. First, the United States urgently needed a stable form of government, one in which the leadership held wide-reaching authority. Secondly, the United States needed to put an end to territorialism. Only a large domestic market stretching from the West to the East Coast, from the Great Lakes to the Gulf of Mexico, could deliver the magic of big numbers. And it was only through the power of big numbers that it became possible to produce the optimal volume of goods in the dawning age of capitalism, which was to become an age of mass production. The third condition was the most difficult to create, but also the most important. Indeed, it was so important that it would become the single most decisive element. For this reason, it was a question that demanded resolution, even if by force.

It was an issue over which there could be no compromises in the long run, while any acceptance of such compromises would mean that the United States could never become a superpower: slavery had to end. This permanent bondage was morally reprehensible, and it produced endless suffering, wounds that remain open to this day. But morality was only a secondary concern. The deciding factor was that slavery was also a mistake economically and politically.

Anyone who opts for a slave state is acting both amorally *and* unwisely. The economic side of this equation was precisely the lesson to be learned from the ailing British Empire: that owning and occupying are by no means a guarantee of decent profits. If they were, why then was the British East India Company periodically broke, despite all the monopolistic rights it enjoyed in the trade between India and Britain? Why did Africa prove to be such a bottomless pit for the imperialists, despite their uninhibited exploitation of the continent's resources? Why did England's economic performance decline relative to that of other Western nations with each new overseas colony it acquired, despite the belief that colonization would bring wealth and power to large numbers of people?

There were more astute people in the United States who recognized the problem, but they were unable to solve it on their own. The North pushed for an end to an oppression, but the South refused to cooperate.

The nation had two choices: partition or war. If it chose war, it would face the most horrible of all conflicts: civil war. And yet it soon became evident that both sides wanted war. The South's war objective was to preserve the status quo, which meant rejection of any ideas that were taking shape in the North. The North's war objective was to create a nation that would be in a position to play a leading role globally. If there was no other alternative, the North was prepared to go to war to establish the necessary conditions—a strong state, a uniform domestic market, and a meritocracy based on economic efficiency. After less than 100 years of nationhood, the emigrants passed through another acid bath. The first time they had marched in as settlers and emerged as reluctant citizens. The second time around, they would abandon the volatile and divided nature of their national existence. In the end, a nation would emerge that was powerful enough to claim a spot among the top tier of nations.

America Liberates Itself

On balance, the North emerged as the clear winner of this almost four-year conflict. When it ended the slaves were more or less free—free to run for political office, start families, and establish businesses. The legal ground had officially been pulled out from under the previous business model of southern agriculture. Public schools were built, including, for the first time, schools for African American children. The United States experienced an educational explosion that agreed with the rising industrial nation. College enrollment jumped from 52,000 in 1870 to a number three times as high within only 20 years. The mentality of the southern states continued to exist, but it had been relegated to the niche of folklore. Their aim of imprinting the stamp of a slaveholder nation on the entire community had not been extinguished, but its light had dimmed considerably. America was united, though not without undergoing a considerable bout of suffering.

Because of the Civil War, the performance-based principle had prevailed against the racist exploitation state, modern industrial capitalism against the feudal system. Only after this shift had occurred were the conditions established for the United States to become a superpower. Since the landing of the *Mayflower*, America had always been a volatile entity, half state, half illusion. It was only now that the structures began to solidify. A state entity had turned into a nation, almost concurrently with Otto von Bismarck's establishment of the German Reich.

The U.S. economy was red-hot from the start. The productive core of the United States was literally fueling itself, quickly expanding in wild bursts. This energy would soon enable the country to rise politically and militarily. The eruptive growth spurts the United States experienced between 1870 and 1914 have only been replicated by post–World War II Europe and modern-day China. In this period, the gross domestic product tripled and industrial production quadrupled. The United States joined the global trade system at such breakneck speed that the British, French, and Germans could hardly believe their eyes. The value of U.S. exports increased from $500 million in 1870 to $1.5 billion in 1900, $2 billion in 1910, and almost $3 billion when World War I broke out.

This United States of America, independent of the outside and united within, became the destination of choice for all people hoping to improve their lot in life. Immigrants came because the conditions for achieving personal prosperity seemed favorable in

America. They stayed because they found work, land, and personal freedom in America. Part of the reason the productive core of the developing superpower could expand so tremendously was that new people with new ideas were constantly advancing into its interior. Their economic output stoked the country's furnace, and their desire for prosperity created, seemingly out of nothing, something that became and has remained the world's largest economy. We cannot measure the willpower that accrued within the country, but we can measure the number of people who rode the crest of its wave, the masses of humanity flowing into the United States. Between 1870 and 1890 alone, the U.S. population increased by 50 percent to 60 million. The new arrivals wasted little time before settling in the industrial zones of Pittsburgh, Detroit, and Cleveland, where they worked in the steelmaking industry and later contributed greatly to the rise of automobile production. The share of foreigners working as industrial workers jumped from about 30 percent in 1870 to 60 percent by the turn of the century. Most importantly the members of this immigrant industrial working class saved their earnings.

Their savings capital formed the investment capital of the United States, the capital that would finance its rise to become the world's biggest industrialized nation. George Westinghouse established one of the leading electrical products corporations, John D. Rockefeller developed his oil empire, Henry Ford built the world's largest automobile company, and the French immigrant family du Pont de Nemours founded a chemical giant more enormous than anything the New World had seen yet. In New York, banker John Pierpont Morgan rose to prominence as the icon of Wall Street. An exemplary economic cycle had been launched in which labor allowed capital to develop, followed by capital creating new labor.

At first the British disavowed what had happened across the Atlantic. Economically, the emigrants had handily outdone those who had stayed at home. The mother country, England, was the global power of the outgoing nineteenth century. America, the offspring, assumed the leading role after the end of World War I.

Without the war, the United States probably would not have surpassed Europe as the world's largest economy until later. By 1919, as the last traces of phosgene, mustard, and chlorine gas had barely dissipated over the trenches of World War I, the new world superpower across the Atlantic was already recognizable.

European global dominance had lasted nearly four centuries, but now a different star had emerged, one with a much larger economic base, impressive in its technological brilliance and of great political unity.

It was only the war that brought the Americans their lucky break. Perhaps they were also fortunate because they did not go into battle with great fervor. They were brutal, rough, and consistently resolute warriors, but they did not wage war for war's sake. They were driven by the thirst for more power, more prosperity, and less vulnerability, but they did not live under the delusion of having to subjugate the rest of the world. Like any nation, they accepted killing as a necessary evil of war. But this did not propel them to embark on an all-out slaughter the way the British did in India or the French did in Africa, nor did they establish murderous killing factories, as the Germans did under Hitler.

Upon closer inspection, we can see that the Americans of the day were reluctant to go to war. They waited and wavered until they had no other choice. The English had instigated the American War for Independence, and the United States had to be drawn into its two major wars overseas.

Nevertheless, America emerged from each of these armed conflicts with more power, prestige, and prosperity than before. The showdown with the British helped them gain their own nation. The wars with the Indians produced new land. Even the gruesome American civil war was ultimately good for the country, welding the state into a nation. A united America grew out of itself into a global economic power. But the ensuing three wars, which, in contrast to the three earlier wars, were waged on foreign territory, brought the country its great political momentum. What had applied in the past was now all the more applicable: each new war represented a rise in power and prominence, as the gains outweighed the losses many times over. This is by no means true of all wars. The Germans, in particular, gained nothing from the two wars they instigated, indeed losing both times. But the wars waged by the Americans paid off. While the generations that waged these wars were undoubtedly the losers, suffering enormous pain and anguish, the nation as a whole enjoyed the tremendous gains in political and economic power that have endured to this day.

America's First World War

As conflict raged in Europe, President Woodrow Wilson warned the Germans to exercise moderation. He severed diplomatic relations with Germany but could not bring himself to declare all-out war. At the end he had no other choice. Shortly after German submarines began attacking American ships, the United States intervened in the battle of the nations. The skies had long since darkened over the various segments of the front. Mobile warfare, static warfare, war of attrition—these were all part of the vocabulary of the day. With each day of the war, Europe was being transformed into a zone of desolation, one in which winners and losers had become almost indistinguishable. If there were one thing the Americans, with their fresh divisions, achieved, it was to demoralize the Germans. The Germans' strong-arm tactics seemed increasingly ridiculous, and the military's efforts to convince the civilian population to endure suddenly fell on deaf ears. After the beginning of 1917, three months before the American declaration of war, Admiral Eduard von Capelle, secretary of state of the Imperial Naval Office, told the German parliament: "The Americans will not even make it to our shores, because our submarines will sink their ships. In other words, militarily speaking the significance of an American intervention is zero, zero and zero."

In truth, however, the Americans' arrival in France proceeded without incident. Intervention signified a triple victory for the United States: militarily, politically, and economically. The Germans no longer had the strength to repel these divisions of troops who, though not hungry for war, were nevertheless deeply committed to waging war. The fate of Germany was sealed the day the Americans committed to war.

And so was the fate of the United States. Because its own territory remained completely unscathed, the United States saw its export motor go into high gear immediately after the fighting ended. War brought the Americans benefits that peace had not produced. Thanks to its destructive power, World War I created an empty space into which the U.S. economic machine could expand. By 1918 the country was producing half of all industrial goods worldwide, and its gross domestic product was equal to that of the world's 23 most affluent nations combined. Over the course of the war, the United States went from being a debtor to a creditor nation, which provided the Americans with the inestimable benefit of earning handsomely from the interest paid by other countries. Of the roughly $13 billion that other countries had borrowed from the United States, $10 billion stemmed from war bonds alone.

The United States continued to profit from its involvement for decades after the fighting ended. "We are no longer the inhabitants of a province," President Wilson told Congress. The war, he said, had made Americans "citizens of the world," which was in fact an understatement. Far from becoming a citizen of the world, the United States had indeed become its mayor.

As a result, the balance of power among the world's major nations had shifted dramatically away from the European industrialized countries. Globalization continued, but under vastly altered conditions. Global industrial production grew by 22 percent from 1913 to 1925, but Europeans were unable to claim a significant share of this increase. American industrial output, on the other hand, grew by close to 50 percent during the same period.

But the Americans were unable to enjoy the fruits of victory for long. Industrial capacity was growing more quickly than the demand for goods. The tumultuous mood of endless possibility after the war was soon followed by a deep depression, with everything that went with it: bankruptcies by the thousands, a stock market crash, and mass unemployment that was disastrous to the lower and middle classes and even afflicted the upper levels of society. Some people even began questioning the superiority of the capitalist system.

The skies darkened over America, and the lightning bolts of a looming worldwide depression illuminated a country that was ill prepared for its new role as a world power.

The mayor of the world reacted like a provincial potentate. The world's economy was global but American politicians were not. Indeed, they were barely able to see beyond the horizon of their nation-state. They reacted to overcapacity within their own country with rigorous protectionism against European exports, increasing import duties by an average of 40 percent. This barrier to foreign imports was detrimental to the world economy, especially after purchasing power at home had collapsed like a cold soufflé. Substantial losses on the stock markets led to a nosedive in consumer spending. Many had speculated on credit and were now forced to dig deeply into their pockets to pay off their debts. The balance between industry and consumers had come unhinged.

Within a few months, the world found itself in a veritable global economic war, together with all its symptoms: threats and ultimatums, new duties, quotas, and purchasing boycotts. The globalization of economies began to decline. World GDP shrank. In 1933, almost a quarter of Americans who were able to work were unemployed: close to 13 million people were on the streets.

America's GDP declined by almost half between 1929 and 1933, taking many families to the brink of poverty. People in residential neighborhoods were starving. Teachers in Chicago, who had not been paid their salaries in more than 12 months, were fainting in their classrooms. People were dying of starvation in the cities, where scenes were reminiscent of Europe in the Middle Ages. Food shipments were raided in many parts of the United States, and there were protest marches within view of the White House. An emotionally cold President Herbert Hoover sent the cavalry with drawn sabers, backed up by tanks and tear gas, to deal with the malcontents in Washington, D.C. The American success story had not come to an end, but it was abruptly interrupted.

How the United States Benefited from World War II

World War II arrived just in time for America. Renewed popular dissatisfaction with the old continent was the best thing that could have happened to the budding world power. The new U.S. president, Franklin Delano Roosevelt, was reluctant to become embroiled in another European conflict. But he did so in the end. The Americans were almost the exclusive economic and political beneficiaries of this war. They hadn't wanted it or encouraged it, and yet they profited from it more than anyone else.

Eventually, the cloud of the Great Depression had been lifted, and the economy began growing at a breathtaking pace before the United States joined the war. The scent of powder in the air only stimulated it even further. The self-doubts that the market crash and mass unemployment of the late 1920s and early 1930s had triggered were suddenly dispelled. The war in Europe triggered an initial reaction that ultimately led to the most powerful upward movement in American history. Almost overnight, the shift from a peaceful to a wartime economy led to full capacity utilization of the factories.

Before the United States officially entered the war, the economic cycle got off to such a powerful start that labor soon became scarce. More and more people were leaving their homes to work in the factories or serve in the army. Unemployment did not so much as decline as literally disappear.

Almost 19 million people, who until then had led lives outside the productive core, were now moving willingly in its direction, and their collective energy helped spur economic activity. A full 10 million people who had previously been unavailable to the labor market joined the roughly nine million unemployed who were now back in the workforce. Housewives and retirees, as well as teenagers and college students, were suddenly working for hourly wages. Economic growth was so strong that the gross domestic product, which had dropped by half at the height of the Great Depression, had already reached its former level by the end of 1940. The production of goods and services had doubled once again by the end of the war.

At the time, no one was concerned that the government was financing this recovery largely with loans. This form of borrowing against future earnings was also considered the latest and greatest in the world of economics. Anyone who didn't wish to be seen as old-fashioned supported government borrowing. The federal debt grew from only $22 billion in 1933 to $50 billion in 1940, $79 billion in 1952, $143 billion in 1943, $204 billion in 1944, and, finally, reached $260 billion by the last year of the war. Never before in history had a government of a democratic nation plunged itself into debt with so little inhibition. In the years between 1940 and 1945, the Roosevelt administration spent as much money as all administrations combined had spent in the preceding 150 years.

But it was a good investment. The U.S. engagement in World War II established the cornerstone for the United States as a global superpower, even if that fact might not have been apparent to, or the goal of, the country's leadership. By the end of the war, nearly one-fourth of all European industrial facilities had been destroyed. Only 20 percent of the German rail network was still in operation. Meanwhile, the United States had remained completely untouched. When President Roosevelt finally decided to fight, Hitler's Germany had long since lost any ability to strike back across the Atlantic.

In the end, America also suffered disproportionately fewer losses of life. For every fallen U.S. citizen, 18 Germans and 58 Russians died. The United States lost 400,000 in the war, the Soviets 23 million. On the whole, Russia bore the brunt of the war, yet in return it received only the economically less significant countries of Eastern Europe. A world power of distinction could hardly be established on the shoulders of Hungarians, Romanians, Bulgarians, Latvians, Lithuanians, Estonians, and about one-third of all Germans.

The world later treated Great Britain as a victorious nation. It was perhaps polite, but it was untrue. The British had lost the world war even before the Russians. With the unconditional surrender of Germany's Wehrmacht, both the British and the French were forced to abandon their once-dominant positions on the world stage. Their seats on the U.N. Security Council are little more than a nod to the past. It was Winston Churchill's combativeness and his country's tremendous resilience in 1940 and 1941 that stood in the way of Hitler scoring a rapid breakthrough there, thereby bridging the time until the United States entered the war. The great, gruff statesman preserved his country's freedom, but it was a freedom that came at a high price.

In return for shipments of weapons from the United States, England was forced to turn over its air and naval bases from Newfoundland to Jamaica and British Guyana to the Americans. Where the flag of the British Empire had once flown, the American Stars and Stripes fluttered in the breeze instead. By the end of the war, the British faced losses that extended well beyond their bombed-out cities. The colonial empire was unraveling, the navy was nearly decimated, the global financial center had moved from London to New York, and the national treasury was forced to make regular payments to the United States. Roosevelt heeded Churchill's pleas, but the deployment of the U.S. military was not free. The price the American president pocketed in return was nothing less than world supremacy.

Totally Global: A Country Blossoms

America was spared the war hangover some people had feared. The government masterfully managed the transition from a wartime economy to a peaceful industrial economy. The country's productive core was bolstered with a powerful dose of new workers and new capital, both of which were now available in abundance. Family income, squirreled away during the war years, was now promptly reinvested in industry. The military's roughly 10 million soldiers, most of whom had been unemployed before the war, were not just sent home, although this seemed the obvious thing to do. They also were not simply pushed in the direction of the factory gates, which was one alternative. Instead, the government proved to be visionary beyond compare. It offered each soldier job training or scholarships, so that the 10 million soldiers could be gradually—and not abruptly—brought into civilian working life. This tactic meant both a delayed reintroduction of workers and the training of millions, which would prove to be an upgrading of the labor force that was unprecedented in the world, at least at this level. On the one hand, America's productive core grew by 10 million people. But more important, the injection of more well-trained and well-educated workers meant that this core would glow far more intensively than before. The great jumps in productivity of the postwar era most likely would have been impossible without this surge in the education and training of the workforce.

On the surface, the superpower devoted its energy to the advance of American corporations, especially after the settlers' land in the West had been distributed and developed. But now the borders could be shifted to far across the Atlantic. The democracies in France, Germany, Italy, Austria, Belgium, Luxembourg, Switzerland, and Scandinavia proved to be the ideal targets for U.S. investors, whereas the postwar dictatorships in Spain and Portugal would find themselves waiting a while longer. A worldwide capital market developed, and its foremost goal was to bring the states of Western Europe into the United States' value added cycles. Sums running into the double-digit billions were sent across the Atlantic as reconstruction aid or, to be more precise, as a sort of connection fee. The Russians complained, but it did them little good. The West increased its productivity and the East its propaganda. Vyacheslav Molotov, Moscow's foreign minister, called the U.S. economic aid "imperialist," which it undoubtedly was. Its principal purpose was to serve the interests of the United States. The motto behind America's economic takeover of Western Europe had already been expressed by U.S. president Calvin Coolidge the 1920s: "The business of America is business."

By the end of World War II, the United States was a large and successful country, and yet it was not a global nation. The country still derived more than 90 percent of its income from within its borders. Foreign trade had stagnated at a low level after the world economic crisis, and foreign investment by American companies was insignificant. But in the world war against Hitler, the military had paved the way for U.S. corporations. The global field was prepared and the men and women of the business world merely had to storm down a readied path, which they did. They brought along the Ford Mustang and the dollar, they put on their rock 'n' roll records, and they had already preproduced dreams in Hollywood's film factories. German filmmaker Wim Winders would later call it the "colonization of fantasy."

The continents are still called America and Europe, but economically, politically, and culturally speaking, a new continental drift began with the end of World War II. A territory developed that without being united geographically, did in fact result in more than half a billion people sharing a similar intellectual landscape and economic operating system. An enormously attractive stateless entity had taken shape, one that we now commonly refer to as "the West." A world became apparent to all in which material prosperity and individual freedom soon became inseparable.

Once again, the destruction of the old became the basis of the new. Although Europe's claim to world supremacy had dissipated after two unsuccessful attempts, the Americans came on the scene as liberators of a continent that was unable to live in peace with itself. In virtually every facet of life, the Americans had something to offer the Europeans that proved to be an improvement over what had been there before and capable of enduring for centuries to follow. Their concepts of democracy were as welcome as their pop culture. They trained the Europeans to consistently separate powers and to pay closer attention to the provinces, and they installed the ground rules for a worldwide capitalism based on performance and competition.

It would be doing the Americans an injustice to define their march into Europe as nothing but a takeover by heartless capitalists. In truth, the second attempt at globalization was considerably more moderate than the first, for which the Europeans were solely responsible. The new, American-style capitalism was less rough-and-ready than the European version that had existed until then. Its political leadership was less megalomaniacal, and for the first time there were reliable checks and balances. The aggressive element in business and government had not disappeared, but it was less apparent.

The American people also benefited from this second round of globalization. The Americanization of Europe was undeniably accompanied by a Europization of America. This provided the impetus for the development of a social welfare state that had more to offer than soup kitchens and donated clothing. Despite having lagged behind other Western nations when it came to social services, the United States quickly caught up. From the standpoint of the less fortunate members of society, the 1950s, 1960s, and 1970s could be considered the golden years. From 1950 to 1960 alone, America's national product increased by 41 percent, adjusted for inflation. The welfare state experienced its greatest expansion to date. Whereas in 1960 monetary payments to the needy comprised only 7 percent of the national income, by 1975 this rate of social expenditure had more than doubled, with the country's economic power expanding even further in the process. If we add employers' contributions, such as pension plans and health insurance, the United States had achieved an impressive rate of social expenditure of 21 percent by 1975. This placed the country at the same level as most European nations. Even Denmark, the world's leader when it came to social benefits, which was spending 24 percent of its gross national product (GNP) on social benefits at the time, was not far ahead of the United States. Not all Americans had health insurance, but 90 percent of employees did qualify for social security benefits. Just shy of 40 percent of the working population was able to supplement their small social security pensions with employer pension funds.

During this time, a member of the American upper classes, John F. Kennedy, became a pioneer of compassionate capitalism. In his first State of the Union speech, President Kennedy painted a dim picture of the economic situation in the United States. ("Our economy has been in the doldrums for the past three and a half years, growth has been reduced for the past seven years and farm incomes have been declining for the past nine years.") What was truly remarkable, however, was not the statement itself but his response to it, diverging, as it did, so significantly from the official government response in the days of the world economic crisis.

Kennedy was not interested in promoting savings and cutbacks, nor did he appeal to the American people to tighten their belts. He wanted to use government funds to help rebuild regions hard hit by unemployment instead of leaving their fate up to market forces. He promised to "increase the buying power of the lowest-paid workers." His goal was to "bring more food to the families of the unemployed and offer assistance to their needy children." It sounded like a socially oriented policy, but what Kennedy was up to was in fact economic policy. He tried to stop economic decline by increasing the buying power of the masses. At the time, at least, it was a successful strategy.

Kennedy's words continued to ring true after his death. The minimum wage and unemployment compensation were increased, and the government-backed retirement program was enhanced. In the end, Lyndon B. Johnson, Kennedy's vice president and his successor after his assassination, continued Kennedy's legacy by introducing free hospital care for all needy Americans. Johnson told his supporters that his goal was to establish a "Great Society" that would unite all social classes. The federal government's spending on social issues almost doubled during his term in office. The country, which had had virtually no social safety net before the Great Depression, was transformed into a social state that offered its citizens legal rights instead of charity. American capitalism had acquired a heart.

This new direction for America offered impressive arguments to challenge the grim prophecies of communist propaganda. As capitalism showed its human face, the suffering of workers some had predicted failed to materialize in the West. Corporate profits and the well-being of workers were no longer a contradiction, but in fact seemed mutually dependent. The social partnership had not only eliminated conflicting interests but had also ensured that they could be satisfied. As a result, the postwar West was able to offer its citizens noticeably more than the nervous capitalism that had prevailed before World War I and between the two world wars. In the space of only a few years, Europe and the United States had been transformed into a zone of peace and prosperity.

Kennedy and Keynes: The Dream Team of the 1960s

Kennedy and Johnson were no romantics. In fact, they found themselves confronted with a situation that offered little reason for reverie. It was the early 1960s and the specter of unemployment had descended on the country once again. The economy was sputtering, incomes were stagnating, and 7 percent of the working population was unemployed. The United States lost market share in the global exchange of goods, partly as a result of Europe regaining its strength. Factory automation also contributed to rising unemployment.

To address these ills, Kennedy summoned a group of prominent academics to the White House shortly after taking office. One of them was Massachusetts Institute of Technology professor and later Nobel Prize winner Paul Samuelson, who had already helped the Roosevelt administration convert the U.S. economy into a wartime economy during World War II. Samuelson was an adherent of John Maynard Keynes, the British economist who concluded, based on the experiences of the world economic crisis, that the state must take a more active role during a crisis, a role that would involve loosening monetary constraints and injecting capital into the economic cycle.

Both Kennedy and Johnson were fascinated by the new theories. And they approached the challenge of putting theory into practice with a thoroughness that would be virtually incomprehensible today. It took government bureaucrats two years to prepare for what would then be the biggest tax reduction in the history of the Western world. The plan called for tax breaks for everyone, including corporations and individuals in the highest income brackets.

To achieve their goal of jump-starting the economy, Kennedy and Johnson had to ensure that the desire to consume was universal. In other words, there could be no exceptions for anyone. The public—and critics—were to be given no occasion to search for winners and losers of the reforms. The goal was not to fund the tax reform by siphoning off the necessary funds elsewhere, because any cutbacks in other areas would have destroyed the program's real and perceived impact. And so the government returned $14 billion, or about 2 percent of the U.S. national income at the time, to society.

The effects were impressive, just as the theory predicted. The national mood improved, consumer spending was up again, industrial corporations increased capacity, and the economy began to revive. The unemployed almost magically disappeared from the streets. But the most astonishing thing about the reform program was that it also benefited the state. Despite tax reductions, public revenue increased. It was as if citizens, to express their gratitude for the government's generous tax gift, had returned the favor with a much larger gift in the form of consumer spending.

The Democrats were thus able to bridge the slump between the Korean War and the Vietnam War. On December 31, 1965, the hero of the recovery, John Maynard Keynes, was featured on the cover of *Time*. In the cover story, Milton Friedman is quoted as saying, "We are all Keynesians now." But the quote by Friedman, not exactly a fan of Keynes, was in fact taken out of context. In reality, he said, not without irony, "In one sense, we are all Keynesians now; in another, nobody is any longer a Keynesian." He meant that Keynes's economic principles—pragmatically applied in this manner—hardly differed from his own views. Since then, tax reforms have been part of the repertoire of left-leaning and conservative politicians alike when it comes bringing the economy up to speed. Only the theoreticians continue to argue over whether such a step tends to strengthen the demand side of the equation, because it relieves the tax burden on citizens, or is more beneficial to the forces of supply, because businesses benefit to the same extent.

Something else was significant in the brief Kennedy era. During the crisis in the early 1960s, America experienced the downsides of modern globalization for the first time. Leather goods, textile, and shoe manufacturers began to feel the pressure of imports, as did U.S. farmers. The country started to become restless. There was talk in Congress of unfair trade, especially with a view toward the Europeans' activities. Kennedy was the first U.S. president to recognize a relationship between the worldwide liberalization of trade and the loss of jobs in U.S. industry. He was unquestionably in favor of free trade, reducing duties and eliminating import quotas like hardly any other president before him. But he wasn't interested in free trade at any price.

"Just as the government helped our troops to become reintegrated into society, and just as it helped convert peacetime production to wartime production and back again, it is its obligation to help everyone who suffers from trade policy," Kennedy said in January 1962. He said that he did not want to see the government telling businesses what to do, but to support those who were being squeezed out of economic life by pressure from imports. This led to the enactment of a law that promised to help reintegrate those who had been locked out. Most importantly, however, an early sensitivity developed for the other, less sunny side of free trade. Kennedy, in probably the earliest stage possible, addressed something that many in the West continue to gloss over today: globalization doesn't benefit everyone to the same degree. It also produces losers.

Kennedy was assassinated, but the issue remained relevant. Imports, which made up only 3 percent of gross national product when Kennedy was alive, increased fifteenfold by 1980, and have permanently exceeded exports since 1976. The balance of trade had shifted, and it happened in the middle of a presidential election campaign. The two major parties took up the issue. "If industries and their jobs are detrimentally affected by foreign competition, adjustment assistance should be offered," the Republicans wrote in their campaign platform. The Democrats demanded "fair trade" and promised their voters that they would work to improve the standard of living in many countries which, "as a result of low wages, attracts American capital, thereby damaging our economy." Both parties zeroed in on the Japanese and Western Europeans, who they claimed were sealing off their markets and coddling their own industries with export subsidies. Trade had become a political issue.

Under pressure from a worsening balance of trade, the government felt compelled to take political action in the early 1970s. President Richard Nixon launched a series of negotiations with the Japanese government over trade practices and the customs regime that would last for years. In August 1971, without further ado, he canceled the global currency system in place until then, which was tied to the dollar. The system, created in the turbulent postwar years to help avert fluctuations and put a stop to speculation, had worked well until then. But Nixon wanted something different. He wanted freedom for the dollar, so that he could devalue it unilaterally if necessary. His objective was twofold: to make U.S. exports cheaper and to increase export volume.

But Nixon had miscalculated. Exports became cheaper but the anticipated growth failed to materialize. Businesspeople the world over remained unimpressed by Nixon's risky maneuver. The pull of imports even intensified. The government began to publicly attack the Japanese and their rigid import laws, while the Central Intelligence Agency (CIA) warned that the American defense industry could become dependent on Japanese memory chips. But the Japanese were tenacious. They listened, nodded their heads, and promised relief, but they did nothing to achieve it. They stubbornly held on to to their import duties, which surrounded the still nascent Japanese computer and electronics industry like an invisible wall.

The Ministry of Trade and Industry (MITI) in Tokyo had set its sights on IBM and Texas Instruments, the icons of U.S. industry. Mitsubishi Electric, Fujitsu, Hitachi, and Toshiba were chosen to become global leaders, while foreign competition was kept out of the domestic market. Japanese citizens paid a high price for initially low-quality electronics, but this was precisely the purpose of the government's policy, which was tantamount to a special tax for the development of national industrial empires. The Americans were indignant, to say the least. "Without changes in foreign trade," said then U.S. secretary of the treasury George Shultz, "we can change exchange rates until hell freezes over, and we still won't get anything in return."

Washington was having trouble adjusting in a world of heightened competition. Europe was stronger, parts of Asia were coming to life economically, and the brief era of American dominance in global markets was already coming to a close.

American industry was the first to react to the changes. It withdrew from many parts of the United States, while at the same time investing heavily abroad. Capital also left the country, to Asia and Europe, where a large domestic market developed. Samuelson saw America moving in the direction of a nonindustrial "office economy" that would be tough on those unable to live on the returns of their foreign investments. The nation had stopped being the frame of reference for everyone else, Robert Reich, a Harvard economist and later secretary of labor in the Clinton administration, wrote in the early 1990s. "The government, companies and citizens," he wrote, "are no longer in the same boat."

But the winners' profits were still enough to offset the losers' losses. To this end, the social welfare state had become indispensable. Many conservatives had initially believed that it was an invention of the Democrats and could be cut back or even eliminated during the next recovery. But when economic stagnation reduced government revenues in 1967, as a presidential candidate, Nixon was opposed to government cost-cutting measures. In keeping with Keynes, as president, Nixon took countermeasures. He allowed the national budget to shoot into deficit territory, thereby reviving the flagging forces of the private sector and giving a boost to purchasing power. His term in office saw a major expansion of the social welfare state. A national system of welfare for the elderly and disabled was introduced, and Nixon increased government social security payments by more than any other president. From then on social security was indexed to inflation.

In January 1971, a confident Nixon stood before the U.S. Congress and admitted: "Now I too have become a Keynesian."

His economic advisor Herbert Stein, an academic from Chicago and avowed opponent of Keynes's theories, could hardly believe his ears. Stein later wrote that he spent days responding to letters to the president from outraged fellow Republicans. Despite the fact that he too was angered by Nixon's words, Stein felt that it was his duty to defend him. He perceived his boss's confession as an obscene display of opportunism. "Nixon," Stein wrote, "wanted to be seen as modern; he wanted to please the intellectuals and liberals."

Ronald Reagan wanted the opposite. He loved provocation and took every opportunity to be contrary. In the collective memory, Reagan has survived as the man who restrained the social welfare state. "The state is not the solution to the problem, it is our problem," he said in his inaugural address in early 1981. He promised his voters, most of whom came from the white upper and middle classes, that he would reduce social benefits, lower taxes, increase defense spending, and liberate the national budget from the debt trap. Reagan had hardly moved into the White House before he opened fire on the unions. Eleven thousand striking air traffic controllers were fired. Reagan turned them into a symbol of his resolve. His goal, ultimately, was to bring about a "conservative revolution" in both foreign and economic policy, which his supporters self-importantly dubbed "Reaganomics."

This was probably Reagan's greatest talent, one in which he surpassed all contemporaries: he could be theatrical, he knew how to be symbolic, and he was sharp and clear, or at least his words were. In truth, however, no other president so callously ignored his own ideals, at times even twisting them around completely, as Ronald Reagan. The historic image he left behind stands in occasionally outrageous contrast to actual circumstances. He was, on balance, the greatest debt maker of all time. The budget deficit grew from $74 billion before Reagan took office to $221 billion in 1986. The government's social budget was reduced here and there, and the poorest of the poor were especially hard hit. But there was no massive reduction in the American social welfare state. The rate of social expenditure, that is, the share of national income that businesses and the government spend on social costs, grew steadily during his presidency. Even the government's share did not decrease. And under his leadership annual subsidies for needy farmers were increased eightfold to about $30 billion.

And so the social welfare state even survived Reagan, mainly because it was needed. The economic machine of the United States resulted in the needy becoming ever more dependent on the social welfare state. It had to catch them, treat them, train them, and care for them, because even as the country's wealth increased, not everyone benefited. Unemployment approached 9 percent in the mid-1970s and passed the 10 percent mark in the 1980s for the first time. For many unskilled workers and the legions of the uneducated, the United States remained a country of limited opportunities. When President Johnson was inaugurated, the U.S. share of global exports of goods was still 15 percent, but by the end of the Reagan era it had dropped to only 9 percent.

The opposite effect applied to imports. Imports had increased sharply beginning in the early 1960s, and had more than tripled by 1972. At the beginning of the 1980s, the balance of trade took a nosedive into negative territory, from which it continued to drop in spurts. The source of imports was easy to identify: Asian countries, initially only Japan and the Asian Tigers, and later China. In 1995, 42 percent of U.S. imports stemmed from trade with Asian countries. Europe's share of American imports, on the other hand, stagnated for decades at just below 20 percent.

Many believed that the slow growth in exports and the dramatic rise in imports was initially only a blip in history. We now know that it marked the beginning of a shift in worldwide economic relations, a shift that is still underway. The United States was still the world's largest economy, but its dominance had been broken.

The Optimism Gene: When Strengths
Turn into Weaknesses

The strengths of the United States are also its weaknesses, which is why it makes sense to discuss them in detail. There are essentially three factors that propel the U.S. economy to success. In fact, Americans seem to have cornered the market on these three factors, and their simultaneous occurrence is what enabled the United States to acquire its globally dominant position in the first place.

First, there is no other country in the world where optimism and daring exist in such high concentrations. Americans strive for the novel more than anyone else, and not just since yesterday (like Eastern Europeans), not just for the past three decades (like the Chinese), but from the day they set foot on the shores of North America. Curiosity without trepidation is apparently embedded in the genetic code of this nation.

This resource Americans call daring is constantly renewed by the flow of immigrants who are willing to work hard. Enduring to this day, immigration has helped increase the legions of the employed by 44 million since 1980.

Second, the United States is radically global. Already the story of its origins, when the rebellious of all countries came together on the soil of the future United States, identifies Americans as children of the world. They form an elite of vitality. The American language now dominates in the world, after relegating Spanish and French to secondary status in the second half of the last century. American popular culture, including everything from the T-shirt to rock 'n' roll to e-mail, has peacefully colonized half of the world. From the very beginning, American companies expanded into other countries to engage in trade and build factories. The multinational corporation was not an American invention, but it became an American specialty.

Third, the United States is the only nation on earth that can conduct business worldwide in its own currency. The U.S. dollar became the world's method of payment. Anyone who wishes to acquire dollars must ultimately purchase them from the United

States. All major decisions on the amount of cash in circulation or prime lending rates are made within the national borders of the United States. This guarantees the country a very high degree of national independence. American monetary blood flows through the arteries of the global economy. Almost half of all business transactions are conducted in dollars; two-thirds of all currency reserves in the world are held in dollars. Even Charles de Gaulle, France's postwar president, admired this "exorbitant privilege."

But there is another side of the coin. First, American optimism is so expansive that it sometimes borders on naïveté. The cumulative indebtedness of the state, businesses, and private households exceeds all previous dimensions. Trusting blindly in a future that looks rosier than the present, millions of households borrow so heavily that they jeopardize their ability to attain this future. Savings are practically nonexistent among the lower and middle classes. At the beginning of the twenty-first century, they live from hand to mouth, like some extended poorest-of-the-poor family, without any financial cushion whatsoever.

Second, globalization strikes back. The United States has driven the global exchange of goods more than any other nation, but the result has been an erosion of its domestic industries. A number of manufacturing sectors, especially the furniture industry, entertainment electronics, many auto suppliers and, more recently, computer production have left the country. Most recently, free trade has benefited the countries that are on the offensive, enabling them to slice off a significant chunk of the U.S. global market share.

Third, not only does the U.S. dollar make the United States strong, it also makes it vulnerable. The government has been so busy pumping the dollar out into the world that the American monetary cycle can be brought to the point of collapse from abroad—from Beijing, for example. Bill Clinton called the United States–China relationship a "strategic partnership" and George W. Bush called it a "strategic rivalry." Both terms are referring to the same phenomenon. A dependency exists that obligates the two countries to cooperate—in normal times. But when times change, that same dependency leads to the temptation to engage in a show of strength.

Anyone looking at the United States at the beginning of the twenty-first century still sees a world power. But it is a world power that faces external competition and internal troubles. The repercussions of globalization are so considerable for the cosmopolitan U.S. economy that large sections of the American labor force are now standing with their backs to the wall. So far, the rise of the Asian economies has resulted in only a relative decline in the U.S. economy. But for many workers in the lower and middle classes, this decline is already absolute, because, more than anything else, they have less than they used to: less money, a lower standing, and a substantial decline in opportunities to climb back up the social ladder. They are the losers in the world war for affluence. This is their fate but not their fault. And by no means is it their business alone. Every nation, especially a society that has declared the pursuit of happiness a constitutional right, must face uncomfortable questions when an ever-growing portion of its population is cut off from society's general prosperity.

The Disintegration of the Middle Class: The New Inequality

On October 28, 1998, the U.S. Congress appointed a high-profile commission to study the effects of the trade deficit and the demise of industrial labor. At the president's request, Donald Rumsfeld, who would later become secretary of defense; Robert Zoellick, the then U.S. trade representative; Anne Krueger, later the second-in-command at the International Monetary Fund; and MIT Professor Lester Thurow produced an analysis of the situation. According to the commission's report, all was well in the world of the Americans until the end of the 1970s. In the first three decades after World War II, family incomes at all levels of society increased at close to the same rate, with a slight advantage for the nation's poor. Incomes increased by 120 percent in the bottom fifth of U.S.

society, 101 percent in the next fifth, 107 percent in the third fifth, 114 percent in the fourth fifth, and 94 percent in the top fifth. This was the American dream, expressed in numbers.

But then the trend began to shift. Japan had awakened and the global flow of trade changed direction. Capitalists ventured abroad to seek suitable investment sites. Foreign direct investment skyrocketed. Until then U.S. businesses had invested abroad primarily to promote the export of German, American, and French goods, but soon production began to be outsourced abroad. Goods destined for the global market were increasingly being produced worldwide, leading to a redistribution of capital and labor. Global production increased by more than 100 percent between 1985 and 1995. By contrast, direct investment abroad in the same period grew by almost 500 percent. Along with this migration of the production factor capital, another production factor, labor, began to become restless.

The new jobs were created elsewhere, a circumstance that could not help but affect family incomes in the United States. Within the next two decades, incomes in the bottom fifth of society declined by 1.4 percent and increased by only 6.2 percent in the second fifth, 11.1 percent in the third fifth, and 19 percent in the fourth fifth. But in the top fifth, the peak of the pyramid—home to the driving forces, prophets, and beneficiaries of globalization—incomes grew by 42 percent.

The members of the commission couldn't believe their own numbers. After all, they reasoned, family income is made up of wages, stocks, rental income, and capital gains from the sale of real estate. Those who own nothing cannot possibly earn any returns, no matter how modest. Even if wages remain constant, the fortunes of the rich and the poor automatically develop in opposite directions, because the former own securities and the latter do not. After all, any interest is better than no interest. And so the experts began analyzing wages. Who is earning how much? What is the relationship between incomes in the lower class and those in the middle and upper classes? How have wages changed over the years?

At this point, it became clear what had actually happened to their country. A wage drift had led to the partial devaluation of human labor in the lower third of the income pyramid. Until well into the 1970s, incomes rose at equal levels in all wage groups. But then, from the early to the mid-1980s, incomes declined noticeably in the lower class—by 15 percent among men. Incomes in the upper class increased by 10 percent in the same period. Then things began to go downhill in the middle class. While middle class wage levels declined beginning in 1985, incomes in the upper brackets continued to increase, starting in the mid-1990s. Not much has changed since then. Work and poverty are no longer incompatible. Those at the bottom of the wage scale have remained there, while those at the top have only improved their lot.

Portions of the former middle classes are slowly approaching the lower classes. In many cases, the affluence on display in their living rooms is nothing but a modern form of fraud. And no one should be fooled by seemingly well-to-do suburbs, where banks own many of the cars parked in garages and driveways.

The contrast with the glory days of the American economy, when the country produced prosperity for almost everyone, is in full evidence on the economy's instrument panels. Until the mid-1970s, the country's productive core was so red-hot that its glow permeated the rest of the world. The United States was exporting its dollars and goods everywhere. The core energy of the American Empire helped in the reconstruction of Europe and Japan, both devastated by war. For four decades, the United States was the world's largest net exporter and lender. Everything went the way it had been described in textbooks, as the richest nation on earth pumped money and goods into the less fortunate nations. With the energy it was able to extract from its productive core, the United States helped other countries shine or at least flicker. It was the world's undisputed center of power, from which energy flowed in all directions.

Even without military deployments, U.S. capital was at home everywhere in the world. Many perceived it as a blessing and some as a curse, but in any case it was a profitable business for America. At the peak of its economic power, the leading Western nation's net assets abroad amounted to 13 percent of its GDP. In other words, the country's productive core had grown so substantially that it possessed branches in many countries.

This indisputably superior United States no longer exists. The center of power is still more powerful than all others, but for some years now the energy has been flowing in the opposite direction. Nowadays, Asians, Latin Americans, and Europeans are partly responsible for tending to North America's productive core. The world's biggest exporter has become its biggest importer. Its principal lender is now its most important borrower. In 2006, the latest figures available, the International Investment position of the United States—the financial statement of its external assets and liabilities—reached an all-time-low. Investors overseas currently own net assets in the United States worth 20 percent of American GDP. They own 9 percent of all stocks, 17 percent of corporate bonds, and 24 percent of government bonds. The highest demand for American assets comes from China, which has doubled the amount of government bonds and corporate bonds over the three years between 2003 and 2006.

This new reality is attributable to neither the laziness of Americans nor their indisputably voracious consumerism. Instead, the fault lies with U.S. industry, or at least what little is left of it. It has declined by half in the space of only a few decades. It contributes only 17 percent to the gross domestic product, with all of the world's relevant economies now exporting goods to the United States without importing U.S. goods at the same levels. In 2007, the U.S. trade deficit with China amounted to about $260 billion. America is no longer even capable of achieving trade surpluses with less-developed economies like Ukraine and Russia. Every day ships are unloaded in U.S. ports without the equivalent in U.S. goods being loaded onto outbound ships bound for foreign ports. Many container ships simply return empty.

It is not raw materials or some imported parts that are causing this growing imbalance. Instead, it is the high-quality products of well-developed economies that are making the difference—

cars, computers, television sets, game consoles, and the like—and are being imported from everywhere, while similar products produced in the United States are no longer as successful on the global market.

The United States has even stopped making money with its proven top products. In 1989, the country earned $35 billion in revenues from high-tech products. By 2002 this figure had gone into the red, and it has only continued to decline. Since then the country imports more high-tech goods than it exports. Even if one accounts for the invisible products of a service economy— consulting and project management, installation, and repair—the trend is not reversing itself.

The global economy is not unlike a shop in which regular customers are given the right to shop on credit, at least for a time. But at some point the shopkeeper's—and the world economy's— patience runs out. Imports normally decline, which means that consumers are left high and dry. Or their currency declines, which would have the same effect. The only solution is that the customer with the constant debts must make a tremendous effort, which must be evident to all, the goal being to increase its ability to deliver. Net importers have often turned into net exporters. Postwar Germany did, and so have the Japanese and the Chinese.

But there has been no evidence so far of any such efforts in the United States: no inflation, no reductions in imports, and no concerted effort to preserve the industrial base. Americans today consume almost twice as much as Europeans, and the country purchases goods everywhere with abandon, but without supplying its own goods to the same degree. Consumer spending in 2007 accounts for more than two-thirds of the country's economic activity, a statistic as impressive as it is frightening. An artful version of reality has taken hold, in which appearance and actuality have entered into a partnership of sorts.

Politicians and economists are trying to convince the American people that they have disabled the laws of economic gravity. Businesspeople in other countries would have no other choice, they say. They would be forced to supply goods to the United

States, the world's über-consumer, if only so that they could continue to utilize their production facilities at full capacity. In their arrogance, politicians claim that consumption without production is a sign of imperial strength.

The Dollar Illusion

Let us perform a thought experiment. Let us view the U.S. dollar, no longer as a form of payment, but as a completely independent class of goods. If we equate the sale of government bonds, debt securities, and stocks with the sale of computers, Hollywood films, and steel tubes, the world for Americans suddenly seems a much more easygoing place. The overall balance of goods, services and money is, well, balanced. The Americans are no longer major sellers of industrial products. But they are unbeatable when it comes to selling the dollar.

To understand the success of this selling activity, one must be familiar with the psyche of buyers of U.S. dollars. Every financial investor is interested primarily in two things: high yields and high security. Because one can never have both, investors are by nature individuals who suffer from mood swings. Fear and greed are alternating emotions. The big investors, corporations and governments, for example, clearly prefer security. Their fear is greater than their greed. They readily forgo the biggest profits in order to ensure the durability of their billions. They fear political unrest, despise all-too-rapid currency fluctuations, and are transported into a state of panic with even the thought of gradual currency devaluation.

Given these risks, there are only a few countries that offer the greatest possible measure of relative security, chief among them the United States. This is why the dollar is not only the world's principal trade and investment currency, but also its reserve currency. Almost all nations distrust their own currency and prefer to invest the money from the vaults of their central banks in the United States, and preferably in U.S. government bonds. Political unrest is practically a nonissue in the United States. The U.S.

Federal Reserve takes active steps to combat inflation. The size of the region covered by the currency and the volume of U.S. dollars circulating worldwide prevent speculators from running amok. As a result, the world's investors use their cash to purchase vast amounts of U.S. currency.

The United States holds a virtual monopoly on security as a good. For many investors, acquiring a U.S. government bond is tantamount to preserving their assets. In 2005, only about 20 percent of currency reserves worldwide were held in euros, while about 60 percent were held in U.S. dollars. The introduction of the euro was an impressive feat and should not be downplayed. But the dollar has remained the world's anchor currency. When this anchor lies on solid ground, it signifies great stability for the economies attached to it. But if it is torn loose and begins to drift in the sea of global finance, it can cause far more turmoil than simply affecting the exchange rates of currencies.

But why are the same investors who once purchased American goods suddenly so obsessed with dollar bills? Why do they put so much faith in security as a commodity, even though it cannot be increased at will? Every student of economics learns that a country's currency is only as stable and therefore as valuable as what that country's economy has to offer. Doesn't anyone realize and sense that a tension is building between dream and reality, and that it could be discharged one day and harm millions of people?

Of course people realize this! Investors realize it. They are amazed, they shake their heads, and they even feel a shiver running down their spines. And yet, as if obsessed, they continue to buy U.S. dollars. The greater their misgivings, the more greedily do they order more dollars. What is so insane about these investors and their business practices is precisely the fact that the buyer is not merely a buyer. By purchasing security as a product, the purchaser generates more security. If the buying were to stop tomorrow, confidence would fizzle and uncertainty would grow. The dream would be over, the U.S. dollar would go into a tailspin, and the value of every dollar fortune would decline, which investors, of course, don't want to happen. In this sense, the only antidote to a weak dollar is to strengthen it.

Many investors no longer care whether or not the American currency justifies their confidence in it. The new game, treacherous for everyone involved, works exactly the other way around. The U.S. dollar earns confidence, because if it didn't, it would lose confidence. One buys it so as not to have to sell it. The dollar is strong because its strength is the only antidote to its weakness. Investors continue to dream and buy with great persistence, because this behavior in fact allows the dream to become reality, at least for a limited time.

Of course, the players in this game know full well that currencies cannot be stronger in the long term than their underlying economies. Consumption without production, import without export, growth on credit—ultimately all of these things can only exist in the hereafter, because there is no basis for their existence in real life. It was the former IMF chief economist Kenneth Rogoff, a man with a clear head and a loose tongue, who recently praised U.S. policy while in fact criticizing it. The recovery in the United States, he said, is "the best recovery money can buy."

But if the situation is so obvious, why don't investors back off? Why do foreigners and U.S. presidents of varying stripes, and even the chairmen of central banks known for their level-headedness, fall for such a risky game, one that could end up destroying everything? And why don't the mechanisms of market control take hold, precisely those mechanisms that supposedly make capitalist systems superior to planned economies?

The answer is frighteningly simple. Everyone knows how dangerous the game is, but it seems less dangerous than getting out of the game. How can they benefit from an all-too-hectic reaction? If investors begin tossing their bank notes and Treasury bonds onto the market, they will lose their money, either in small spurts or in one fell swoop. Both are outcomes they prefer to avoid, if only temporarily. Any U.S. president who so much as acknowledges the existence of the problem could very well be voted out of office because the displeasure of voters will invariably seek an outlet. The heads of central banks, despite the ones with the greatest obligation to recognize the truth, missed the opportunity to intervene long ago.

Alan Greenspan, the legendary former head of the U.S. Federal Reserve System, even took a number of steps to feed the dollar illusion. Whenever doubts loomed, he would raise the prime rate, which is also a risk premium for investors. When doubts were voiced over the sustainability of economic growth, the Great Mumbler, who was otherwise exceedingly fond of keeping the financial world in the dark, would suddenly counter those doubts with astonishing precision. "The bottom line is that the private household sector appears to be in good shape," he said in October 2004. The managers of the world financial markets worship Greenspan primarily because he had prolonged their dream for years.

His successor, Ben S. Bernanke, has had no choice but to continue along the same path. He knows that, in his position, there can be no advice without consequences. The minute he warns against a precarious situation it will have already have occurred. Even if he manages to find a gentle way of describing the situation, the financial markets will understand him all too well. Everyone is waiting for a signal of a trend reversal, one that no one wants to happen but, conversely, that no one can afford to miss.

Panic Blooming: The Phantom Successes of the United States

At this point, one could object, and justifiably so, that the financial markets are normally not at the beck and call of the political world. If this is the case, why doesn't self-regulation result in a correction of this activity? Who, or what, is preventing financial investors from taking the same approach to the U.S. dollar that was taken to the stocks of the New Economy?

It will happen, but the question is when. Financial investors are no financial officials. They love excess, and the markets drive them to overshoot the market in recurring intervals. They just happen to be speculators by trade, living with the risk of exaggeration. Their approach to their profession is not unlike that of the Formula 1 racecar driver whose goal is victory, not driving without the risk of accident.

What remains unclear is the scope of this major event, when it occurs. Experts have often envisioned the consequences of a dollar meltdown. Were the downward trend to begin, lending interest rates would rise in stages to avert the loss of value. As a result, within a few days the dollar crisis would jump from the world of currencies to the real world of factories, shops, and household budgets. With interest rates on the rise, private investments large and small would become less profitable, people would start saving, and the economy would stall and eventually begin contracting. Massive layoffs would be one of the first consequences. The government would again and again inject new stimulus packages. But at the end of the day they would no longer work. Americans would be forced to drastically reduce consumption, because the country would be shaken by unemployment and waves of bankruptcies. Millions of households would no longer be able to service their loans. At the same time, there would be a further decline in real estate and stock prices, which started several months ago. With the real estate bubble bursting, consumption would inevitably decline even further, the pull of imports would turn into a trickle, which in turn would cause problems for the countries supplying goods to the United States. By then it would be a matter of days before a long-forgotten phrase would suddenly reappear in newspaper headlines: worldwide economic crisis.

America has fallen into a deep crisis once before, and it was followed by the rest of the world. It was called the Great Depression, because it lasted 10 years and led to mass unemployment and starvation in the United States. The country lost about one-third of its economic strength. In the end, the virus of crisis raged throughout the Western world. At the height of its fever curve, six million people were unemployed in Germany. Adolf Hitler became chancellor.

Today's investors live in a dichotomy no one should envy. They see the relative weakness of the U.S. economy and recognize the tectonic shift in the global economy. They know that enormous statistical effort is expended on extending the American dream into the future. Government statisticians have long been reporting sensational production successes in the U.S. economy and yet, oddly enough, none of these successes has led to a corresponding increase in wages. This is more than unusual. Either the capital side derives the sole benefits from the fruits of rising productivity, which would be a political bombshell, even in the hub of capitalism, or these advances in productivity exist primarily in the statistics, which seems increasingly likely.

Half the world is astonished over the low unemployment figures in the United States. The other half of the world knows full well that these statistics are the result of a voluntary telephone survey. Many of those who purport to be employed are day laborers and people who survive on odd jobs. All it takes to be listed as "employed" is to have one hour of work per week. Because admitting to be unemployed is considered socially unacceptable, the U.S. government statistics are probably more instructive about the prevailing standards of American society than its actual condition. Furthermore, millions of men in their prime are disappearing from the workforce. Today, more than one of every eight men between 30 and 55 has dropped out of work. Despite their great numbers, many of them are missing from the nation's best-known statistic on unemployment. If we combine these people and the officially unemployed, the real unemployment rate of men between 30 and 55 would climb to 12.3 percent.

The supposedly high growth rates in the United States are also not necessarily a reflection of reality. They are also a consequence of high levels of borrowing among the private sector and the government. By no means are they evidence of a self-propelled increase in the production of domestic goods and services. In 2002, the national deficit alone was responsible for almost half of economic growth, and in 2005 that number had increased to 60 percent. The United States, an economic giant, is being artificially pumped up to cover up its actual decline in productivity.

For investors in the capital markets, reality only becomes reality when it has convinced the majority of investors—and when they behave accordingly. At this point, everyone is stalking everyone else. Everyone knows that the dream has come to an end, and yet everyone chooses to keep his or her eyes shut for a little while longer.

As it happens, government bonds and stocks have no objective value, at least nothing that can be seen, weighed, tasted, or eaten. Their value is determined by the blind faith of investors that the purchasing power of one million dollars will still equal one million dollars in 10 years. This blind faith is measured on the markets virtually from one second to the next, and the unit of measure is nothing but the confidence of other investors. As long as the trusting outnumber the mistrustful, all is well in the world of the dollar (and the global economy). The problems begin on the day this relationship begins to shift.

The process is complicated by the fact that it is by no means blind faith that drives investors. Indeed, hard facts appear to be what encourages them to continue to bestow their confidence on the markets. U.S. economic growth, which seems robust and impressive year after year, at least on paper, is an important key figure for investors. If growth is high, they feel confirmed in their confidence in the strength of the American economy. The trade deficit has exploded since it first emerged on the scene in the mid-1970s. And yet the economy, say the dreamers with growing self-assurance, continues to grow at a healthy clip—not as steeply as in China, but certainly twice as fast as in Europe.

But it is precisely this key figure that is not as reliable as it looks. In fact, the confidence of investors has helped produce this number in the first place. This is because the cost of a bond flows almost directly into government consumption, while the price of a stock stimulates corporate consumption and expands the credit base of millions of private households, which in turn boosts consumption. As a result, investors' expectations, including the expectation that the United States will continue to grow, are transformed into certainties. Thus the capital of confidence even spawns the growth rates it requires to justify its own legitimacy. This is because the driving force behind the growth of the American economy during the last boom period was the rise in consumption, which, given industry's shrinking ability to deliver and virtually declining income growth, should seem surprising to anyone. But everyone knows the answer to the riddle. Growing consumption was not based on more production, a sharp rise in wages, or even an increase in exports but, for the most part, on rising debt. But why did the banks keep approving new loans? They did so because they are willing to accept high stock and real estate prices as collateral. This explains how an essentially closed circuit of miraculous monetary growth has developed. The mortage crisis is only the beginning of the moment of truth.

The banks' balance sheets reveal the full extent of this self-delusion. Savings activity has come to a standstill in America. Every business day the U.S. foreign debt grows by the insane amount of about $660 million. It currently totals $2.5 trillion. Private households are now in debt, at home and abroad, to the tune of $11 trillion, and 30 percent of this debt has been established since 2003 alone. Americans are enjoying a present for which they are selling off bigger and bigger pieces of the future. It is entirely justifiable to say that the global economic crisis the world faces is the most well predicted in recent history. Far from disproving the crisis, the American boom of the first seven years of the new millennium is in fact its harbinger.

The IMF, which is responsible in part for preserving stability in the world's financial architecture, has handled the United States with kid gloves until now, doing little more than issue the occasional diplomatic reprimand or dispense advice. The IMF's largest shareholder has so far managed to protect itself against an assessment of the American financial sector. But the grace period is about to expire. At the end of 2009, when the new administration in Washington will have been in office for almost a year, a general review of the U.S. financial system is set to take place in the context of the so-called Financial Sector Assessment Program (FSAP). The audit will affect investment banks, hedge funds, mortgage companies, credit card issuers, and retail banks. In interviews with bank employees and regulators, as well as through the use of computer-aided stress tests designed to simulate worst-case scenarios, the IMF's experts will probe the U.S. financial system for hidden risks. The country's national regulatory system will also be examined—for the first time—to evaluate its stability in times of crisis.

Biologists have observed symptoms in plants that suffer from exposure to pollutants. Before they die, they produce, for one last time, such strong shoots that they are barely distinguishable from healthy members of their own species. The phenomenon is referred to in the vernacular as panic blooming.

But who will be the first to shatter the dollar illusion? Aren't all investors bound together by an invisible bond, because any attack on the lead currency would in fact reduce their own assets and perhaps even destroy them to a large extent? Why should the Japanese or Chinese central banks throw their dollars onto the market? Why would U.S. pension funds be interested in wantonly destroying their dollar riches? What would be the sense of plunging the United States into a serious crisis that could possibly take all other countries along with it?

It would be the same motivation that once turned investors into dollar buyers: fear. This time it is the fear that others might beat them to the punch, the fear that the dollar's strength is ultimately fleeting, and the fear that each day of waiting is one day too many. Finally, it's the fear that a herd mentality could take hold in the world's financial markets and of being left behind.

The U.S. dollar has become sinister to many. One morning many of its owners will wake up to take a new, crystal-clear look at the figures that describe the U.S. economy. It will not be unlike the morning when private investors woke up to take an unclouded look at the stocks of the New Economy and realized that they were looking at companies whose value could not possibly be justified by even the most astonishing jump in profits. On that day, sales forecasts had been developed that exceeded the entire market several times over. The cumulative value on the Nasdaq market for technology stocks had increased by an astonishing 1,000 percent in only a few years, while the U.S. economy had experienced nominal growth of only 25 percent in the same period.

Greed had trumped fear for a few years, but then fear returned. Within a few months technology stocks lost more than 70 percent of their value, and prices remain at less than half of former highs today. Even the Dow Jones Industrial Average, a stock index made up of some of the most important and largest companies in the United States, lost close to 40 percent of its value.

A similar fate awaits the U.S. dollar and dollar bonds. The United States has sold more security than it has to offer. Expectations have been traded that will prove to be worthless because they cannot be fulfilled. Just as the New Economy was capable of delivering neither the growth nor the profits it had predicted to investors, one day the currency traders will have to admit that the economy behind the currency is weaker than claimed.

The commission to examine the negative balance of trade appointed by former U.S. president Bill Clinton came to the clear conclusion that the government must do everything within its power to stop any further widening of imbalance between exports and imports. One of the goals was to bring the public around to finally abandoning optimism in favor of realism. Citizens were to be convinced to start saving, and the state was to gently help reduce imports so as to soften the full brunt of a hard landing.

None of this has happened. In fact, even the opposite of everything the experts recommended has happened. Debt has grown, the pull of imports has been amplified, and optimism no longer compatible with reality has become the national policy. No one will believe that an American balance-of-payments crisis is possible—until the day it happens.

CHAPTER 4

NEW RIVALS
THE ASIAN CHALLENGE

Monster Mao

China's great national "saint," Mao Zedong, really made only one contribution significant enough to survive the centuries. It was to spare the life of Deng Xiaoping, who would become an important reformer, despite all the indignities he was forced to endure at the hands of the Mao regime. Whether Mao allowed Deng to remain alive deliberately or by accident is unclear.

Twice Mao relieved Deng of his party duties, and Deng repeatedly was the object of vicious attacks in public meetings. "Boil the dog's head in hot oil," Mao's Red Guards would call out after him. Anyone who disagreed with the Great Chairman, as Mao liked to call himself, could expect all kinds of responses, but leniency was not one of them. Deng's closest associates were tortured to death, and his brother was killed. Mao's followers even chased Deng's eldest son up to the fourth floor of Beijing University and harassed him until he became so desperate that he jumped from a window. He was wheelchair-bound for the rest of his life.

But Mao left the extraordinarily intelligent and diminutive Deng (he was five feet tall) physically unharmed. He degraded and humiliated Deng, but he didn't have him killed. Mao threatened to do so many times, but he never made good on his threats. This restraint was remarkable for a man with Mao's reputation. He was renowned for his demonic rages, and was particularly brutal to his direct adversaries. He was a vicious leader who killed many of his own subjects. But Mao left his country with a successor of historic stature.

After the death of the Great Chairman in September 1976, China gained the sort of leader with which a country is rarely blessed. The delicate Deng can easily hold his own with the great men and women of world history. He created the global economic power China has become today. Without him the huge country would probably have deteriorated into the world's biggest poverty-stricken nation, and would be competing with disintegrating African countries for assistance from the world's wealthier nations. But Deng organized a political shift that was both radical and successful, and as a result, he changed the course of history like no other Chinese, a fact that many will only begin to realize in the coming decades.

China was already a huge country before Deng's time. Mao liberated it from foreign influence and reunified it, but it was only under Deng's leadership that the country began to develop into a world power. Under Deng, private initiative returned to China, and millions of China's citizens got their first taste of prosperity. By the beginning of the twenty-first century, the number of shareholders in China (66.5 million) had almost reached the number of members of the Chinese Communist Party (69.6 million).

The Great Leap Backward

One of the darkest chapters in Chinese history will prove to be the leadership of Mao Zedong. Mao, a former schoolteacher, rose to prominence as a result of a civil war, which he led with great tenacity. On October 1, 1949, Mao, then 55, appeared before a crowd waiting in Tiananmen Square in Beijing to proclaim the birth of the "People's Republic of China." Mao's southern Chinese accent identified him as a man of the provinces. "The Chinese, who constitute one-fourth of all mankind, have now risen up," he called out to the assembled masses.

These people would also have been pleased to rise up out of poverty, but economic prosperity was not in the cards under Mao. For poverty-stricken China, his almost uninterrupted rule over a quarter of a century meant even further decline, and millions of people paid for it with their lives. The true constant of the Mao era was the fact that whatever he tried, ordered, and implemented, the death toll was always high.

In January 1953, Mao instituted his first five-year plan, a plan that revealed a depth of naïveté rarely found in the leadership of such a large country. Using the Soviet system as its model, China was to invest every means at its disposal to develop heavy industry. According to the plan, China needed steel furnaces, power plants, truck factories, a chemical industry, and a national energy supply network. In another nod to the Soviet system, agriculture was to supply the funds needed to invest in this colossal undertaking. The flaw in this reasoning was that unlike the Soviets, Chinese farmers did not produce any excess crops. In fact, their harvests were barely enough to feed the population, and even then, harvests sometimes fell short of the mark.

So, despite the fact that Chinese farmers produced only one-fifth as much as the Soviets, this poverty-stricken agricultural system was supposed to provide the funding to develop the country's heavy industry. This simply meant that in order to meet the goals of China's five-year plans, millions of farmers were routinely forced to live so far below the subsistence level that their lives would ultimately be the price of fulfilling the government's plans. Mao later admitted that he had misjudged the situation. The supposedly enlightened leader summed up the problem when he said that his government had attempted to "dry out the pond in order to catch the fish."

But the real madness was yet to come. Once it became apparent that agriculture was incapable of fueling industrialization, Mao tried to forcibly industrialize agriculture itself. This is how Mao, the leader of the Chinese Communist Party, the government, and the military, envisioned that his plan would work: the farmers were to spend winters building small factories and paving roads in the countryside. Mao hoped that he could transform the underutilized labor potential of the rural population, including women, into capital. Once again, he believed in the miraculous multiplication of fish.

When his critics in the Politburo criticized his policies as a "leftist adventure," he became even more determined to succeed. China's farmers, he declared, were to prepare for the "Great Leap Forward." With the help of small power plants and small steel furnaces, Mao reasoned, farmers would be capable of building roads and bridges on their own. In May 1958, a party congress gave its seal of approval to Mao's Great Leap Forward strategy. At that time, the general secretary of the Central Committee of the Chinese Communist Party was Deng Xiaoping. During the Great Leap Forward, Deng was able to complete an apprenticeship at Mao's side. The most important lesson he learned was that nothing was working.

Accompanied by marching music, farmers throughout the country built roads and dams, attended evening courses to become steelworkers, and, at village meetings, spurred one another on by chanting fiery slogans. While the women worked in the fields, the men fed a million small blast furnaces. The party leadership reasoned that China would join the club of important, industrialized nations in a "battle for steel." According to one of the standard slogans of the day, it was "possible to overtake Great Britain in 15 years." But in reality China only declined further.

Mao's Great Leap Forward was in fact a great leap backward because every Chinese citizen was used in the wrong position. The steel the farmers produced was practically worthless. Meanwhile, harvests were shrinking because women lacked the necessary farming experience and, most of all, the strength needed to perform the heavy physical labor of farming.

The effects were astounding. Beijing's central planning committee forecast a grain harvest of 375 million tons in 1958. The real number was only 200 million tons. The next year the harvest declined even further, to 170 million tons, and in 1960 to 143 million tons, where it remained for the following year. Because party leaders stubbornly insisted that farmers deliver the amounts specified in the plan, people were caught in a deadly and vicious circle. The state demanded grain deliveries strictly according to plan. But because productivity of the soil was declining, farmers were unable to produce enough food, after delivering their allotted amounts to the government, to feed the rural population.

Starvation had returned to the villages. Cattle and pigs died of hunger or were slaughtered first, which only further aggravated the food situation. But, the Chinese state, which had imprudently guaranteed grain shipments to the Soviets, continued to relentlessly demand that farmers meet their quotas. Mao was determined not to show his failure to the Soviet leader, Nikita Khrushchev.

As a result, villagers delivered the grain to the government that they in fact needed to stay alive. Instead, they went hungry, developed malnutrition, and ultimately starved to death. Emaciated rural inhabitants were collapsing all over China—while walking to the market or working night shifts at blast furnaces or farming the fields. A mass of deaths began that was never mentioned in Chinese newspapers and initially was kept quiet in the West. According to current Western estimates, up to 40 million Chinese paid for the Great Chairman's great leap with their lives. It was the biggest manmade famine in history, and it took several years before photographs of dead farmers lying by the roadside or in their fields reached the Western public.

In an attempt to put a positive spin on the situation, Mao told the Politburo, "There are still many problems at the moment, but a radiant future lies before us." But the party was no longer interested in his rallying calls. Mao, considered a failure, was forced to withdraw from politics and for the first, brief time, economic expert Deng Xiaoping came to power. His successes gave the country, which Mao had brought to the brink of ruin, the respite it so urgently needed.

Deng, who had worked at a Renault factory in Paris in the 1920s, introduced pragmatism as a new, life-affirming virtue into the previously ideologically calcified party life. His declared goal was to strengthen the nation once again. He talked about economic growth and stability, not about equality and propagandist campaigns. He made it clear that private initiative was not just an empty phrase, but instead an indispensable and fundamental condition for strengthening the nation.

"It doesn't matter if a cat is black or white, so long as it catches mice," he told the delegates at a party convention in 1962. He was so pleased with his metaphor that he later had a painting of two cats made, one black and one white. He displayed the painting in his home.

But Mao was still alive, and he was incensed. To him, the new openness seemed arbitrary. He saw the modern methods of using performance incentives to encourage greater productivity as a betrayal of his principles. He sat in his self-imposed exile in Shanghai, watching the goings on in Beijing with growing displeasure. His detachment didn't last long. Just as suddenly as the revolutionary hero withdrew, he reemerged into public life. Almost as if nothing had happened, he attended a party convention in January 1962 and declared war on Deng and his supporters within the party leadership. The country was about to experience yet another test of its ability to withstand suffering.

Mao's return ended in triumph and with the social and political exile of his adversary. Deng Xiaoping survived, but he was forced to work as a laborer in a tractor factory. By the end of the 1960s, Mao had turned the one-party state into a military state.

Red China: An Assessment of the Damage

Mao was a talented military leader and propagandist, but a miserable custodian of the economy. He had little understanding of economics, which explains why he failed to bring prosperity to China. Of all socialist states, his was the worst.

By the end of the Mao era, roughly one-third of all Chinese were living well below the poverty line. Sickness was endemic, life expectancy was short, and hunger was ubiquitous. The situation was especially dire in the countryside, but Mao also failed to bring progress to the cities. Between the early 1950s and the mid-1970s, an urban family of four saw its living space shrink from 185 to 155 square feet.

Because China's industrial production was based primarily on the exploitation of people and raw materials, Mao sought to boost both factors. Families were required to have children, and in a campaign dubbed "War Against Nature" Mao declared environmental destruction a Chinese virtue. The results were impressive. During the Mao years, the population grew by 70 percent and destruction of the environment progressed, eating through the soil, groundwater, and forests and leaving behind ugly scars all across China. Rarely has such a powerful man so stubbornly ignored the laws of economics.

Remembering the Mao era teaches us two things. First, the Chinese are accustomed to misery. We should not underestimate their capacity for suffering. Second, they are deeply determined to put this dark past behind them. None of today's affluent Western nations can look back on such an economically difficult past. The Chinese today know that they have looked poverty in the face. This history of suffering is what fuels their burning desire to get ahead. The entire population is practically glowing with energy and ambition. China today is the world leader when it comes to a population's willingness to work hard and succeed.

Deng Xiaoping: A Small but Great Man

When Deng came back to power in 1978, the country did not know it, but it was about to be led by an exceptional politician. His background alone was impressive. A former Jesuit scholar and the son of a large landowner, he left China for Europe at the age of 16. As a student in France, he became familiar with the Western lifestyle and its ideas, but he was so disillusioned with this experience that he decided to become a communist.

After studying Marxist-Leninist theory in Moscow, he returned to China at 22 to become an underground fighter. He joined the rebels in the mountains, where he served the Red Army as its political commissioner and a commander in various battles. Deng joined the Central Committee of the Chinese Communist Party in 1945. By 1955 he was a member of the Politburo, but in the late 1960s, when Mao led his Cultural Revolution against the leadership in Beijing, Deng was stripped of all his positions. He became a persona non grata, but he reappeared six years later, when he was named deputy prime minister and was later reappointed to the Politburo. In 1975 he was made the Great Chairman's deputy once again.

This time the peaceful collaboration between these two former fellow rebels lasted only a year. Mao, who was already ailing, dropped his deputy once again. Deng was forced to flee Beijing, and it was his great fortune that Mao finally died a short time later, on September 9, 1976. Mao was mourned for a short time, but his death came as a relief for the party leadership. Deng, who was brought back into power once again, aptly called himself a "skipjack."

At an age at which many people are barely able to perform the simplest tasks anymore, Deng achieved an unparalleled feat of strength. He opened up China, long isolated from the world. For decades, foreign visitors arriving at the Beijing airport were greeted with a banner that read: "Peoples of the world unite, defeat the U.S. aggressors and all their lackeys." Shortly before Deng came to power, the Chinese defense minister had even threatened the Americans with a "people's war of the world's villages against the world's cities."

But when Deng returned, the "aggressors" were waved in, and the airport banner was taken down. From then on, Westerners were welcomed with open arms, not as friends but only as business partners. Reasonably normal relations with the United States served as the basis for development of a Chinese export industry. China rejoined the global community, and it eventually became a member of the United Nations Security Council.

Initially unnoticed by the global public, Deng put a stop to the country's decline and began a race to catch up to the rest of the world, an effort that decades later would earn China a place at the table among the world's most powerful nations. Within an extremely short time period, a state formerly based on agriculture and heavy industry became an export machine, producing textiles, computers, and automobiles for the world market. It is no exaggeration to describe the aging Deng Xiaoping as the founder of China as a global power. This tiny man managed to remain at the head of the giant country for almost 20 years, and it was not until his death on February 19, 1997, that his term in office ended.

Hardly any of his contemporaries recognized Deng, known as a reformer, for what he really was—a revolutionary. No one sensed the depth of this man's reservoir of political energy, a man who was already walking with a slight stoop by the time he came into power. The *Wall Street Journal* called him a "man without any vision whatsoever," and former U.S. secretary of state Henry Kissinger, a man rightfully respected for his judgment, saw Deng as "a tragic figure that will be unable to emerge from Mao's shadow today."

China: The New Beginning

When Deng assumed power, he went straight to work. He had a low opinion of the ideals of equality, asceticism, and the permanent class struggle. Instead, he believed in the power of egotism and the yearning for distinction. "The purpose of socialism is to make the country rich and strong," Deng said. But he could only conceive of the country's wealth as one in which the individual was also permitted to become affluent. He was not interested in a nation of paupers. "Becoming rich is glorious," he said with the clarity and straightforwardness needed to make an impression on China's one billion people. Deng wanted to change the way people thought, revitalize the egotism Mao had suppressed, and make use of the human desire for affluence and wealth. He never denied the fact that wealth would also mean inequality. In fact, he would occasionally say, "Let a few become wealthy more quickly so that they can help the others."

He also made his position clear to China's military leaders. He told them that it was impossible for the military's needs to be met at the beginning of his reconstruction period. The money to modernize or even build up the armed forces had to be earned first, which was why a powerful Red Army was an important but, at the time at least, not the overriding goal of his policies.

Deng wasn't shy about acknowledging his lack of experience with these processes of transformation. He was aware of his shortcomings. In fact, Deng was unique among Chinese political leaders in that he admitted his ignorance in public. After decades of being ruled by someone who was supposedly infallible, this revelation alone was a sensation for China. Deng had no theory of transformation and did not seek to replace it with some new utopia, nor did he even resort to utopia's cousin, vision. He was a man who felt his way forward, taking small but powerful steps. To a people who had been raised on the mother's milk of ideology he now preached the benefits of pragmatism. "No one has taken this road. This is why we must proceed with caution," he warned. He never composed a volume of his principles, because even this would have seemed too dogmatic for him. He rejected both the personality cult of his predecessor and the tendency among all previous Communist Party leaders to pose as great theoreticians. He was also against the idea, suggested by some of his fellow party members, of putting his body on public display in a mausoleum after his death. Instead, he instructed them to scatter his ashes over the ocean from an airplane.

Personal documents that were found after Deng's death reveal his unique blend of modesty and craftiness. When he instructed a leading party member to establish, for the first time, an investment company that would attract foreign capital into the country, he wrote a few simple sentences describing the principles of his policy transformation: "You will be the head of a company that will be an open window to the outside world. Do not build a bureaucratic enterprise. Accept what is rational and reject what is irrational. You will not be punished if you make mistakes. You should manage the business using economic methods and conclude agreements from a commercial perspective. Only sign your name to agreements that will bring profits and foreign currency. Otherwise do not sign."

Deng was a patriot who wanted to return his country to world leadership. He was also a good judge of human nature. Probably without ever having read Britain's national economist Adam Smith, he stressed the importance of unleashing the power of human egotism. Like Smith, Deng believed that the individual, with an inherent yearning for affluence and a unique thirst for profit and recognition, would inadvertently but methodically promote the rise of the entire nation. He gradually abandoned the instrument of central planning and granted regions, companies, and individuals more and more independence. *Responsibility* was one of his favorite words. He wanted all individuals to take responsibility for their own affairs—the farmers for their land, the managers for their factories, the mayors for their cities, and the ordinary individuals for themselves.

A look at reformers elsewhere reveals how astute Deng's policy of taking small steps was. The shock therapists in Moscow, who, under the guidance of professors like Jeffrey Sachs, suddenly abandoned the planned economy for capitalism, have the remnants of a former superpower, Russia, on their conscience. Ironically, the Russian system was launched under better conditions than the Chinese. China is a country with comparatively few natural resources, with only significant amounts of bauxite, iron, and copper ore. Russia, on the other hand, sits on a wealth of vast petroleum and significant natural gas reserves. Industry in the Soviet Union had seen better days, and yet it was still worth far more than Chinese industry. Both countries were ineffective, but the Soviet Union was an ailing industrialized nation while China was an incompetent agricultural state.

The Moscow leadership's abrupt decision to change the Russian system transferred the country's undisputed riches into the hands of a small number of people. The result was a predatory capitalism not seen since the days of the Gold Rush in the United States. Without much thought, the Russian leadership had switched its convictions and converted from communist to capitalist. Ten years after the implosion of the Soviet Union, the standard of living in Russia was still below that of the Gorbachev era.

Seen against the background of the Russian experience, Deng Xiaoping's economic development achievements have been brilliant. It is now clear, almost 30 years later, that Deng managed to find the right measure of depth and rate of reform. He challenged the Chinese without overburdening them. He downgraded party officials but did not chase them away. He put off but did not forget the military. He opened up the country, but not to everyone. Trade was liberalized, but the currency was not. Of course, we should not overlook the dark sides of Deng's policies. Private enterprise was given free rein but democracy was not allowed. Deng did not oppress his people, but he responded harshly to anyone who dared to question the role of the party. He is responsible for the 1989 Tiananmen Square massacre, when tanks were ordered to attack protesting students. Tiananmen Square is blood on Deng's hands. It will fade over the years, but it will never disappear.

One of the reasons that Westerners had so little confidence in Mao's successor is that they thought it was impossible for a market economy to function without democracy. Here in the West, we believe that democracy and the market economy are connected like Siamese twins. But perhaps capitalism and an authoritarian state are a better fit than we would like to believe. Indeed, majority rule is just as alien to the world of business as it is in China, where management is also top-down. It is not the white-collar and blue-collar workers in a company who have the power, but management. Opposition within the company can only exist until it reveals itself, at which point management quickly puts opposition in its place.

Additionally, a successor to the head of a company is also occasionally chosen according to the rules of feudal succession. Compensation systems within companies are even geared to achieve precisely the opposite of the modern social welfare state's goals. The welfare state seeks to achieve equality, whereas the corporation deliberately promotes inequality among its employees. It uses bonus systems, profit sharing, and sales commissions to encourage better performance, not to reduce inequality.

Deng utilized the rules of modern business management and set about undoing the country's past under Mao. He gradually liberated China's collectivized farmers. At first they were permitted to sell small parts of their harvests on the free market, and eventually their entire annual harvests or livestock inventories. In the end, the government even gave them back their land. In 1983, only five years after Deng's reform policies began, 98 percent of agricultural land was back in the hands of the farmers. Beginning in 1988, Chinese farmers were allowed to do as they pleased with their land. They could lease it, sell it, or leave it to their heirs.

The new autonomy worked wonders. At the beginning of the 1980s, agriculture was growing at more than 9 percent a year. For the first time in the history of the People's Republic, rural incomes increased at a faster rate than those of city dwellers.

Made possible by the cleverness and corruptibility of local party leaders, communal enterprises also experienced a resurgence that no one had expected. Mao himself had already given the local leaders the authority to manage about 700,000 smaller industrial and service companies. Their purpose was to serve the needs of agriculture, providing it with fertilizer, tractors, various types of agricultural machinery, building materials, and electricity. But it was only Deng's reform policies that turned these companies into a profitable industry. He eliminated government subsidies, but in return he did away with the government's policy of collecting the revenues of the communal businesses. From then on, local party officials produced profits for their communes—and for themselves. The communal companies served as the framework for the development of the country's first truly private enterprises, which remained government owned in name only. The owners paid protection money to local party officials, who, in return, did everything they could to provide these new businesses with access to markets. Self-interest began to stir under their protection. Capitalism—camouflaged in red—had been born.

As communal corporations developed, they began to penetrate into the core business of China's huge state-owned concerns, companies that produced consumer goods. Employment in rural small industry grew from about 30 million at the beginning of the reforms to almost 170 million in 2000. A middle class, in which private businesspeople and party officials existed side by side, had developed almost inadvertently. Everyone involved was primarily interested in profit. Private business owners took advantage of the protections offered by the state and guaranteed by party officials. To this day, this system assumes the role of the body of rules and regulations a functioning market economy needs. Anyone who finds this outrageous is certainly justified in saying that local party officials are corrupt. Put differently, however, these officials perform the multiple roles of an antitrust agency, economic development office, and court, all in one. They have breathed life into private enterprise, thereby ultimately applying pressure to the government leviathans until Beijing's planning commissioners gradually could withdraw. Chinese capitalism could not have developed without their participation.

Eventually, China's state-owned, but essentially private, companies were opened to Western investment, and the country's export business started running like clockwork. These companies produce everything from electronic toys to mobile phone accessories and engine parts, and they are now responsible for nearly 30 percent of Chinese exports.

But Deng's most monumental decision was to end the isolation Mao had imposed on China. The Chinese economic miracle was made possible only by the country's entry into the global economy. This step allowed China to tap into the tremendous amount of money circulating in world markets, money to which China had had no access in the past. The financial capital on the stock markets and direct corporate investment had bypassed China until this point. Mao, who didn't like capitalists, barricaded his country to keep them out. The capitalists didn't like China, because the fundamental goal of capitalism of turning capital into more capital was strictly forbidden there.

Deng looked for ways to connect his country to Western capital. China's export industry, which was developed from scratch, became the power plant for the new economy. Suddenly, the most successful joint venture in world history went into operation. All participants contributed what they had in abundance. The Chinese put in their labor, and the West put in its capital and purchasing power. The joint venture began with less than $7 million—the amount foreign investors invested in China in 1980. That initial investment had mushroomed to $21 billion by 1990. The sum of all foreign investment in China today is about $250 billion. The combination of Chinese labor and Western capital has produced the export machine that is now attracting so much attention in the war for wealth.

India: The Burden of the Past

The British in India were just as thorough in doing to India what the later emperors and then the communists did to China. They kept the country in an artificial coma for almost 200 years—politically, militarily, and economically. The leaders of the British Empire did a great deal to thwart industrialization. The British government, for its part, did nothing to prevent its businesspeople from pursuing their avaricious goals, nor did they have any interest in a strong India. Imperial ambition and commercial interests were combined to form an occupation regime that increasingly isolated the Indians from the rest of the world.

Economically, the Indians didn't stand a chance of making it on their own. Whenever they tried, there was always someone or something to stand in their way. The British occupiers systematically thwarted Indian efforts to make the transition from an agrarian to an industrialized society. Looking back, this was an achievement that was as impressive as it was malicious. The British forced Indian farmers to pay a high land tax, thereby preventing any significant development of capital. One needs money to make money. But money was in chronically short supply in the Indian economy. Farmers were also required to turn over 50 to 60 percent of their harvests to the authorities. Nearly half of all Indian tax revenues were sent to England.

The farmers had two additional, more powerful adversaries to contend with. The first was the monsoon, which would occasionally ruin their harvests and then inundate them in its torrential rains. The second was the British, who relentlessly insisted on their land tax, which was computed based on average values, even in years when there were no crop yields to speak of. As a result, the farmers slipped into a deep dependency on their creditors that not even hard work could alleviate. Free farmers had been turned into agricultural slaves. A feudal system had developed that made the fundamental condition for the rise of industrial capitalism—capital formation—impossible.

In Europe the English were seen as the inventors of the modern age. But in India they were its greatest obstacle. Britain, with a population at the time of roughly 30 million, prevented the 250 million Indians from even being touched by the wave of industrialization. Partly as a result of new production methods, Great Britain became a political, economic, and military giant, while India remained a dwarf dependent on arid soil and centuries-old handicraft traditions. India's per capita economic output actually declined between 1600 and 1870. Between 1870 and Indian independence on August 15, 1947, the country's per capita growth economic output increased by an average of only 0.2 percent year. The subcontinent was in fact completely disconnected from European economic growth. In the early days of industrialization, both population and per capita economic output exploded in England, Germany, France, and Italy. But in India, the gap between the mother country and the colony became wider with each year of the British occupation, until it became clear that the former was a member of the First World and the latter of the Third.

Today we know that poverty in India was not an act of God or even the product of coincidence. Indian poverty was intended by the British and was artificially prolonged, with great perseverance, into modern times. Life expectancy among ordinary Indians declined by 20 percent between 1871 and 1921.

It was obvious that the British government did not want to nurture a partner. Instead, its goal was to maintain an inventory of natural resources and labor halfway around the world and to keep the Indian population's standard of living well below that of Western civilizations. The British were intent on increasing cotton and indigo production, exploiting diamond mines, and quietly siphoning off the labor force, preferably without setting off resistance among the locals. The deeper purpose of the British colonial adventure was to make more money than was invested. The vast estates in faraway Asia were meant to produce healthy profits without imposing a burden on taxpayers at home.

The strategy worked, at least initially. London used the taxes collected from Indian farmers and merchants to pay for its officials and soldiers stationed on the subcontinent, and even managed to reserve a respectable take for the British national budget. The Queen was right when she called her Indian estates the "crown jewel" of the British Empire.

In close to 200 years of British occupation, India remained what it had been before, an economic midget, rich only in culture and tradition.

When the British granted their crown colony independence in August 1947, the country they left behind was closer to the Middle Ages than the industrial age. Industrial production made up only 3 percent of India's total economic output, and less than 2 percent of the Indian workforce worked in factories. Millions of people remained hungry, sick, and uneducated under British reign. The Western world had extracted itself from the stranglehold of epidemics and wrenching poverty, but India had not. The average life expectancy was 32 years, and almost 90 percent of

Shelton State Libraries
Shelton State Community College

the population was illiterate. Famines continued to plague the country at irregular intervals, killing millions. The British Crown left behind a society with many scars, including a scar on its soul.

The Colonial Complex: India's Fear of Selling Out

The Indians had hardly gained their independence before they turned their backs on the West. They were determined that the country would never again be dependent on its former tormentors, nor would they ever allow the West to establish itself on the subcontinent. Western capital was seen as a threat, and the free market economy, based, as it were, on the freedom of business owners, as a system of oppression. Even trade relations with Europeans and Americans were frowned upon.

For the Indians, Western values reeked of blood. To them, the fact that civil societies invoked values like freedom, equality, and camaraderie was the height of hypocrisy. Concepts like freedom of opinion and the inviolability of the human being, and his or her living environment, health, and dignity seemed to the Indians like little more than the latest Western propaganda trick—and one that was easy to see through. Indians were so suspicious because they had had direct experience with precisely the opposite of these sentiments. For them, the West stood for bondage and inequality, and for powers that sometimes punished their challengers with death.

During the rule of the British Empire, a slightly built Indian lawyer named Mahatma Gandhi made a name for himself. He referred to London society as "satanic" and called upon his fellow Indians to engage in nonviolent resistance. As the concept of freedom surged through the country, Gandhi hurried from province to province to awaken the spirit of resistance and force it politically into his direction, that of nonviolent resistance. He visited indigo farmers, and he stood by striking textile workers as they demanded higher wages and better working conditions.

Gandhi told the British to "quit India," which they eventually did. But first they divided the huge territory into two parts. The southern portion of British India became today's India, which adopted a democratic, nonreligious constitution, in which discrimination on the basis of religion, race, gender, and caste was outlawed. In the northern portion, the Islamic state of Pakistan had a constitution that required that "no law may stand in contradiction to the requirements and teachings of Islam."

Pakistan has not embarked on the path to prosperity to this day. India, for its part, set out on a decades-long, energy-consuming detour. Just when it had entered its hour of freedom, the country threw itself into the arms of Stalin's Soviet Union. The lost years of the British occupation were to be followed by several more decades of decline. India may have gained its independence, but it didn't know what to do with it. On the day after celebrating its independence, the new country's leaders stood there like a group of just-released prisoners in front of the prison gates. India was free but empty inside. The Indians loved their freedom, but whether this newfound freedom would respond in kind was uncertain. They wanted progress but were not entirely sure where to find it.

This desire afforded the Soviet Union the perfect opportunity to present itself as India's great protector and mentor. It was with great delight that the communists greeted India's new premier, Jawaharlal Nehru, in Delhi. He had studied in England and was as enamored of aristocratic life as he was fond of democracy. But since the days of his youth, Nehru was also fascinated by socialism. He rejected Stalin's brutal repression, but he was attracted to Stalin's methods of economic planning. The scion of an aristocratic family from Kashmir, Nehru believed that the command economy was vastly superior to the market economy.

For Nehru, the men in the Kremlin were in many ways the inverse of India's negative image of the British. They were leftists and, at least according to their rhetoric, were antiimperialistic and anticapitalist. Nehru, along with many Indians, believed that he could safely trust the Soviets.

When India's first five-year plan came into effect in 1951, it brought gray, prefabricated Soviet-style apartment towers and a new disregard for the natural environment. In the ensuing Indian industrial age, the environment was no longer just a source of raw materials, but was also used as a free garbage dump. A labyrinthine bureaucracy developed, and its apathetic stance toward the country's problems was to become perhaps the most serious legacy of the era. In 2002, about 50,000 cases had been pending before India's higher courts for more than 10 years, a number that jumped to one million when it came to the lower courts. One trial that ended in 1990 lasted 33 years and became increasingly complicated as 16 witnesses died in the interim.

India had chosen a third path, one that ran between capitalism and communism. This path soon proved to be a dead end. The subcontinent had listened to the wrong teachers.

But the Soviets were pleased, so much so that they no longer left the Indians' side. The country became the most important recipient of Moscow's economic aid and military assistance. The Indians and the Soviets had become both trading partners and brothers in arms. When China parted ways with the Moscow leadership in the early 1960s, India clung all the more tightly to the Kremlin's rulers. At least the Indians could depend on the men in Moscow. India would not have been able to build its first nuclear weapons without Soviet help. Its friends at the Kremlin also helped explore India's oil reserves.

For their part, the Indians were fiercely protective of their new partners. Even the Red Army's invasion of Afghanistan was incapable of pulling the Indians out of Moscow's shadow. Former U.S. president Richard Nixon was impressed. Prime Minister Indira Gandhi, Nixon told friends, was apparently even more unscrupulous than he was.

The Wakeup Call: How Gorbachev Turned the Indians into Reformers

India has no less a person that former Russian president Mikhail Gorbachev to thank for its second liberation. With his policies of glasnost and perestroika, Gorbachev dealt a deathblow to the ailing Soviet influence and gave new life to India. It was only the loss of its ally and mentor that gave India the latitude it needed to act and, more importantly, think. The Indian elites were forced to pull themselves together and take stock of their situation. Suddenly they noticed something they had disavowed until then: the technical foundation of their own economy was even more decrepit than that of the Soviets. The Indian economy, which was virtually sealed off from the world market, lacked the necessary capital for investment.

The government sector had tripled in size from 1960 to 1990, and its inefficiency had grown just as quickly. Many of the 240 corporations controlled by the central government were companies designed to create jobs that would remain forever irrelevant in competitive international markets. But even that had gone unnoticed until 1990, because the Indian leadership had nurtured its colonial complex for decades and had been uninterested in the global division of labor. The importing and exporting business was frowned upon as a relic of the British occupation. Foreign trade was seen as a particularly malicious tool of domination, to be shunned if at all possible.

As a result, the Indians did their best to keep out international capital. At their peak, import duties amounted to more than 300 percent of the value of imported goods. Neighboring China was already attracting investors while India continued to discourage foreign investment. The leaders in Delhi had different aspirations than their counterparts in Beijing. The Chinese dreamed in dollars, while the magic words in India were still holdovers from the Soviet era: planning, control, and self-reliance.

It wasn't that the Indians failed to see the disadvantages of their eccentricities. The downsides were obvious, but they were accepted. Many members of the Indian establishment had carved out a comfortable niche in the midst of the country's crowded economic circumstances, a niche that, to them at least, guaranteed an easy life because it was free of surprises and required little exertion. Tensions were low. Everything went according to plan, especially their careers, while the impoverishment of the masses continued. In 1974, the Indian parliament held a debate over hunger that shone a glaring light on the agonies of life in India. Those who had died of starvation were quickly buried so that their bones could later be unearthed to make soup, one member of parliament reported. B. Sudhakar Shenoy, a professor of economics and former member of the government's planning committee and Indian delegate to the IMF and the World Bank, was deeply critical of his own government. "We are not even a developing country," said Shenoy. "We are a society, an economy in decline."

After four decades of experimentation, it was clear that the instruments of India's planning bureaucracy were incapable of turning it into an economic power. Even the country's achievements seemed by no means secure. The Indians sensed that an era was coming to an end. They turned their attention to China, which they had become accustomed to viewing as an enemy, not as a country worth emulating. Long-neglected questions were now asked. Why could China do what India could not? Why was the Central Committee of the Chinese Communist Party trumpeting its victories while India teetered on the brink of bankruptcy? Why was the West so interested in China? Why was the U.S. president, Richard Nixon, in such a hurry to travel to Beijing and not Delhi? Where was all the wealth in China's coastal cities coming from, and why were the Chinese elite, and not just the establishment, suddenly driving Western cars while Indians negotiated their way across bumpy roads in aging Hindustan Ambassadors or even on oxcarts or bicycles?

The Southeast Asian countries had also rushed ahead of India. Skyscrapers and state-of-the-art industrial complexes were built in Singapore and Taiwan. South Korea's economic strength was less than one-fourth that of the Indians in the early 1950s. Forty years later, its per capita income was already six times higher. More than four decades after its independence celebrations and almost 15 years after China's first free market reforms under Deng Xiaoping, India finally came to life. The man responsible for the change in attitude was someone whose political career had in fact already ended.

Rao the Reformer: A Retiree Turns Up the Heat

At age 70, Narasimha Rao could look back on a fulfilling career in the second tier of Indian politics. He had worked as a translator and spoke a dozen languages. He had even tried his hand at poetry. Finally, Prime Minister Indira Gandhi appointed Rao general secretary of the Congress Party and later to the positions of both foreign and interior minister. The most remarkable thing about Rao was his unobtrusiveness. As his mistress's loyal servant, Rao remained in the shadow of the great Indira Gandhi, who returned the favor by treating him poorly and sometimes even roughly. But Rao was also an extremely patient man and not one to revolt or speak out. He had been raised in the Indian caste system, which assigned a specific role to each member of society. He was married, in a marriage arranged by his parents, at the age of 10.

In 1989, after the assassination of Indira Gandhi and the election defeat of her son, Rajiv Gandhi, Rao left the government. He was old and sick, and he was being called a political has-been behind his back. He was a vegetarian and opposed to alcohol consumption, but his healthy lifestyle did little to prevent him from having heart disease. After undergoing open-heart surgery in Houston, Texas, Rao finally retired, determined to complete a literary work he had begun while in office.

But, another murder got in the way of Rao's plans. Rajiv Gandhi, who had assumed the leadership of what was then the opposition Congress Party, fell victim to an assassination himself. His mother was shot in her own garden, by her own bodyguards. Rajiv was killed in a bombing attack at a campaign rally. After overcoming its momentary shock, the Congress Party nominated the retired Rao to the position of prime minister. Rao, a man of few words, offered three advantages for the position: he was old, he was presentable, and he was considered unassertive. The party had initially intended Rao to be nothing but a transitional candidate, a man who, in the eyes of younger politicians, fulfilled the most important of all criteria: he would not stand in their way.

But fate had chosen a different and far more important role for Rao than merely to serve as a puppet prime minister. After winning the election, Rao decided to attempt in India what Mikhail Gorbachev in Moscow and Deng Xiaoping in Beijing had begun. India's circumstances left him with no other choice than to push for the long overdue and repeatedly delayed reform of India's economic system.

Rao could no longer expect anything from the Soviet Union—neither assistance nor opposition. The former ally fell to its knees before the eyes of the global public. In the end, its last Communist president said a few sentences about democracy, the transparency of a society, and economic transformation. One of them went like this: "The new way of thinking, as the Soviet Union understands it, is based on the realities of this century."

But the realities were faster than Gorbachev. They overtook him and threw him to the ground. Gorbachev was forced to look on as the Soviet Union, which he had hoped to save and guide into a new era, slipped out of his hands. He wanted everything at once, both democracy and a free market economy, but he got none of it. During the traditional May Day parade in 1990, the crowds booed and catcalled the Soviet leadership for the first time.

India was even worse off economically than its big brother. Its $70 billion in foreign debt made India the third world's third-largest debtor nation, next to Mexico and Brazil. Its hard currency reserves were barely sufficient to cover the cost of imports for the space of two weeks. Seeking help, the government turned to the West. But Western bankers could only shake their heads. The Indians had long since lost the one quality that a debtor nation needs to survive: financial standing. By the summer of 1991, India's international insolvency was imminent.

Even the Washington-based IMF was only willing to provide emergency funding under the strictest of conditions. There are many ways a country can lose its sovereignty. Having a weak economy is one of them. In June 1991, roughly 20 tons of gold were removed from safes at the Indian Central Bank and flown to Switzerland. This was the condition under which the IMF was willing to provide emergency financial assistance. The proud Indian nation was forced to lay its treasures on the counter as if it were in a pawnshop. The country's future alone was no longer seen as sufficient collateral. A truly complicated situation had developed. India had lost its connections in the North and exhausted its goodwill in the West. It was as if the positive and negative poles of two power cables had come into contact for several seconds. The initial spark for an Indian reform policy had been created, but no one was able to get away from it.

To continue along its current path would probably have been more draining for India than turning back. As a politician of the old order, the complacent Rao was essentially the wrong man for the massive reform project. But he was the wrong man at the right time and in the right place. In the end, Rao's reform policies went well beyond the IMF's requirements.

Perhaps all he had to do was release the bureaucratic brakes with which his predecessors had slowed down the economy. He reduced import and export duties to expand trade with other countries once again. He eliminated the licensing system, which had applied to almost every class of goods, triggering domestic competition on the basis of price and quality. He attracted foreign capital with tax rebates instead of scaring it away with duties. The first state-owned companies were auctioned off in an initial stab at privatization. The Indian rupee has been more or less freely convertible since 1993, allowing foreign companies to take home their earnings from India.

Two men with international standing helped Rao bring about his reforms. Finance Minister Manmohan Singh had studied economics in Oxford and Cambridge. Minister of Trade Palaniappan Chidambaram came from a leading family of industrialists that had sent him to Harvard. Both men were eager to rejuvenate their country. They wanted to bring India closer to the West politically and integrate it into the world economy, step by step, without overtaxing domestic industry, if possible. Rao promised his compatriots "change without trauma." His finance minister added that there would be no Indian shock therapy. And yet, Chidambaram told his fellow Indians, many things would have to change: "I saw how meddlesome, oppressive and inefficient the state had become, how it was suffocating entrepreneurial spirit, killing every idea and giving back nothing in return."

To all those who feared that they were "selling out India," the trio responded with a policy of many subtleties. Their greatest achievement lay in the perseverance with which they pursued the goal of reform. Their changes, which made deep inroads into the lives of the population, were not an overnight success. The majority of Indians are devout Hindus and therefore more likely to be tolerant than short-tempered. They believe in fate, and many even submit to it.

But now a rumbling had begun within the population. Higher ticket prices had hardly been announced before crowds were throwing rocks at trains. The roughly 200,000 employees of the customs offices became agitated when they realized that their jobs were becoming less important. In June 1992, a general strike was staged to protest Rao's reform policies.

But Rao did what he had always done—he remained resolute. He presented straightforward and simple arguments, and he seemed only moderately impressed by his vocal critics, even though they had penetrated deeply into his own Congress Party and were out to destroy his political life. "The reforms cannot be turned back," he repeatedly told the Indian public. In a nationwide radio address, Rao announced that he planned to "tear apart the spider webs getting in the way of rapid industrialization." His finance minister quoted the great French author Victor Hugo when he said: "There is nothing more powerful than an idea whose time has come."

In many respects, the Indian reformers proved to be more astute than the men in the Kremlin. Rao and Singh never forgot to mention everything that would remain untouched by their reforms. They acknowledged the yearning of human beings for traditions, even though this was not particularly glamorous and was all but ignored internationally. While Gorbachev whipped up his fellow Russians to the applause of the West, Rao and Singh sought to appease and calm the Indian public.

As it turned out, luck was with the gentle reformers. Foreign investors became interested and began knocking on India's door. Many Indians also became enthusiastic once the country's permit-oriented bureaucracy had given them more breathing room. Industrial growth rose to a peak of 12 percent during the five-year creative period of the Rao administration. India managed for the first time to generate a stronger economic dynamic than the Asian Tiger states. According to predictions by investment bankers at Goldman Sachs, by 2050 India will be the world's third-largest producer of affluence, behind China and the United States and ahead of the European Union.

A clear acknowledgment of inequality—and a lack of simul-taneity—was critical to the success of India's reforms. Based on the example set by Singapore, Taiwan, and China, special eco-nomic zones—that is, small productive cores—were established and carefully nurtured by the state. The slums remained, and to this day smoldering fires cause heavy pollution during the sum-mer in many places. The doubly cursed slums are inundated with mud in the winter, but in the special economic zones capitalists from all over the world are spoiled beyond compare.

Now, India has large numbers of workers who are well trained in the technological fields. The government also does a great deal to ensure a steady flow of new blood. In the Bangalore region alone there are 3 universities, 14 engineering schools, and 47 spe-cialty schools and research institutes. More than 400,000 new engineers enter the job market each year, half of them trained in computer engineering. Western corporate executives privately, and irreverently, say that "brain shopping" is what attracts them to India. Hardly anywhere else in the world is a freshly trained engineer's brain available for as little money as in India. Not sur-prisingly, the conversion rate is simple: 10 Indian software devel-opers can be had for as much as 1 in San Francisco.

By far the country's most important natural resource lies in the brains of its still-young population. The Indians are experts in the development and use of software. They help American tax accountants, operate call centers for half the world, and develop software for global corporations like Siemens, General Electric, Samsung, and Nokia. India's exports of software and IT services more than tripled from $4 billion in 2000 to $12 billion in 2005. While today's China is the world's factory, India is setting up a global service center. The governmental leaders of both countries recently met and agreed to closer cooperation, which is, most of all, an indicator of one thing: they take each other seriously.

The Chinese still come out on top in a performance comparison between the two giant countries. Deng's reform policies, begun in the late 1970s, gave the country a significant head start. The Chinese highway network is 60 times larger, the country has 6 times as many Internet connections, and, in 2005, China received 10 times as much foreign direct investment as India. Both countries have doubled their export rates relative to their national products, but Chinese goods already make up 6.5 percent of world trade, compared with India's 0.8 percent share.

India looks to its industrious neighbor to the East with envy and admiration, especially given the determination with which the Chinese worked their way out of the misery of the Mao years. China, in turn, looks with amazement and alarm to India, where the leaders are attempting, in a single bold step, to take the country from an agrarian state directly into the world of the modern service industry. Compared with the West, the two giant Asian countries are conspicuous for their enthusiastic, larger-than-life growth. China's communist-controlled economy has grown by 300 percent since 1990, while the Indian economy has added 130 percent. By comparison, the U.S. economy grew by just under 60 percent in the same period.

As the economy grows, so does India's self-confidence. In June 2003, the Indian government wrote a letter to all Western governments requesting that they discontinue all bilateral development aid when the current projects come to an end. At the annual World Economic Forum in Davos, Switzerland, it was the Indian government that distributed gifts to the wealthy. All attendees found a cashmere shawl and an Apple MP3 player waiting for them in their rooms. It was a clear message from the Indian government to the West: people of the world, look at this country. The days of need are gone, and now India is throwing away its crutches and walking on its own.

But history has not been kind to Rao. After his five-year term in office, Rao's Congress Party lost the elections. Rao lost his reputation a short time later when he became embroiled in a corruption trial that lasted years. On October 12, 2000, he was sentenced to three years' probation in a verdict reached on scant evidence. He was accused of having paid off members of parliament and government officials in a bid to hold on to power, principally to secure his position and his reform policies. Rao died in a hospital in Delhi four years after his conviction. He was 83.

The Attacker Nations: Asia Rumbles

Today's up-and-coming global powers are already significantly more impressive than the Soviet Union ever was. Their recipe for success is based on the productivity of people, not on the propaganda of party officials. Millions of people are working, saving, and creating capital, the fuel that will propel them to global power. The most important productive energy of these populations is nothing more and nothing less than their determination to add a new, more radiant chapter to their histories.

Their politicians are not only supporting them but are in fact spurring them on. Instead of struggling with symbols and final communiqués with the devotion of Soviet leaders, they pay all the more attention to the share of wealth allotted to the populations they govern. The results of this collective endeavor are unmistakable. Those who were once underprivileged and underdeveloped are rising up before our eyes. Millions of yesterday's poor are suddenly flexing their muscles. We are looking into the eyes of an adversary that has made the ambitious and indisputable resolution to no longer live at the lower end of the world's scale of affluence.

An entire continent, which many erroneously considered less than capable of performing, is rising up with the expectation of becoming the West's equal. Since 1970, the region's entire econ-omy, excluding Japan, has grown more than sixfold. Growth rates have been steep for decades, and all the fears of Western indus-trialized nations—fears which were in fact hopes—that social unrest or environmental decline would slow the region's rapid growth have not materialized.

The West can either treat the Asians as competitors or con-tinue to refer to them as developing nations. It would be more honest to see them for what they are also: attacker states. The Chinese, the Indians, and most other Asians have made signifi-cant gains in the war for wealth. What began in Japan, then jumped to the city-states of Singapore and Hong Kong and finally reached the tiger states, South Korea and Taiwan, has transformed the continent into an economic zone with a tremendous concen-tration of energy. Each of these countries has embarked on a road to wealth that will change the world's political, economic, and, ultimately, military architecture.

The populations reaching for the stars in Asia are, for the most part, extraordinarily large. If its efforts to develop continue more or less without interruption, China will replace the United States as the world's biggest economic superpower within the next 35 years. India will be close behind. Almost two and a half billion people, more than five times the population of Europe, are attempting to turn their histories in a positive direction.

Unlike the Soviet Union, the Asians' secret is that they are launching their attack from the opposite corner. The Soviets tried to embroil the West in an ideological conflict, while the Asians are attacking with economic weapons and avoiding ideological conflict. They do not conduct debates with the West over equal-ity and justice, nor do they level any accusations or issue threats. The rising global powers are not interested in a battle of cultures. They are ignoring issues of religion and ideology. They are quiet adversaries who are placing their bets on economic efficiency. The West, they reason, can be defeated with its own weapons.

While the Soviet Union was a loudmouth among nations, the representatives of today's ascending major powers prefer modesty.

Moscow's communists were quick to portray their interim economic successes as final victories. In contrast, the Chinese and the Indians would rather keep the world guessing when it comes to their true strength. According to Chinese statistics, the Chinese economy was the world's seventh largest in 2004. But if we add together the figures for China's 31 provinces, which are readily available, we discover that the country's true economic strength was significantly greater. Shortly before the beginning of 2006, the National Office of Statistics in Beijing decided to adjust its numbers upward. The director of the agency claimed that the figures it had published previously were too low. Now China sees itself in sixth place, ahead of Italy and behind the United States, Japan, France, Great Britain, and Germany. Western intelligence agencies assume that China continues to publish official growth figures that are lower than actual figures—so as not to cause alarm in the United States.

Requiem for the Soviet Union

The rise of India and China is accompanied by the relative decline of the West. Americans and Western Europeans are still richer and more powerful than any of their rivals. For this reason, distinguishing between attacker states and declining states does not describe the status quo, but the rate at which and direction in which the distinctions are being overcome.

The ascending states, after having escaped a dark past, are storming ahead at an impressive rate. In many cases, young people in these countries are even prepared to break with the ideological and cultural traditions of their parents' generation.

Using a simple cost-benefit comparison, the South Koreans, Chinese, Indians, and, before them, the Japanese have made a clean break with the previous realities of their lives. Anything that has stood in the way of acquiring wealth has been jettisoned: agrarian societies that still bear traces of the Middle Ages, the planned economy, the ideology of equality, the party's control over factories and traditional lifestyles, and so on. Religious sentiments have endured, but in muted form.

Far Eastern spirituality has been privatized wherever it once shaped daily public life. The overriding goal of the leaders is to change the status quo to their benefit. The state acts as the center of energy, not the society as a whole. This is why we refer to these nations as attacker states, because their governments and parties are the standard bearers of an economic transformation that has only reached portions of their societies.

The declining societies, on the other hand, would be happy to extend the current reality a short while longer. They are fighting, but only to preserve yesterday's achievements.

In the face of their Asian challengers, the self-confidence of Western populations, especially among ordinary people, has suffered noticeably. Westerners seek comfort in looking back at days gone by. It is not, as the left claims, the total marketization of life that weighs so heavily on people. In fact, it is the end of this marketization and the beginning of marginalization, their growing exclusion from the value-added cycle, that worries people. Millions are ceasing to be economically valuable and financially useful to the state. Many have the feeling that America still needs them as consumers but no longer as workers.

Both the attacker state and the declining society are reflections of each other. The dream of the former is the nightmare of the latter. The established economic powers feel irritated by the self-confidence of the rising stars and threatened by their ascent. The great hopes of the attacker states stand face to face with the equally great fears of the declining societies. Both are perfectly aware that they live in a relative world. The attacker states are breathing down the necks of the declining societies, which are already scared because they lack the confidence to even attempt to achieve the high-growth rates of their early years.

Laying the blame at the feet of the current generation of politicians would seem the obvious thing to do. Portraying them as powerless, without vision, and unsuccessful has come into vogue. This criticism is as cheap as it is wrong. In a democracy, there can be no policies against the people, nor can there be any policies that extend far beyond the people. Attempts to redirect society all too forcefully are perceived as a breach of the peace. Nowhere in the West does a government possess the legitimacy to fundamentally transform the state and economy. Many voters' expectations of a return to the past cannot be fulfilled, not even when it is the majority voicing these expectations.

The attacker states are no longer poverty stricken, but they are also not truly wealthy. Their populations are young and ambitious, and the elite and the middle classes, at least, have turned to the future with great decisiveness. Laptops and mobile phones are the most sought-after accessories of their time. The attacker states are determined to slice off a bigger piece of the world's wealth for themselves. To do so, they are prepared to perform extraordinary feats of strength, and they do not shy away from the necessary unscrupulousness that has always been the mark of the climber.

The Western industrialized nations are not disappearing into obscurity, but their importance is waning. The United States and Europe are losing jobs that cannot be replaced with jobs in the new service economy. The political and cultural dominance of the West is being increasingly questioned, just as the amount of territory it controls militarily has been shrinking. The Americans are no longer occupiers in Europe, but only partners. In Asia they are principally tolerated. Western nations are fighting a losing battle almost everywhere in the Arab world.

Economic strength is not a guarantee but a condition of the ability to become a world power. All other forms of superiority, including military and political, are derived from economic strength. Even the gesture of moral superiority can only acquire true weight if the economic behind it is flourishing.

Many in the West will soon remember the Soviet Union with nostalgia. The communist superpower, which vanished almost silently from the face of world history in the early 1990s, was always an appreciative adversary. The rulers at the Kremlin were occasionally moody and loud, but they were not hunters. In fact, they embarked on no more than a few regional military campaigns in Hungary, Czechoslovakia, and Afghanistan. Lenin was the hard-hearted architect of the empire, while Stalin was its only true despot. The men who followed sought a balance with the West. They were more fond of vodka than of conflict.

The system struggled economically from its inception. The planned economy, which was most reliable when plans were ignored, couldn't keep pace with the free market economy. The socialist state also proved to be a poor cousin of the Western welfare state, and its most salient feature was its boastfulness. The so-called people's democracy proved to be a dictatorship of bureaucrats, displaying its greatest vitality whenever it was time to spy on and lock up its critics.

The West began to like this feeble adversary. The countries east of the Iron Curtain posed a threat until the very end, but they were no longer a challenge to the West. The competition between systems was decided before it was won. The cold war survived on both sides of the line of demarcation as little more than a ritual, until Mikhail Gorbachev finally put an end to this game in a mercifully straightforward way.

The Soviet Union died quietly, leaving Russia behind as a wounded state. We will still be hearing from this great loser of the last century, which has yet to find peace. There are rumblings in the country, and no early warning system on earth is capable of measuring whether, and when, these rumblings will lead to tensions on the surface. Russia remains a source of unrest, but the country is unlikely to reemerge as a global power in our lifetimes, although it does stand a chance of remaining a top player as an energy superpower.

The decline of the Soviet empire and Asia's simultaneous ascent were only noticed after these events had occurred. No one saw the Soviet collapse coming, at least not at first. No one heard the Asians coming. And even when both were happening at the same time, very few understood the relationships between the two. The West dreamed of a peace that was long in coming. Men like Francis Fukuyama, then the deputy chief of the State Department's policy planning staff, were quick to declare their political dreams a reality: "What we may be witnessing is not just the end of the cold war, or the passing of a particular period of postwar history, but the end of history as such; that is, the end point of mankind's ideological evolution and the universalization of Western liberal democracy as the final form of human government."

But precisely the opposite was happening at the same time. A new chapter in history had begun. A sleeping giant had been awakened. Since then, Asia, far from Western liberal democracy, has set about rewriting world history. No one knows whether the rising Asian powers will manage to advance into the top echelon of nations, and at what price to others. But to anyone capable of seeing and perceiving, it is obvious that Asia is rumbling. History goes on. The departure of one superpower is accompanied by the rise of another. Asia is in the process of ending its more than 500-year cycle of backwardness and poverty. The Asian century is not ahead of us. We are already in it.

The growing strength and influence of Asian factories and universities may change America more than the cold war ever did. The cold war united the country, bringing together citizens of widely diverging backgrounds behind a common cause. Faced with the communist threat, the great adversaries of any Western economy, the capitalist and the worker, came closer together than Karl Marx could ever have imagined.

After World War II, all countries on this side of the Iron Curtain rose up out of the ashes like phoenixes, with their new friend across the Atlantic blowing powerfully underneath their wings. People saw themselves as Americans, Italians, Britons, or French, but most of all they considered themselves the winners of history, a self-image that lasted several decades. They pitied the peoples of the southern hemisphere, who were trying to escape slums, floods, and corrupt dictators to at least save their hides. It seemed to be a law of nature that no other zone of prosperity could exist outside the established industrialized nations. Billions of people, essentially the entire portion of the population fit for work in China, the Soviet Union, Bulgaria, Romania, Hungary, East Germany, Yugoslavia, and India were virtually nonexistent as competitors in the product markets or participants in the labor markets. They lived and worked, but in another galaxy that was foreign to us.

Whenever the talk turned to these populations, people would lower their eyes and express their compassion, which often masked their inability to comprehend the foreign and crude life, a life full of political constraint that lived on the other side of the earth. One of the reasons everything was the way it should be in the world of the West was that life elsewhere was not. Westerners perceived their lives to be whole because those of others were so obviously broken. Now the Western world is broken itself.

CHAPTER 5

THE FLAT WORLD IS BROKEN

Shanghai Salutes Detroit: The Emergence of a Global Labor Market

C apitalists go where they expect the highest return on their investment. The specifics of what they do are irrelevant. They can build a factory under palm trees or drill for oil in Siberia. For capitalists, the only important thing is that they have more money at the end of their ventures than they did at the beginning. Whether we like it or not, the most important objective of capital is growth. If the opposite were the case, that is, if capital started to shrink, no one would benefit, not even workers. When capital shrinks, layoffs are never far behind. Soon the word *mismanagement* starts appearing in the *Wall Street Journal*, quickly followed by words like *crisis*, *restructuring*, and *unemployment*.

In the end, the staying power of jobs consistently depends on a surprisingly simple question: Is it possible to turn capital into more capital? Does the initial investment grow or does it fade away? No capitalists are fond of watching their investment shrink from one day to the next. If it does, unexpectedly, they soon cease to be capitalists.

Workers enjoy a better reputation, even though they are as disloyal as the capitalists. If they are given free rein to travel and settle wherever they please, they will automatically go where they are most likely to find high pay and a secure standard of living. Southern Italians migrate to the north of their beautiful country, Germans from east to west, and people from Latin America to North America. Indeed, millions of people are prepared to traverse oceans and continents, if only to bring themselves closer to what they perceive to be a promised land.

The great injustice in this equation is that capital is welcome almost everywhere, while foreign workers are not. All kinds of tricks and schemes are employed worldwide to attract investment, but most countries fear migrating workers and often slam the immigration door in their faces. Some even bring in the military to defend their homeland against the perceived threat of migratory workers. Governments worldwide are determined to stop, or at least limit, the global migration of workers.

The fear of uncontrolled movement of labor exists in every political and economic system. The communists were afraid that their workers would emigrate, and so they built a wall and fences straight across Germany. Europe is concerned about an influx of migrating workers and keeps a tight watch on its southern borders—toward Africa. The United States only issues visas to foreigners who can be of use to American citizens—specialists, students, scientists, and people with enough capital to run a business. Others are caught at the United States–Mexico border like flies on a glue strip. Europe, the United States, and the countries of the former Soviet bloc have been successful at controlling their borders, albeit in different ways, and in so doing have demonstrated that it is possible to control the immigration and emigration of people. Anyone who is willing to order his soldiers to shoot at his own people will manage to keep his people together for some time.

Labor and capital differ in another important way. Capital and the capitalist form a unit. One cannot exist without the other. It is as if they were joined at the hip. Countries that have used nationalization as a means of separating capital from its private owners have deeply regretted it and learned the most important principle of economics first hand: if capital is separated from capitalists, it soon starts to disintegrate. The capitalist has no purpose without capital, nor does capital make much sense without the capitalist. It becomes eroded, melts away, and ultimately evaporates like a drop of water on a hot griddle.

François Mitterand had hardly been voted into office as France's first socialist president when he began to make good on a daring campaign promise. He had told voters that he planned to make a "break with capitalism"—which was precisely what transpired. In the early 1980s, the French government nationalized the country's major banks and 13 of its leading industrial corporations. But the change did not sit well with the companies. Profits shrank, and the public became alarmed when the first reports of losses began rolling in. In a cabinet meeting an agitated minister of finance Jacques Delors told Mitterand: "All you talk about is lending money. If we end up in International Monetary Fund receivership, you will lay the blame at my feet."

Sure enough, the new state-owned companies soon began losing money, prompting international investors to withdraw their investments from France. The franc became subject to speculative attacks on the financial markets. The government, whose solvency was already being called into question, managed to obtain an emergency loan from Saudi Arabia to fend off speculators. How humiliating for the Grande Nation! The magic of Mitterand's socialist experiment had quickly gone up in smoke. Mitterand himself initiated measures to bring the country back on course, beginning with the reprivatization of state-owned enterprises. "The state must be capable of restraint," said the newly enlightened president. The experiment and would-be debacle ultimately had a happy end—because capital and the capitalist were reunited.

Eastern Europe's planned economies, unwilling to take this step, were headed for a slow demise. Companies remained state owned until they were little more than shells. Karl Marx and

Friedrich Engels make no mention of the essence of capital: that capital and the capitalist are as inseparable as a tree and its bark.

Jobs and workers were at a disadvantage from the start because they did not enjoy the same symbiotic relationship. The movements of workers back and forth across national boundaries can be interrupted. But border guards are incapable of preserving their country's jobs. The fact that the countries of the West managed to keep their labor markets by and large closed to outsiders seems to be the true miracle of the postwar years. The nations of the world traded all sorts of goods, exporting and importing bananas and television sets, gasoline and steel plates, and money also traveled freely across borders. But there was still no exporting or importing of workers and jobs. The word *offshoring* had not been coined.

There is a simple explanation for the prolonged, peaceful coexistence of workers and jobs: the labor markets in Europe and America were not significantly different. Businesses on the two sides of the Atlantic were competitors, not rivals. They paid wages but not charity. Children were allowed to remain children, not forced to serve as cheap labor. The Western world was a generally uniform world. Everyone had the same values—freedom, democracy, gender and racial equality, private ownership, unfettered trade unions, and much more—and everyone played by the same rules. The experts spoke of a "level playing field." We call it a "flat world."

Eastern Europe's communist leaders had no place on the West's playing field. They exchanged goods and raw materials with the West, but they stayed away from its labor and capital markets. They created their own playing field, the complex and ineffective contract system common to all planned economies. The third world also lived on a different planet. Its powerlessness and the fact that the West was interested primarily in its natural resources ensured that it would remain excluded from the process we now call globalization. Western capital made a wide berth around the galaxies of the poor, treating third world countries as a source of raw materials but not investing in them. This explains why there was little incentive for jobs to migrate away from the West.

All of this has changed fundamentally. The flat world is broken, at least for workers. Their playing field is out of whack, and millions of people have embarked on a downward trajectory. The peaceful coexistence between jobs and workers has come to an end. The old order no longer exists, but a new one has yet to take its place. Capitalists can use this lack of a cohesive world order on the labor markets to their benefit. They tour the most remote spots on earth with the declared intention of setting up shop there. Their factories pop up everywhere, and jobs follow without hesitation.

In 1980, the sum of all direct investment, that is, the funds a country invests outside its own borders, amounted to only $500 billion. Old-school capitalists tended to be stay-at-home investors.

Their successors are frequent flyers with bonus cards. Direct investment has jumped to $10 trillion, an increase of close to 2,000 percent in only 25 years. Capitalists and their capital have become flexible, in many cases even restless, and they expect jobs to be equally prepared to travel. Modern capitalists are both at home and strangers everywhere in the world. No longer inclined to be patriots, they now call themselves "global players."

The jobs have followed the capitalists as they have invested around the world. They leave the West and pop up elsewhere. They surface in an Indian software company, or we encounter them in a Hungarian toy factory or a Chinese engine assembly plant.

An outrageous—and largely unanticipated—state of affairs has developed. A global labor market has evolved that expands every day, palpably changing the lives and work of billions of people. People who don't know one another and, in some cases, are not even aware of the existence of one another's countries are now linked by an invisible system of conduits. Asia, America, and Europe have moved closer together and now form a global market for anything that can be traded. Financial experts pump capital through the economic cycle, businesspeople ship their products around the world, and billions of ordinary people suddenly find themselves face to face on the global job market.

This is what distinguishes today's globalization from that of the early trading nations, the colonial empires, and the industrial capitalism of the mid-nineteenth century. For the first time in history, an economic system has taken shape that encompasses all production factors, without exception. Nowadays, capital, raw materials, and human labor are traded the way silver and silk were in the past.

The difference is that a wide range of conditions prevails in different parts of the current system. Some places are hot, some cold, some densely populated, some not, and even individual systems encompass the most varied of worlds. The rough and brutal rules of the early capitalism of the 1930s still apply in some places, while the practices of the modern age prevail in others. Never before has the world of workers been so fragmented as it is today. Their former flat world had become skewed and slippery.

Many of the things we once believed were firmly entrenched have come unhinged. The power and wealth of nations are being redistributed, as are the opportunities available to the individual. Everyone sees the same world, but sometimes from vastly different perspectives.

The new arrivals on the global labor market approach life with optimism and high hopes for the future. Many of them are now able to bring home more than paltry wages for the first time. For them the worldwide labor market holds previously unheard-of promise. And for them the end of poverty is no longer a dream but a realistic prospect.

But the new era comes with a different lesson for millions of American workers, which explains why the optimism of the country's early years has all but dissipated. Many will be eliminated from the working world altogether in the coming recessions. Even where Western employees will presumably be able to hold on to their jobs, they are forced to look on as their wages decline, not abruptly, but bit by bit, year after year. Social contracts that were once seen as a certainty are losing their validity. An unprecedented level of uncertainty is taking hold in the lives of many ordinary people. Some lose their sense of stability while others lose their bearings altogether.

The world is by no means at the end of this development, but in fact it is at its beginning. "Globalization is expanding along the

entire value-added chain, even when it comes to the once sacro-
sanct jobs of white collar employees," say people like Stephen S.
Roach, chief economist at Morgan Stanley. Many of Roach's fellow investment bankers still insist on calling this a win-win situation, an outlook that seems nothing short of a parody of reality.

For both the attackers and defenders of the status quo, the
emergence of a global labor market is a process of historic proportions, a process that becomes all too obvious when one considers the unusually large numbers of people it now encompasses.
In the 1970s, nearly 90 million workers from Hong Kong,
Malaysia, Singapore, Japan, and Taiwan became part of an economic system that until then had been reserved almost exclusively
for Western Europeans, Canadians, and Americans. The Asian
Tigers were greeted with great surprise and the Japanese with the
deep respect they deserved. Michael Crichton's novel *Rising Sun*
was a wake-up call for Americans—and rightfully so. But the new
arrivals on the global labor market were merely the advance guard
of what was to become a new, modern age.

The Chinese followed on their heels a short time later, and with
the demise of the Soviet Union, the world labor market was suddenly confronted with a veritable tidal wave of Eastern European
and Indian workers. Within a period of time that would amount
to barely a blip in history, 3 billion additional people and therefore 1.5 billion new workers joined the world's labor force and
helped bring about an unprecedented shift in the balance of
power. The West's 350 million well-trained but costly workers,
who until then had been responsible for a large segment of world
production, became a minority almost overnight.

Clyde Prestowitz, founder and president of the Washington-
based Economic Strategy Institute, speaks of three billion new
capitalists, but this seems to be a misunderstanding. He has it
wrong. A vast group of people who were everything but capitalists appeared on the global stage: workers, who have always been
the counterparts to capitalists. If three billion new capitalists were
to suddenly descend upon the world, profits would decline and
cash would be overabundant. The American capitalist could then

be called the loser of modern times. Of course, astronomical investment returns can only be achieved if capital is scarce in the first place.

So, it's exactly the other way round: the expansion of the labor supply to include 1.5 billion new workers—essentially the injection of a large group of people with no capital into the world economy—was in fact most harmful to simple, unskilled laborers, whose livelihoods depended solely on their ability to work and not their capital. The traditional workers are the losers, while the traditional capitalists gain as much as never before in history.

Today Brazil, Russia, India, and China combine to provide more than 45 percent of the world's labor supply, compared with 19 percent for the entire area covered by the Organization for Economic Co-operation and Development (OECD), a forum where the governments of 30 democracies work together to address the challenges of globalization. But the question is, have workers in advanced economies become increasingly vulnerable to the impact of globalization? In its Employment Outlook 2007, the OECD reports:

> *Foreign competition—especially, imports from non-OECD countries—tends to reduce employment in the most exposed industries. . . . Offshoring changes the skill structure of labour demand by reducing the demand for low-skilled workers. This suggest that some of the workers displaced by offshoring lack the qualifications required to move into the new jobs being created in the same industry. By raising skill demand, offshoring also contributes to the trend increase in earnings inequality observed in most OECD countries.*

This expansion of the global labor supply alone would be more than impressive, if that were the extent of it. What's more, high birth rates in the emerging nations mean a constantly growing supply of new people eager to join the global labor market, which translates into 80 million births each year, most of them in Asia. That continent's population is expected to grow from 4 billion today to about 5.2 billion by 2050. These people will want work, no matter what the cost. The economic machinery must constantly produce new jobs, if only to keep these burgeoning masses of people reasonably fed, clothed, and housed.

Despite the fact that no new countries have been added to the world labor market, it has grown by an additional 400 million people within the last decade. According to the Geneva-based United Nations International Labor Organization (ILO), another 200 million people are eager to work but unable to find even the lowest paying of jobs. They are unemployed, which makes them workers in waiting.

Many of these people have never held down a normal, full-time job. They eke out a living as day laborers and pickpockets and live in slums. For obvious reasons, they are only too pleased to leave this miserable existence behind by joining the global labor market. They seek out factories, warehouses, and major construction sites, accounting for growth in worldwide labor potential of 200,000 laborers a day since the early 1990s.

An expansion in the labor supply of this magnitude is unprecedented in history. This expansion of the labor supply far outpaces the demand for workers. In its 2007 Economic Outlook, the IMF calculates that the number of available workers on the global labor market has quadrupled since 1980. This explosion in the labor supply has led to a decline in the value of human labor. Labor becomes cheaper or, in some cases, even worthless. The bottom segment of Western labor markets is now subject to what is in essence a hyperinflation not unlike that which descended on the world's financial markets in the wake of Black Friday in October 1929, when overnight the U.S. stock market started its meltdown.

As was the case in the ensuing world economic crisis, this new form of hyperinflation forcibly wrenches ordinary people from their once well-ordered lives. Money retains its value, but people lose their jobs or must make do with lower wages than before. The social net to which they are accustomed vanishes and, to make matters worse, they lose their dignity and their sense of self-worth. The root cause of labor inflation is economic, but its effects penetrate deep into the cultural, social, and political fabric of America.

Nobody today has a true grasp of the full extent of devaluation of the American workforce. It has the potential to divide the country more than ever before. The new frontier runs not between North and South, black and white, men and women, but between those who derive profit from today's globalization and those whom globalization harms. All Americans are still swimming in the same pond. But some are sharks and others sardines. It's not fun being a sardine in an ocean full of sharks.

Businesses, on the other hand, can hardly believe their good fortune, with governments treating them like visiting dignitaries while their old rivals—workers—will do almost anything to survive. Companies have never had such a lavish selection of willing and cheap workers at their disposal. They are courted wherever they go. Meanwhile, workers in the West find themselves surrounded by the desperate masses struggling to become part of the global labor market—their new rivals in a battle for economic survival.

The Market's Iron Fist: Lower Wages or No Wages at All

Prices on the world's stock exchanges flicker across computer screens at banks and brokerage trading floors. American, Asian, and European quotations are adjusted within minutes, sometimes even seconds. If wages in various countries were displayed on giant screens installed in prime locations throughout the country—on Times Square in New York or in front of the White House in Washington—many would be surprised at what they would see.

The same price adjustments take place in the global labor market, but in slow motion. The addition of billions of new potential workers has set a process in motion that will soon radically change the central foundations of Western societies, as both the wages and the standard of living of unskilled workers approach a common denominator.

Wages are rising in Eastern Europe and Southeast Asia and declining in the West. About half of the roughly three billion people currently active on the global labor market earn less than $3 a day. This means, of course, that these people are dirt-poor, but also that their poverty-level wages are pulling down the wages of everyone else. In other words, those at the lowest level of the wage scale are fatefully linked to those in the middle.

One of the greatest mistakes we make today is to believe that the millions of migrant workers in China and the employees at Ford and General Motors in Detroit have nothing in common. But this impression is misleading. We separate the two in our minds because the workers in China have probably never heard of Detroit as a center of automobile production, while the latter have only a vague notion of what it means to be a migrant worker hanging around in Shanghai. Nevertheless, their biographies are inextricably linked.

The migrant worker from Shanghai, who comes from the Chinese countryside and now lives in a hut and works, without any legal safeguards whatsoever, for a supplier to a Chinese automobile plant, competes with the full-time but unskilled employee at this Chinese plant. The two workers are fully aware of each other's wages, because the migrant worker has a burning desire to take away the full-time factory worker's job. Local companies are constantly tempted to play off the two groups against each other. And, whether they like it or not, the migrant worker and the full-time factory worker are locked in a bitter competition for wages.

The unskilled factory worker, of course, does his best to escape this wage competition. His goal is to be promoted to at least a skilled worker position in the Chinese auto plant. To achieve his goal he is willing to do almost anything: work overtime, attend training courses, and accept low wages. The migrant laborer is to the unskilled factory worker what he, in turn, is to the skilled worker: a fierce rival. The unskilled worker is willing to accept even the lowest entry-level pay to rise through the ranks, especially in China, where there are no trade unions willing or able to fight for the rights of individuals.

Once the unskilled worker has ascended the factory ladder and has a few years of experience under his belt, he in turn becomes a rival to an autoworker in Detroit. The two have never met, and yet they are intricately linked. U.S. automakers Ford, Chrysler, and General Motors keep computer records documenting the wages and performance of the two competing groups: skilled workers in the United States and those in countries like China. Their statistics appear on the same page. They encounter each other as numbers. The force this interdependent relationship exerts on the global labor market is nothing less than the market's iron fist, and it remains unrelenting until a balance is achieved.

The differences in wage levels are not determined by living conditions, even though an apartment in Detroit is substantially more expensive than one in Calcutta. Instead, the key factor is the "relative scarcity" of what an individual has to offer the world. If that individual is an exceptional phenomenon like Bill Gates or Yahoo's Jerry Yang, the sky is the limit. If the individual is one of a small group of people offering his particular skill, he will always do well. But if he is one of many, his wages will always amount to a pittance. As more and more people offer the world the same service, their labor becomes devalued. Experts call this phenomenon a "loss of equilibrium," that is, the condition of the labor market before it regains equilibrium. Everything the worker does from this point on is just as strenuous as it was before. It costs him the same amount of sweat, energy, and stress, and he is as exhausted as ever at the end of his workday— but his efforts are worth less, because he himself has become less scarce.

There are two forms of wage adjustment in the West, but only one is visible to all: the standard practice of cutting the wages of blue-collar workers and lower-income white-collar workers, who are then forced to provide the same amount of work for less money and reduced benefits. Meanwhile, their taxes remain the same or are even increased. Within the last decade, the wages and salaries of lower-paid workers have been gradually shrinking in every Western country. This process has been especially pronounced within the lower third of the labor market, creating a new underclass known as the "working poor." Americans were "working harder for less," President Bill Clinton, concluded at the beginning of the 1990s.

The second form of wage adjustment is more treacherous, because it is not mentioned in any income statistics. We tend to underestimate or, worse yet, ignore it. In this case, a worker's wages suddenly plunge to zero, the worker vanishes from all income statistics, and from then on society focuses solely on those left behind. This is comforting for the general public. The number of workers may have declined, but the productivity of the remaining workers rises and, in some cases, so do their hourly wages. Unemployment is in fact the most brutal form of downward wage adjustment.

People at the lower ends of the wage scale are the ones most likely to be forced out of the market. Most of them will never see the inside of an office or a factory floor again. What British sociologist Richard Sennett calls "the specter of uselessness" will accompany them throughout the rest of their lives, which in most cases will follow a downward spiral. In the early 1970s, when the global labor market was essentially a hermetically sealed Western labor market, full employment prevailed in most places. Wages were on the rise, and remaining in the same job for life was the rule, not the exception.

In a new global labor market characterized by an excess supply of labor, the initial consequences are all too obvious. Eighteen million Europeans are already unemployed. Add to that the women who have been forced back into the role of homemaker and the older workers sent into early retirement against their wills, and the unemployment figure in Europe jumps to 30 million. This army of the unemployed is equal to the combined populations of Berlin, Paris, London, Madrid, Brussels, Rome, Lisbon, and Athens.

U.S. unemployment will also increase significantly in the next economic downturn. The end of the 2002–2007 boom, which owed its strength to increased consumer spending, has spelled economic ruin for many and could yet wreak havoc on the financial situations of many more. Even after a five-year economic upswing, writes the U.S. Census Bureau in a survey published in August 2007, average wages in 2007 were lower than they were in 1999.

The global labor market is experiencing a decline in wages that no one in the West saw coming. The promise of the postwar years was that rising wages would bring rising prosperity. But workers cashed in practically overnight on any gains they might have made in the first place. The graphs depicting wages on the imaginary monitors in Times Square and in front of the White House now point downward.

No one should expect to see a rapid rise in incomes in the Far East or Eastern Europe. The fact that millions of farmers and slum dwellers are literally waiting in the wings for their chance to join the industrial labor market has a depressing effect on wages in these regions. Indeed, wage levels in the Far East are climbing at a much slower pace than the West would like to see. Given the disparity between pay in the United States and emerging economies, even an immediate wage freeze in the United States would be relatively ineffectual. If the rate of wage growth in Asia remains constant, it will take another 30 years before Asian incomes are only half as high as in the United States.

Past experiences with trade unions' efforts to resist wage decline have been sobering for employees. Those who have sought to slow down the process have in fact accelerated it. The choice today's workers face is not whether to accept high wages or low wages. Indeed, the alternative for millions of people in blue-collar professions is much more stark: low wages or no wages.

The world is by no means running out of work, as some claim. As long as the number of goods that are produced, sold, and consumed increases, there can be no loss of jobs. At the beginning of the twenty-first century, the global economy is experiencing one of its biggest growth spurts in decades. Despite the advent of the Internet and industrial automation, the sheer volume of jobs continues to increase. What has changed, however, is the distribution of labor in the context of a global labor market. This labor market is unlimited—but not for the Western worker.

A Ship Will Come: Workers Go Abroad

The departure of American jobs can be measured in precise quantities. Every job lost somewhere between Florida and Seattle returns to U.S. shores in the form of imported products. These products are merely a reflection of the fact that someone's job has been outsourced to someplace else in the world. From our vantage point, we may not be able to peer over the shoulders of workers in Asia or Eastern Europe, but the fruits of their labor are all too apparent.

They send them to us by truck, airfreight, or container ship, and our customs agencies keep detailed accounts of the nature and scope of these shipments. This is what economists call "import penetration," which is nothing more complicated than the phenomenon of foreign products penetrating our home markets. In America, the rate of penetration has increased tremendously, while domestic production has declined at virtually the same rate. Some industries already report import penetration at rates of more than 80 percent, which essentially spells the demise of these domestic industries in favor of new growth elsewhere in the world.

The worldwide migration of jobs is generally devoid of symbols. No one sheds a tear, nor are eulogies spoken for companies like Polaroid, Bethlehem Steel, Sunbeam, and WorldCom as they slowly die off, only to be replaced by others with names like Mitsubishi, Sony, Samsung, China Mobil, Haier, Kia, and Lenovo. We are witnessing the demise of the British auto industry, which once made automotive history with its legendary makers—Jaguar, Rover, British Leyland—only to be confronted with the rising stars of Korean and Japanese carmakers. The Chinese are trying to follow suit.

Only the small labels identifying the manufacturer are evidence that big things have happened beyond our field of vision. Stuffed animals are as cuddly as ever, but it's the labels that reveal the long journey our children's bears and lions have completed: "Made in China."

More complex products are also ideal candidates for outsourcing. We have only to glance at the back of Apple's latest computer model to see where it comes from: "Designed by Apple in California. Assembled in Taiwan." Many companies that we believe to be American, British, or French have already become businesses with nothing but skeleton staffs in their native countries. These are the people who inspect, develop, test, package, ship, and do the accounting for products that have been produced elsewhere. This may be comforting to all the inspectors, developers, testers, packagers, shippers, and accountants, but not to the people who were actually making the same products not too long ago. This is complicated by the fact that it isn't easy for a factory worker to suddenly be retrained to work as a designer or accountant. Designers and accountants probably would have a similarly tough time switching gears to work on an assembly line, where it's hot and the work is hard.

Experts say that the depth of production is decreasing, which sounds like some inevitable law of nature. But the truth is that nothing is really decreasing. Products are still being produced, and the depth of production is unchanged, but the people responsible for production live in other countries and work for completely different wages. The same experts have long predicted the end of industrial society. But it's obvious that nothing is in fact ending. On the contrary, there has been a sharp rise in industrial employment. It has grown by 16 percent worldwide in the last decade, amounting to about 600 million people working in the world's factories today. In other words, precisely the opposite of the experts' predictions has come about: industrial society is experiencing a renaissance, but far away from the West's cities and small towns. The blue-collar worker is the symbol of a new era, but one that is taking shape far away.

Globalization is a process that polarizes and divides, producing winners and losers alike—both in large numbers. Anyone who had hoped that the enormous manufacturing operations in the Far East and Eastern Europe would quickly become integrated into the global economy will certainly be disappointed in the first decade of the twenty-first century. The integration of millions of people in Asia goes hand in hand with the disintegration of millions more in the United States and Europe. Some are climbing the global ladder while others are on their way down. Instead of complementing each other, workers from the declining countries and those from the emerging countries are mutually exclusive. It may be true that the global labor market, after years of adjustment, offers enough jobs for all workers. This is a dream worth dreaming. But it would be foolish to view it as today's reality.

For the past 10 years, globalization has been accompanied by job losses in Europe and declining incomes in America. The development of new productive cores in Eastern Europe and Asia is currently linked to what amounts to a core meltdown in America and Western Europe, primarily affecting the traditional industries.

The establishment of new jobs in new industries could not make up for job loss in the old sectors of the economy, despite the fact that this is exactly what politicians and their economic advisors had promised. They would be well advised to abandon these self-created illusions and take a look at today's realities. The furniture industry; clothing manufacturers; steel mills; the producers of semiconductors, TVs, and computers; and, more recently, the pharmaceutical industry and genetic engineering firms have joined an exodus from America's shores. Shoes are now imported in large quantities, and even the mundane refrigerator comes from another country. Most of the memory chips in computers are imported.

China is securing an impressive global market position in many industries, made all the more striking by the fact that it remains a recipient of Western aid. Two-thirds of all photocopiers, microwave ovens, and toys are made in China, as are half of all digital cameras, textiles, and bags of cement sold on the market, as well as one-third of computers. One-quarter of all mobile phones and car radios, and one in four tons of steel comes from China.

We import more than just traditional industrial products from China. The country is now seeking a leading role in the production of genetically modified (GM) cotton. With the help of Monsanto, a major producer of GM seeds, millions of Chinese farmers already plant GM strains of cotton in their fields. The Chinese government has also approved the use of GM tomatoes, peppers, and petunias. In 2005, China increased its national research budget for biotechnology in plant production by 400 percent, to just under half a billion dollars. China's biotech industry is only in the preparatory stages of a coming export offensive. If nothing changes, the U.S. pharmaceutical industry will go the way of the textile industry.

India currently focuses on the production of drugs and software. The country offers major corporations a well-trained, English-speaking workforce with relatively modest earnings requirements. Indian workers are only too eager to take on the work once performed in the West. Who can blame them?

Indians nowadays operate the telephone call centers for many companies in Great Britain and the United States, analyze X rays for Western hospitals overnight, put together presentations for the advertising industry, prepare annual financial statements, provide human resource management services, develop software programs, and offer their expertise in information technology to major accounting and law firms. In a study titled "The Pouncing Tiger," economists at a major bank explain to the bank's customers how outsourcing to India is worthwhile for almost all industries, despite high initial investments and additional telecommunications costs. "Savings of up 20 to 40 percent can be achieved through wage arbitrage."

The counterpart to the strengthening of Asian and Eastern European companies is the waning of industry in the Western world. A process that began with the disappearance of individual departments, followed by entire factories, has now engulfed entire branches of industry. America's productive core is shrinking, which has a trickle-down effect on the weaker fringes of society, where retirees, children, the sick, and the unemployed depend on support from those charged with producing wealth.

Wal-Mart has become a symbol of the meltdown in U.S. industry. While company founder Sam Walton may have believed, until his death in 1992, in the superiority of domestic products and the American workforce, his successors introduced radical changes. They curtailed the company's important supply relationships with

U.S. producers and began waving in container ships from Hong Kong and Shanghai. Nowadays, 80 percent of Wal-Mart's 5,000 suppliers are from China. If Wal-Mart were a country, it would be ahead of Germany and Great Britain in China's export rankings. The jobs behind Wal-Mart's products did not disappear; they were simply shifted to new suppliers halfway around the world.

One of them is the Shenzhen Baoan Fenda Industrial Company, which pays its workers less than $1 an hour and openly threatens underperforming workers. A sign on the wall at one of the company's plants reads: "If you do not work hard today you will be working harder tomorrow when you look for a new job."

Wal-Mart is more radical than other businesses (and therefore more successful), but it is not an isolated case. Economic pressure has brought noticeable changes to many parts of the West. Liverpool and Manchester, in England's industrial northwest, as well as the West Midlands region, are replete with scenes of decommissioned factories and warehouses. Germany now registers unemployment rates upwards of 25 percent in its former industrial strongholds along the Rhine and Ruhr rivers.

In Berlin, a former industrial center, more people today live off of government assistance payments than their own wages. In Italy, the textile industry, which still provides jobs to 17 percent of all industrial employees in the country, is on its last legs. Unless EU trade officials continue to negotiate import quotas with the Chinese, not much will be left of the 543,000 textile jobs remaining in Italy today. Fashion czar Ermenegildo Zegna and the country's left-leaning textile worker unions have already staged a number of joint protests.

Deindustrialization has progressed further in the United States than in Europe. The growth of imports has led to an unprecedented shrinking process in American industry more severe than many phenomena seen in Europe. Factories first moved from the north to the lower-cost south before production was finally sent overseas. In many places, domestic value added was replaced by foreign value added in the textile, iron, steel, furniture, electronics, and computer industries.

Thirty-five percent of the American workforce worked in industry in the 1950s. By the 1960s, that number had dropped to 32 percent, and in the 1980s it slid below 20 percent. Today less than 15 percent of American workers are employed in industry, a 50 percent decline within a single generation. And now the American auto industry, once the beating heart of the U.S. economy, is fighting for its survival. For several months in 2007, for the first time ever, sales of imported cars in the United States had surpassed those of U.S.-made cars. Detroit's auto giants have reported losses in market share and profit during the last few years.

Outsourcing isn't the same thing as dismantling factories. If that were the case, those affected by outsourcing could witness it taking place. They would hear screwdrivers and chainsaws and see crates being packed and loaded into containers. Indeed, ordinary, run-of-the mill outsourcing of jobs is invisible and practically inaudible. All it takes is a gray, green, or pink purchase order, the sort of standard form most companies use every day. The only difference is that the shipping addresses change as companies redirect their flows of materials.

Instead of ordering steering wheels, tail lights, and cable harnesses from internal divisions or domestic suppliers, U.S. companies now place their orders in Asia. A year later, brakes, transmissions, and bumpers are added to the purchase order. Eventually much of what goes into a car ends up being shipped to Detroit from someplace else. To put it in simple terms, the outsourcing of jobs is reflected not in what is leaving our shores but in what is being unloaded at our container ports.

The business executives have a tendency to cross their arms and press their lips together at the mere mention of the word *offshoring*. Some see it as an accusation, others as an attempt to intervene in their companies' internal affairs. The new jobs overseas will help them develop new markets, they say, partly to dispel growing fears at home. Outsourcing represents nothing more than an expansion of foreign revenues, which, as they claim, is in the country's general interest. How else, they ask, can we market our products locally unless we have local workers?

Developing new markets and growing revenues abroad are certainly desirable and necessary. They help secure jobs at home. And yet these objectives fail to explain the phenomenon of large-scale outsourcing of the production factors of labor and capital away from Western countries.

By analyzing the balance sheets of a group of well-known multinational companies—BASF, Electrolux, Fiat, General Motors, IBM, Philips, Siemens, Sony, and Volkswagen—the McKinsey consulting firm was able to demonstrate that a form of job outsourcing is taking place that has nothing to do with developing new markets. The combined sales overseas of these conglomerates increased between 1990 and 2002, but only by a moderate 8.5 percent. However, their assets abroad and their foreign workforces grew by 20 percent in the same period. These numbers show that Western companies are trying to earn profits from their new customers. This is something they readily admit, but it's only half of the truth. They would rather not discuss their other, overriding goal: to profit from the new, low-wage competitors of Western workers.

But capital isn't in as much of a hurry to go offshore as many would assume. At times, capital can even function as a deterrent to outsourcing. From the standpoint of senior executives and company boards, excess workers are the least of their problems. It is often much easier for businesses to dispose of workers than their aging buildings and the toxic chemicals polluting the soil and groundwater beneath their factories. The costs of laying off workers are less of a concern to businesses than one might assume, because government and families end up shouldering these costs. In essence, Western society's system of values becomes a saving grace for businesses, because it allows them to transfer the responsibility for newly unemployed workers to society and the state.

Existing factories present the real problem for these companies, because no one wants property to depreciate at a faster rate than necessary. As a result, companies continue to operate their assembly lines at full capacity, even when they are no longer competitive. They are loath to demolish existing buildings and

send equipment to the scrap heap, because this requires executive boards and market analysts to take action. Instead they
attempt to squeeze as much benefit as possible out of yesterday's
investments, which have already been sunk into painting lines
and welding robots in their factories. They attempt to hold on
to their main plants and key employees for as long as possible,
the objective being to prevent total devaluation of domestic capital stock.

The countries that become home to the newly outsourced
industries also attempt to curb outsourcing, at least initially. Many
former developing nations are not yet in a position to handle the
entire automobile production cycle on their own. In China, for
example, companies that are building modern cars still import
about half of their parts from abroad. But the value-added chain
is gradually being completed as these countries build their own
production facilities and as Western suppliers outsource their production. With each new link in the chain, China comes one step
closer to becoming a full-fledged automobile producer. Once
Asian producers start making car seats, steering wheels, and transmissions, not far behind are car bodies, electronic components,
and engines. Experts call this self-propelling process, which is
already underway, the "network effort."

Another restraint on outsourcing production is the need to ship
goods around the world. Container ships and aircraft are not in
short supply, but shipping is costly, complex, and time consum-
ing. The textile industry, for example, continues to operate factories in the United States so that it can react quickly to fashion
trends. The carpet industry has an aversion to wall-to-wall carpeting from the Far East, because some carpeting is so heavy that
it loses its shape during lengthy shipping. Some books are printed
in China but most magazines are not, because they would be out
of date by the time they had been shipped.

New technologies are also changing the world of shipping.
Breakthroughs in railroad technology, aircraft construction, and
shipbuilding, as well as advances in the art of food preservation,
will provide new impetus to developments already underway. A

gold-rush mentality has dominated container shipping for some time, with the advent of giant container ships and automated loading and unloading substantially bringing down costs. Indeed, the cost of sea transport at the beginning of the twenty-first century was less than 1 percent of what it was in 1830, close to two centuries earlier. Meanwhile, shipbuilders and shipping companies are steadily developing ways to reduce transit time even further.

Industrial Workers in Retirement

Asian and Eastern European economies are currently scoring their biggest successes by performing the West's basic industrial activities. This outermost layer of the productive core, where workers produce little profit, sometimes even generating losses, is the most accessible to these emerging economies. Work processes in this sector of the economy require little training, education, or even dexterity. This segment of the value-added chain is where the most monotonous jobs are performed such as feeding material into a textile machine, assembling plastic parts to make toys, and operating semiautomated printing presses.

One of the reasons for the declining value of the West's low-wage workers to their employers was that they were producing little in the way of profits. They were cheap, but not cheap enough. With foreign workers willing to work for less than a dollar an hour, American workers' hourly wages of 6 or even 12 dollars per hour are suddenly nothing short of astronomical. Companies are completely uninterested in their workers' religious faith, gender, skin color, or age. Indeed, anyone who can promise lower costs for the same service is more than welcome in their factories.

In the end, even the increased use of machinery to offset wage differences has done ordinary blue-collar workers little good. Most low-wage countries have already caught up with the West and have also increased their capital investments, so much so that there is now little difference between some of their sparkling new industrial facilities and ours. Wages, despite the fact that they constitute an ever-shrinking share of production costs, ultimately remain the deciding factor.

Labor costs make up 23 percent of the retail price of a television set made in the West; the cost of labor that goes into the primarily Asian-made parts is low, but the assembling costs in the West are much higher. If the television set is completely made in China, labor costs make up only 4 percent of its retail price. It is precisely this wage gap—all other production costs being nearly equal—that will ultimately shut out ordinary American workers. This is commonly downplayed as "production site competition." In reality, it is nothing but competition among workers vying directly with one another on the global labor market. In this wage competition among workers on different continents, which has never existed in this form before, workers are in effect fighting tooth and nail for the same jobs.

Capitalists have no choice but to take full advantage of this enormous supply of low-wage workers. If they don't, their competitors will. Those who fail to grasp the importance of using wage competition for their own gain, those who refuse to invest in production locations marred by substandard working conditions, and those who scoff at inexpensive imports are more than likely to go out of business. It does no one any good, not least themselves, if they refuse to take these steps. Clever businesspeople will take full advantage of globalization before it starts to destroy their businesses. They are not driven by greed, but by necessity.

The Customer Is King—With or Without the Welfare State?

The welfare state is basically a cartel. The difference between it and corporate cartels is that the welfare state benefits many, while the cartel benefits only a few. The welfare state benefits all citizens who qualify for government or company pensions, who take advantage of government health-care programs, and who send their children to public schools and universities. But even those who do not derive financial benefit from the welfare state enjoy the protections it guarantees: the right to experience childhood, the right to form labor unions, the right to race and gender equality, and the right to legal minimum wage.

Put simply, the modern welfare state has made us all parts of its cartel. We benefit from its protections and its financial perks. We enjoy the luxury of having company bathrooms for both men and women, as our labor laws require, we are only too willing to take advantage of our federal holidays, and if our lives suddenly fall apart we can always fall back on government assistance programs. We may think government assistance is poor in the United States, but from the standpoint of a worker in China or India it is nothing short of big government.

If this protective cartel, which imposes social costs that make the price of labor more expensive, competes with countries where these protections and the corresponding monetary costs to society are nonexistent, the cartel is suddenly no longer protective but threatening. One of the reasons for the differences in labor costs between the old and new members of the global labor market is this very welfare state. Workers in the West enjoy its fruits while it remains distant and unattainable to those in Asia and Eastern Europe. Nevertheless, those who currently benefit from the welfare state, in one way or another, now face the constant threat of losing their livelihood. A system that only yesterday was seen as one of civilization's great achievements now seems like a millstone around its neck.

The opponents of the welfare state welcome global labor inflation with open arms, because it has proven to be the most effective method of whittling down the welfare state. They no longer need to promote or actively engage in its dismantling, because it appears to be disintegrating entirely of its own accord. For them, the easiest approach is simply to ignore the welfare state, and one way of achieving this is to order goods and services from Asian suppliers, countries where the welfare state is close to nonexistent. Doing so is practically a vote against the many benefits and achievements of the welfare state and, of course, in favor of lower wages.

In free markets with free consumers, the friends of the welfare state are in fact the greatest threat to its very existence. Most of us who walk into a supermarket or a department store are unwilling to pay what we might call a social surcharge. Normal shoppers at Target, Wal-Mart, or even a car dealership are in fact avid fans of globalization. They compare prices and performance, but they couldn't care less about nationalities or social welfare systems. Everyone wants a good deal, but no one wants to pay a markup—for anything—nor does anyone want to hear about the unsavory way of doing business elsewhere in the world that makes the good deal possible in the first place. Consumers looking to buy a new sound system will compare the performance and features of different systems, but not the wages of the workers who produced them. Those consumers may consider themselves to be idealistic, but they are in fact card-carrying materialists who only occasionally are overcome by moral qualms. They even feign surprise at the seemingly phenomenal bargains to be had—the large, handmade rugs for ridiculously low prices and the computers and mobile phones available at bargain basement prices.

With each purchase of a product from the Far East, consumers are driving yet another nail into the coffin of their domestic social welfare state. They compare products on price and performance while ignoring the true costs to their domestic economy. Today's globalization wouldn't stand a chance without the active participation of consumers in every Western country. Western consumers are, in a sense, the unwitting allies of the emerging nations in the war for wealth. We call ourselves smart shoppers, but our purchase decisions are in fact not nearly as clever as we believe them to be.

Unless someone stops us, we will destroy our domestic industries with our cool-headed purchase decisions. Practically everything on store shelves nowadays is available in a form that lacks the welfare state rate.

We can choose to buy a car from General Motors, in which case the sticker price includes $1,600 in social costs, as the CEO of General Motors mentioned in a recent speech to his employees.

But it would be cheaper to pay a visit to the local Kia dealer. The price of a Kia will not include a comparable markup, because South Korean workers aren't guaranteed the same benefits as their counterparts in Detroit. We can feel good about buying a Whirlpool washing machine, because it reflects American values and has the American social cost—higher wages and trade unions—built in. But standing right next to it is a row of washing machines made in Taiwan, China, or Poland—low wages, no legal cap on weekly working hours, and few if any environmental restrictions—that are pretty much washing machines and nothing else. There is no built-in welfare state in a Chinese-made household appliance.

Today, 75 percent of the world's population still lacks any form of unemployment insurance—clearly a disadvantage to workers, but a boon to the products they make and to the companies that employee them. The workers shoulder the risks of illness, poverty, and old age, but the products they make do not. The opposite is true in the West.

Workers have no representation in the Far East. Instead, they work under the watchful eyes of factory foremen who, in the best case, will choose leniency over the rule of law. The law is not the worker's friend in the factories of low-wage countries. Workers are permitted to work, but they are barred from demonstrating. Their wages are set, not negotiated. The family, not the company, provides their social safety net. The practice of "reeducation" in China's roughly 300 labor camps also helps bring down prices. According to the Hong Kong–based organization China Labour Bulletin, about 300,000 forced laborers help boost China's exports. By bringing down labor costs even further (to zero, in this case), the practice makes Chinese products even more competitive on the global market.

We should think twice before we condemn company executives and consumers. It would be foolish to blame them for seeking to maximize their own benefit. The political decision to allow the countries of Asia and Eastern Europe access to the global labor market was reached in both camps, theirs and ours. They wanted to become part of the Western production network and stake out their piece of the pie. We encouraged and supported them, sometimes even egging them on. There is no wrong or right in this situation. It is, however, important to recognize that the global labor market, at least the way it has been structured until now, has created sovereign territories accessible to labor worldwide. Demand for labor changes from one country to the next. Capitalists, of course, prefer countries that can offer them the lowest possible wages and do not impose the pesky burden of additional social costs.

Those who have believed that a market economy with a human face and compassionate capitalism represents a final stage in our history are now recognizing their colossal error. With the help of a global labor and financial market, capitalism has regained its former brutality while many of the constituents of the welfare state have been weakened. The market has picked up speed and, apparently, a certain sense of inevitability. Meanwhile, yesterday's social achievements have faded. Capitalism, which undoubtedly will have generated more wealth worldwide by the end of this process, is returning to its roots, at least for now.

Who's Next?

Who, in fact, decides which jobs stay and which ones go? Who is allowed to swim with the sharks and who will perish with the sardines? Why is it that some workers can be out of a job from one day to the next, while others will always be in demand? To put it in concrete terms: why can a barber in Los Angeles charge former U.S. presidential hopeful John Edwards $400 for a haircut, why does it take months to get a good carpenter, and why do plumbers behave as if they were doing their customers a favor by merely showing up, if such an unprecedented shrinking process is underway in industry?

The barber is in a good position, because his job is not connected to the global economy. His counterpart in Bombay gets only a fraction of what Los Angeles's celebrity hairdressers charge for the same service. But someone like John Edwards would rather pay the high cost of stepping into a salon in Los Angeles than travel to Bombay. Hairdressers are incredibly fortunate. Globalization has left their profession virtually untouched. They hover on the sidelines, scissors in hand, watching momentous events unfold, listening to their customers gossip about outsourcing, secure in the knowledge that it will never affect them.

The same applies to many other professions, which is why they will neither die out nor be outsourced. Electricians are hardly likely to travel far. Few people would make an appointment with a doctor or dentist if a day's travel were involved. There is a lot that can be done on the Internet: processing software, canvassing for new customers, placing orders, holding conferences, and disseminating the news. But so far no one has figured out a way to install plumbing in this virtual world, or apply makeup, water plants, build houses, and haul away trash. For this reason, the future will not be significantly different from the past in many professions. The members of these professions may have the world of globalized labor at their doorsteps, but they are not an active part of it. Their world is flat, and it will continue to be so in the future.

And then there is everyone else, who can be divided into two classes. First we have the lucky dogs of globalization, the financial experts, the aircraft designers, and the novelists. The fruits of their labor are unique, because they are experts in a world of novices. They design airplanes, a skill of the very few. They have a nose for the right investment, at the right time and in the right country. They write novels that are so insightful, wild, or funny that their readers are constantly begging for more. This new, expanded world needs even more aircraft. Financial experts are experiencing a boom in their profession. Novelists can look forward to a whole new class of people having unfettered access to their works, and they can hope that at least some of those people will blossom into avid readers. For all three, the expanded global market may not spell guaranteed success, but it certainly improves their prospects. They hold two lots in their hands while others have only one.

And then there are the unlucky souls who may find themselves shut out of the global lottery in the future. Their jobs are suddenly part of a global competition, which makes them part of the global workforce. Toys can be produced anywhere, as can clothes and shoes, television sets, and washing machines. Even computers, automobiles, and drugs are ultimately so devoid of production-based specialization that anyone with the right set of plans can quickly set about producing them.

The one thing almost all consumer goods have in common is that it doesn't matter where they are made, be it in the Midwest, on the shores of Lake Michigan; in the Yangtze delta near Shanghai; or in Győr, a picturesque little Hungarian town on the banks of the Danube River. All it takes is for governments to patch together a halfway reliable legal structure that enables capitalists to take their profits home. Roads, seaports, and airports are needed so that products can be shipped around the world. People, of course, are necessary, and they must satisfy only three criteria to be hired. First, they must have the will to work, the hungrier the better. Second, they must be capable of performing the task at hand, which requires a minimum set of skills. Finally, they must be willing to do so at the best price possible. If their drive and ability do not compare favorably against those of workers elsewhere, they automatically give up the right to demand higher wages.

As soon as a product concept begins to show its age—the ordinary washing machine, the conventional TV, the traditional Christmas tree lights—price, which includes the cost of labor, becomes the overriding factor. Just as entrepreneurs seek to buy their steel, oil, screws, and rivets for the best possible price on the world market, and are not willing to pay a cent more, they also scour the global labor market for the best possible cost of labor. Workers who are part of the global economy are subject to different conditions than electricians, hairdressers, and aircraft designers. No union representatives have negotiated or even signed off on their wage scales. The price of a global worker establishes itself globally based on the archaic rules of supply and demand, which does not bode well for the worker in times of such greatly expanding supply.

Hardly anyone follows developments on the global labor market as attentively as McKinsey. The company has developed a computer program that, within seconds, can show clients where any type of production facility can be developed most cost effectively. The software is constantly updated with information critical to investors: How high are wages elsewhere? What are the qualifications of workers in a given location? Are there suppliers nearby? How big is the market in the vicinity of a potential new factory? What will happen in 10 years? Is the workforce expected to grow or shrink in the anticipated target region?

The program includes simulations that allow users to walk along a virtual production chain anywhere in the world. It reveals that Mexico is probably the most opportune place to produce cast-iron auto parts, and that India might be the ideal place to make plastic struts. The computer becomes a radar screen of globalization, enabling users to pinpoint where they can find the optimal combination of capital and labor at any given time. Once that combination of relevant factors has been found, lights begin flashing on the computer screen. The lights rarely flash in America or Europe anymore. The program routinely scores rave reviews among corporate executives. A McKinsey analyst explains why: "We help companies emigrate their problems."

The Great Knowledge Transfer

Experts once said that only the lowest-paying, unskilled, routine jobs would leave our shores, a loss that no one would really mind. These jobs, they insisted, were mind-numbing and dull, and not particularly profitable. They were convinced that the future lay in skilled work in the modern service professions, and that the old manufacturing jobs were hardly worth the trouble.

After all, they argued, every participant in economic life possesses advantages, which he or she uses in a way that benefits society as a whole. One is a skilled fisherman because he lives by the sea. Another has mastered the art of textile processing, because she lives in a cotton-growing region. A third knows the ins and outs of trading in spices and carpets, because he lives in a country that has long been at the intersection of ancient trading routes. According to this way of thinking, if each person makes full use of her or his skills and advantages, this will result in a division of labor in which everyone does what she or he does best. The fisher will catch fish, the weaver will weave cloth, and the merchant will trade.

Because the emerging nations can produce at the lowest cost, the theory goes, it would be logical for them to handle the West's primitive manufacturing jobs. They could make themselves most useful by performing the menial, unskilled work of Western corporations. The extended workbench (from the West's perspective) would provide them with urgently needed work, while the West would finally have the chance to attend to what was truly important: research, marketing, and sales. In other words, the Chinese could go ahead and produce toys, the Bangladeshis could keep on sewing together cotton dresses, and the Indians could make jewelry, freeing up the United States to devote all of its attention and resources to the higher-level stages of production: pharmaceuticals, investment banking, and aerospace. Thanks to new factories, the agrarian states of the South would become industrialized, making them consumers of the higher-quality products from America.

The countries of the West, after having shed the ballast of the industrial age, could finally make the leap to becoming true high-tech societies. This way both sides— the West and the emerging economies—would climb the ladder of human history in an orderly, sequential fashion.

There is only one problem with this line of reasoning. The emerging nations aren't in the least bit interested in the West's idea of the division of labor. They would rather jostle their way up the ladder. The Chinese, Indians, Malaysians, Taiwanese, South Koreans, and large numbers of Eastern Europeans set their own pace. The step from an agrarian to an industrialized state is too small for them, and so they push to speed up the process. "Reality no longer conforms to the theory," a disappointed International Labor Organization concluded in its annual report. When analysts at the U.N. agency reviewed Asian statistics, they noticed one thing in particular: "Many workers are moving directly from agriculture to the service sector."

The new market economies want to avoid, at all costs, becoming stuck in the low-productivity zone. Their upward trajectory started in low-wage production, but that was only the beginning. Today, the world's emerging economies are attacking the core of the Western productive society, training academics in large numbers so that they can perform the same, modern tasks that have been performed in New York, London, Paris, and Berlin for decades, tasks once considered reserved for the West. They develop software, design cars, manage the accounting systems for major corporations, and, of course, develop and sell anything with a promising future: telephones, computers, and all manner of drugs and remedies.

Until 2004, the United States was the world's largest exporter of information technology (IT) products. This distinction has since gone to the Chinese. They now export high-tech products worth a total of $180 billion, compared with the United States, which now exports $150 billion worth of the global economy's premium products. The U.S. share of global IT exports has declined by half in the last 15 years. To attain its leading position worldwide, China has quadrupled its share since 2000 alone.

Automobile production follows the same trend. This year China is expected to overtake Germany, traditionally a key car-producing country. Experts predict that it could take less than 15 years for China to unseat the United States as the world's largest automobile-producing country.

The triumphal procession on the product markets will also leave its mark on the white-collar labor market. Not all the jobs of managers, designers, marketing strategists, financial experts, and design engineers are being outsourced, but more will be than many believe today. Employment growth, in particular, is taking place elsewhere. This represents the beginning of an attack on the core competencies of the West.

The political will of the Asians and the new technology of our day—satellites, broadband cable, video transmission, and Internet communication—will have a disastrous impact on millions of people who today have only the slightest idea of what they are in for. If everything remains as it is, nothing will be as it was. Alan Blinder, a professor of economics at Princeton University and former vice chairman of the U.S. Federal Reserve, predicts that the next great wave of offshoring will affect up to 40 million American white-collar workers.

It came as a shock to many economists when, in the spring of 2007, Blinder, a dedicated free trader and world-renowned expert, issued a public warning against the consequences of today's free trade:

> *American workers will still face a troublesome transition as tens of millions of old jobs are replaced by new ones. There will also be great political strains on the open trading system as millions of white-collar workers who thought their jobs were immune to foreign competition suddenly find that the game has changed—and not to their liking.*

In a moving appeal to his fellow economists, Blinder asked them to rethink free trade in its present form. In an article in the *Washington Post*, published on May 6, 2007, he solicited their understanding or at least encouraged them to devote more thought to the issue:

> *When I say this, many of my fellow free-traders react with a mixture of disbelief, pity and hostility. Blinder, have you lost your mind? (Answer: I think not.) Have you forgotten about the basic economic gains from international trade? (Answer: No.) Are you advocating some form of protectionism? (Answer: No !) Aren't you giving aid and comfort to the enemies of free trade? (Answer: No, I'm trying to save free trade from itself.)*

We should not blame the Asians for their intentions. But we should certainly see through them. Indian and Chinese leaders know all too well that being the world's factory is ultimately unappealing. Only those who make their money with techno-logical miracle devices, the devices we reverently refer to as high tech, can lay claim to having reached world class. But those who continue to sew the Americans' athletic shoes based on the Amer-icans' patterns will always remain their servants, and those who do little more than assemble products based on someone else's designs will never be able to call themselves global powers. Not a single country in the world wants to end up as someone else's colony, even if the colonial master proves to be as generous as Bill Gates.

All the Indians and the Chinese have to do is look back at their own unpleasant histories to know what it means to be dependent. This time they want to work for themselves and live by their own rules. The gargantuan amount of effort we see being exerted in the Far East is to boost their efficiency, not ours.

China and India are not the only ones with burning ambitions. Many countries that until recently were considered to be parts of the third world are now forging ahead into the world of high finance and cutting-edge research. A race to recruit the best minds, including those of the West, is underway in Asia, where billions of dollars are being spent to entice researchers and com-panies to relocate from one country to another. Last year Dutch electronics giant Philips moved its Asian headquarters and a large share of its research facilities from Singapore to Hong Kong's newly opened Science Park.

This is surprising, because Singapore has probably the most dar-ing vision to offer businesses. The city-state is on track to become the world's leading center for the biomedical sciences. Under its current five-year plan, Singapore has doubled government fund-ing for research compared with the previous five-year plan. Phar-maceutical giants Pfizer and Glaxo SmithKline have already set up shop there, and the Scottish creator of Dolly, the world's first cloned sheep, has also found a new home in Singapore.

Exports of high-tech products have been growing for years in practically every Asian country. Malaysia was an agricultural country in the 1970s. Nowadays one-half of its exports are electronic products. Thailand, until recently the region's biggest food supplier, has shifted much of its export economy to the production of machine parts and other industrial products. Even the Philippines is now a major world supplier of a wide range of electronic products, which already make up two-thirds of the country's exports.

Though lagging somewhat behind countries like Singapore and Malaysia, China and India have also begun developing this innermost zone of the productive core. McKinsey's software program now shows scores of red lights flashing on the territory of these two Asian giants, because they represent the greatest concentration of energy. They offer the strategic jobs that are critical to the continued development of their economies.

China and India are now home to product developers and scientists conducting basic research, the men and women who, with their improvements, innovations, and groundbreaking inventions, are steadily conquering tomorrow's markets. This is where genetic material was decoded, the first cloning experiments were conducted, stem cell therapy was fine-tuned, and solar technology was invented. It is within this innermost layer of the productive core that the future of every society is decided: whether it will lead or follow, produce originals or copies, and whether it will be able to maintain or enhance its position in the global race for wealth and power.

As the countries of the Far East develop their knowledge-based economies, the amount of money they are investing in the future attests to the scope of their ambition. China's research spending is already close to one-third of the amount spent on research in the United States and almost half of European spending. Government and private research expenditures have been growing by up to 20 percent for years, at almost twice the rate of overall economic output, in some cases. This is a rate never before seen in history.

The Chinese go about their work with great resolve and impressive astuteness. In addition to their financial expenditures, they have introduced a new form of currency into international economic relations to help accelerate their ascent: knowledge or, more specifically, the knowledge of the West. The Chinese are interested in all sorts of blueprints. In return for being allowed to build factories in China and gain access to Chinese markets, Western companies are required to relinquish their secrets, large and small. How do you build microchips with extreme memory? What are the secrets of stainless steel production? What makes a magnetic levitation train levitate? Chinese and Indian politicians have realized that thoroughly training their skilled workers is more important than turning a quick and easy profit.

They now understand that only by developing this vital infrastructure within the core of their economy can they acquire the energy they need to leap forward in the direction of modernity. Only when the core of its economy is red hot, when it has managed to attract inventors and creative spirits, and when the pioneers of a new age produce groundbreaking thought and research can a nation advance into the inner circle of global powers.

Knowledge used to be handed down from one generation to the next. Nowadays knowledge is being transferred from one part of the world to another. Never before in history has there been such a massive transfer of knowledge—without war or conquest—from one social group to another.

Western companies are doing their best to help the Asians develop, but their assistance is by no means voluntary. Business executives are loath to discuss the humiliating conditions they must sometimes satisfy to get ahead in foreign countries. In some cases, they must reveal knowledge they have accumulated over decades as a precondition for market entry. Within weeks, Western companies sometimes lose the know-how they have acquired through years of research, research that makes them capable of designing and building modern steel mills, magnetic levitation trains, and automobile engines. This price of access to Far Eastern joint venture companies is not shown on any balance sheet.

Many businesspeople, in their constant quest to grow their capital, are guilty of ignoring the big picture in which they do business.

They are convinced that money is there for the taking in the Far East, on the streets or at least in factory buildings. In return, they are willing to pay the entry fee demanded of them, even if payment comes in the form of handing over this valuable knowledge.

The Indians and the Chinese were astute enough to force the West to help them develop their own research facilities as a condition for outsourcing production. General Electric currently operates the world's largest research institute outside the United States—in Bangalore, India. Within three years of its establishment, the Bangalore facility had already generated 95 patent applications. Many of the biggest players among Western corporations have set up shop in India, including chipmaker Intel, German electronics giant Siemens, U.S. aircraft manufacturer Boeing, oil multinational ExxonMobil, and Anglo-Dutch consumer products maker Unilever. All of these companies are passing on their knowledge in order to acquire new knowledge. U.S. corporations' Indian research facilities produce more than 1,000 new patent applications a year, a number that attests to the fact that a productive core is growing in India that, once sufficiently powerful, will also be capable of turning against its sponsors.

And then there is the illegal form of knowledge transfer, which the West has been particularly reluctant to combat. The modus operandi of many young Chinese engineers is simple: better try than buy. China today is the world's epicenter of product piracy. A company in Shenzhen was recently caught making exact duplicates of network technology by Cisco Systems, a California-based company that designs and sells networking and communications technology and services. A company in Inner Mongolia produces a knockoff of Procter & Gamble's top-selling Head & Shoulders shampoo. Not content with printing black-market copies of British author J. K. Rowling's Harry Potter series, the Chinese have come up with their own version of the fictional character—except that the Chinese Harry Potter has nothing more in common with the original than his name and a number of key personality traits.

This illegal knowledge transfer is incredibly damaging to the West. According to the United States Patent and Trademark

Office, Western automobile manufacturers could employ an additional 210,000 people if China would stop making illegal copies of auto parts. Eighty percent of the motorcycles sold in China are imitations, say officials at Japanese motorcycle manufacturer Yamaha. About 90 percent of music CDs sold in China are believed to be pirated versions.

The structure of many intellectual property laws actually promotes piracy. For example, it can take up to two years from the time a patent application is filed before the corresponding patent is granted. Chinese companies know how to use this time to their advantage, and even those who continue to copy or imitate after a patent has been granted are unlikely to face any serious consequences. Chinese officials do conduct raids occasionally, but at irregular intervals and mainly to appease Western companies. In the worst of cases, the offending Chinese company faces the threat of confiscation of its goods. Because the government has not imposed any production bans or significant fines in recent years, a certain sense of shamelessness has developed, so much so that denouncing such activities is seen as impolite in China.

The practice is so widespread that entire steel mills or individual production lines are copies, sometimes even within view of the joint-venture companies that provided the knowledge in the first place. Even such high-profile projects as the construction of a maglev railway in Shanghai are not immune. The Chinese partners of Siemens and ThyssenKrupp—the inventors and license holders of magnetic levitation technology through their joint venture company, Transrapid—had long urged these companies to disclose the details of the system's control and propulsion technology. When the executives refused, the Chinese apparently opted for a less-than-savory way of gaining access to the technology they wanted.

On a Friday night, Chinese engineers broke into the Transrapid's maintenance station to measure parts used in its propulsion system. Their activity was recorded by a security camera, which led to a discussion with Wu Xiangming, the head of the Shanghai Transrapid project. But Wu reacted coolly, refusing to admit that the nocturnal break-in had been a mistake. Instead, he told his joint-venture partners, the purpose of the nocturnal escapade was to promote research and development.

The Chinese are essentially fueling the innermost core of their economy with energy generated elsewhere. They buy time by acquiring Western companies and, more importantly, they steal time by demanding free use of the concepts others have developed. "A problem of this magnitude can only exist as a result of the direct or indirect participation of the state," says Daniel Chow, a professor at the University of Ohio and one of the United States' leading legal experts on intellectual property. China's accession to the World Trade Organization and the corresponding obligation to comply with the rules of free trade have done little to change the country's practices.

According to a study by consulting firm Booz Allen Hamilton, countries like China now are able to use the knowledge they have acquired, legally and illegally, to stage "successful attacks." Philipp Vorndran, senior investment strategist at Credit Suisse First Boston, says, "The Western industrialized nations have transferred much of their know-how to China, thereby fulfilling their purpose. They won't be needed much longer. An attack from China is only a matter of time."

The Next Einstein Will Be Indian

In the Far East, Western knowledge is encountering the largest generation of students that has ever existed on earth. This year alone, three million people will attain university degrees in India and four million in China. Asian countries have noticeably increased the numbers of students graduating from their universities since the early 1990s. Even if we ignore Japan's traditionally knowledge-oriented society, almost four times as many people graduated from universities in the Far East than in Europe in 2005. China practically mass-produces engineers, with 10 times as many newly minted engineers entering the market each year as in Germany. It spends an enormous amount of money educating its workers, a commitment that is all the more impressive for a country that until recently was part of the third world. China has the world's third-largest national budget, next to the United States and Japan, for research and development.

China's political drive to overtake the United States is unmistakable. The official goal of the current state and party leadership is to achieve a harmonious society. In truth, however, the country's leaders, communists in name but nationalists in practice, would rather cut back on social spending than research. The Chinese want to be the best, not the cheapest. They want to lead, not to follow. All of this has roots in the country's history. Tsinghua University in Beijing, one of China's top educational institutions, is directly adjacent to the imperial summer palace, a building once destroyed by the British and the French. It was here that colonial masters began a long process of humiliation and repression, and it is from here that China's economic resurgence is being launched. The harmonious society is little more than a placebo for the impatient within the country.

Many U.S. universities have begun to resemble branches of the Chinese and Indian knowledge industry. One-fourth of all U.S. doctoral diplomas in science and engineering are handed out to Chinese students. Close to half of these graduates return home to China to devote themselves to the development of new knowledge centers for biotechnology, genetic engineering, and nanotechnology. Jeffrey Garten, the former dean of the Yale School of Management in New Haven, Connecticut, is impressed by this development of knowledge, which he says he has never witnessed happening at such a fast pace anywhere in the world. Garten predicts China's emergence as a "technological super-state."

But even the Chinese are no match for the one million Indians living in the United States, who are hungry for any form of training and education because they have figured out that knowledge promises prosperity. Nowadays, the path to power and wealth leads directly through the lecture halls of universities. Three-quarters of working-age Indians in the United States have a bachelor's degree or higher. Thirty-eight percent have a master's degree or a doctorate. The close relationships Indians living in the United States maintain with families and businesses back in India result in an ongoing transfer of knowledge. Indians who have lived and worked abroad manage 95 percent of international companies in Bangalore, for example. India already boasts more than 700,000 IT specialists, which is twice as many as Germany, still considered a major exporting nation.

The Indian specialists are just as well trained as their Western counterparts but earn only a fraction of Western pay. A highly qualified professional in Asia, who comes complete with the university degrees considered a standard requirement today, earns less than a cleaning person in Chicago.

Politicians seek to downplay the enormous number of Asian academics by pointing out that these countries also boast very large populations. This is merely an attempt to shed a positive—but ultimately misleading—light on America's academic track record. But such references are irrelevant in economic terms. As it happens, the Asians possess the advantage of strength in numbers, which no amount of statistical qualification can diminish. Their success depends on the notion that whoever is able to make the most attempts stands a greater chance of taking home the grand prize. The next Einstein will more than likely come from China or India.

We can call the power of numbers the Asians' greatest boon, qualify their large populations as an unfair advantage, and insist that comparing the two systems is like comparing apples and oranges. We can also point out that the average age of Asia's millions is significantly lower than that of the residents of our latitudes. But there is one mistake we must not make, and that is to underestimate the enormous power of big numbers. While certainly no guarantee of success, a large, well-educated population does guarantee significantly better chances of success. Members of skilled professions that can be pursued anywhere in the world are already realizing that their jobs are not as safe as they once believed. Globalization is unbiased, in a manner of speaking, because it also devalues some at the center of Western economies.

A doctor who analyzes an X ray can just as well be located in Bangladesh, but a nurse cannot. Software developers will soon be at home anywhere in the world, while salespeople will remain local.

Western governments acknowledge the enormous efforts underway in emerging nations. They may admire or fear these upstart economies, but their response to the threat they pose is inadequate. Since the Chinese and Indians made their debut on the international knowledge markets, no Western country has significantly increased research and education spending. In fact, many are doing the opposite, seeking to cut costs and maximize shareholder value. Businesses may be busy saving money, but they do so at the expense of their own futures.

Microsoft founder Bill Gates points out that there is a "crisis in the American education system" and spends millions to fund schools and training seminars, hoping to counteract the problem. Gates senses—perhaps more acutely than others—that the West is on the verge of falling behind technologically. "I'm surprised by the forces that are being released in China," Gates said at the World Economic Forum in Davos, Switzerland, adding that the United States' technological leadership position is by no means secure indefinitely. He told his audience that he had recently been introduced to the 10 most-talented Microsoft employees. "Only one of them had an American name. The rest were Asians," he said.

Quiet Departures: Capitalism without Capital?

Capital is restless and capricious. At first, when it was interested in steel and coal, blast furnaces and coal mines were developed. Soon it turned its attention to the electronics and textile industries, before moving on to entertainment electronics and computers. From there, it devoted itself to companies in the service industry, and then developed a liking for the advertising industry, law, and tourism. This culminated in the development of an independent financial industry, which was soon more powerful than the conglomerates of the early industrial age.

A strong, energetic migration of capital from one economic sector to the next is dubbed "structural change." Old jobs die so that new ones can be created. From its very beginnings, the history of capitalism is a great tale of the development and demise of economic sectors, while capital always migrates from one economic sector to another. If this were not the case, steam engines would still be in use today and large numbers of workers would come home from work covered in coal dust.

While the fickle and constantly wandering nature of capital is nothing new, the tremendous expansion in its range of action is. Modern capitalists hold a map of the world in their hands. Their interest extends to billions of people in countless countries on all continents. The cycle of development and demise continues, but it is no longer a foregone conclusion that it must take place exclusively in the Western hemisphere. Structural change is underway once again, but this time it eclipses anything that has preceded it in human history.

We should not envision capital's wandering nature as an abrupt coming and going. Capital, once invested, is no longer as mobile as its representatives would have the public believe. They love to carry on and threaten us with outsourcing, but their threats are often little more than posturing. Capital changed its constitution from liquid (money) to solid (factories) long ago, a process that takes enormous effort to reverse. This explains why capitalists rarely choose to dismantle machinery, pack it up, and move it elsewhere. Severing the roots laid down by invested capital is no easy task.

Young capital, on the other hand, is mobile. This is why the statistics for new investment are a more precise indicator of the future prosperity of a nation. Each new investment is a declaration of love for the future. Only those who expect great things of the future—new customers and additional profits, for instance— are willing to invest in it. Thus, by taking a look at new investment, we gain a better understanding of the factors leading to Europe's decline. For the first time since the Industrial Revolution, there is no new passion to take the place of waning interest in old industries. The migration of capital from one sector to the next—structural change—has become a rare phenomenon in Western Europe, partly evident in the fact that no significant new businesses have been added in at least 20 years.

Corporations are merging, concentrating, and slimming down wherever they can. But the act of building business from scratch has become a rarity, and only in exceptional cases do new companies attain the size of their aging counterparts. The top 100 corporations in France, Great Britain, and Germany are almost all well-known household names. Occasionally, when a successful merger has taken place, the name on the door and the composition of executive boards are changed, allowing the media to convey the impression that what we are witnessing is evidence of change and revitalization.

A look at the instrument panel of European economies confirms the first, still fleeting impression of a noticeable drop in pressure in recent years. No new energy has been fed into the system. The net rate of investment, that is, the ratio of new acquisitions to total economic strength, has declined by half since 1970. This is the first time since World War II that there has been so little investment in new businesses. No one is willing to take the plunge, nor is anyone deriving any benefit from new business ventures. Europe's once-impressive economic history appears to have arrived at one of its final chapters.

One problem is the continent's shrinking population, which, unlike the U.S. population, is not being boosted by immigration. Germany alone, Europe's largest economy, will lose about 10 million of its 82 million inhabitants in the next four decades. This disappearance of people will also bring with it a loss of capital.

A capital base that is shrinking in relative terms cannot serve as the basis for growth and renewal. Other nations and continents where the capital base is growing in relative terms are quickly catching up. Well-trained people and the investment capital necessary to put them to work are the propellant needed for economic revival. The street sweeper needs a broom, the fisherman a rod, and the bartender a tap and bar, but automobile and aircraft designers and members of the biomedical professions are of a different caliber. They need large amounts of capital to be able to be productive in the first place. Without this capital, the knowledge stored in their brains simply goes to waste. Without a laboratory and a computer network, members of the biomedical professions are even less valuable on the labor market than bartenders, because they lack the experience to tap beer and mix drinks.

There is a significant difference between the United States and Old Europe when it comes to the balance of investment. Industrial production may be steadily departing from Europe's shores, but capital has already said its goodbyes. Structural change remains intact, but investors have moved on to American software developers and the giants of the financial and pharmaceutical industries. Within the last decade alone, the United States has seen a number of new companies—eBay, Lucent Technologies, Biogen, Google, Yahoo!, and Apple—emerge and quickly develop into major players. They have managed to dominate the markets just as pioneering American industries like Standard Oil and Ford led by industrialists John D. Rockefeller and Henry Ford once did. The rate of investment in America has increased rather than decreased. Investors mistrust Europe, despite its considerable efforts to attract investment. Conversely, investors love America, despite its problems. The United States is still the world leader when it comes to attracting major investment.

But the new thing is, Southeast Asia is quickly catching up. The new players are surprising the world with their ability to attract foreign direct investment, which began at a strong pace and is only getting stronger. Taken as a whole, Asia's growth markets have already surpassed the United States, with China, Hong Kong, and Singapore attracting the largest volume of foreign direct investment among Asian countries.

"Go Out!" The Asians Are Buying Time

To speed up their ascent, the Chinese, Indians, Koreans, and Malaysians are penetrating into the inner cores of Western economies. They do so by acquiring Western companies outright, or at least investing in them, and then injecting the capital they have earned in their export trade with Europe and the United States back into the economies of the West. They deploy their own managers to examine the effects of their capital injection. Beijing's edict to China's corporate executives is called "*Zou chuqu!*" which translates as "Go out!"

The flow of investment from all Asian countries to the West has grown almost tenfold in the past 15 years. In 2005, Asian investment in the West reached $64 billion and increased to $103 billion in 2006. At the time of this writing, data for 2007 were unavailable.

The government in Beijing, which until now has invested China's trade surpluses primarily in U.S. government bonds, is now becoming a major investor in its own right. Using Dubai International Capital LLC and Temasek Holdings, a Singapore investment company, as its models, the National Council of the People's Republic recently established its own investment company. The new company will use the central bank's treasure chest, which, with its more than $1 trillion, has the largest currency reserves in human history, to finance a politically motivated double strategy: On the one hand, the Chinese plan to buy up foreign companies, focusing on high-tech and natural resources. On the other hand, the state, by acquiring shares in domestic companies, aims to protect them from the same fate.

The Chinese central bank, the People's Bank of China (PBOC), is already the world's most influential and, in good years, the most profitable bank of our time. The difference between the interest rates paid on U.S. government bonds and the significantly lower rates the PBOC offers China's own commercial banks from its reserves amounted to nearly $30 billion in 2006. By comparison, Citibank and Bank of America earned combined profits of $21 billion in 2006.

Achieving quick profits with their investments tends to be a secondary goal for most Asian government investors. Asian investors are primarily interested in three things: the knowledge of Western scientists and researchers, the well-established global brand names of Western companies, and the network of dealers that has developed over decades, which they intend to use for their products.

The journey to the center of Western economies is costly and risky for the Asians, as evidenced by their many failures. Nevertheless, it is worthwhile, because it enables them to circumvent decades of painstaking development work. The Asians are buying time. Anyone who begins at zero technologically and never ventures abroad will never become a world leader. That is why India's Tata Group is seeking to acquire Jaguar and Land Rover, two brands the Ford Company wants to spin off. That is why Beijing is so interested in American computer companies. And that is why Singapore has acquired shares in dozens of biotech companies.

The idea of laying down roots within the cores of other economies is nothing new. In fact, it is something the Asians learned from the West in the first place. Major American corporations have been taking this approach for decades. By linking their domestic operations with factories in other countries and setting up subsidiaries and research facilities around the world, they become fixed components of the various economies. This guarantees them distribution clout and political influence, helps them grow market share, and produces earnings that can quickly be pumped back into their home operations. Promoting the advance of multinational corporations has long been a political priority in the West, particularly at the White House.

The steady advance of foreign companies has always been a source of turmoil, at least in the countries they target. When the United States began populating the world with its major corporations, the phenomenon was dubbed "Coca-Cola colonialism." But none of this troubled U.S. citizens—until their own country became the target of big foreign investment. Japanese investors began buying up U.S. television studios and real estate in the 1980s and 1990s, and the acquisition of New York's Rockefeller Center was perceived as a desecration of American soil. The U.S. Congress only recently put a stop to the proposed sale of U.S. port facilities to an Arab management company: Dubai Ports World. A Chinese bid for California-based oil company Unocal was also doomed to failure.

This doesn't stop Asian governments from trying again and again. In the past, communists were bureaucrats, often stupid and lazy. But today's descendants of Marx and Mao are clever and indefatigable. In the summer of 2007, the Chinese raised concerns in Washington once again when they tried to acquire another U.S. company, Seagate Technology, the world's largest maker of hard-disk drives.

"This is clearly a critical component of a computer system, and the purchase by the Chinese or other nations merits a full review to determine what our risks are," said Michael R. Wessell, a commissioner of the United States-China Economic and Security Review Commission, a group that monitors the national security implications of trade with China for Congress. It is still unclear whether the deal will materialize.

They will keep trying, because anyone who desires to ascend to the pinnacle of the global economy has no other choice but to go offshore and energetically penetrate into the hearts of his greatest rivals. Only those who manage to inject their capital into the productive core of other nations can join the club of the world's major powers. The Chinese government has made its goal to bring 50 of the 500 largest corporations in the world into Chinese hands within the next 10 years. Beijing plans to be the world leader in the microelectronics sector by 2015.

Strategists at China's Ministry of Foreign Trade and Economic Cooperation have prepared a document titled "List of Countries and Industries for Overseas Investment." It lists countries and industries the government believes to be worthwhile targets for investment. According to the document, the Chinese are interested in British biomedical companies and French producers of air conditioners, vacuum cleaners, and microwave ovens, among others. On a global scale, China plans to invest in countries with large reserves of oil, natural gas, iron ore, and copper. The country's state-owned utilities are investing billions to satisfy Chinese industry's thirst for energy. All of Africa has become a shopping mall for the resource-hungry Chinese.

China's approach to industrial corporate takeovers in the West follows a pattern that is worth closer inspection. The Chinese aim to link their low-wage domestic production to the distribution networks of the West so that they can add lucrative trade margins to their current production profits. One of their goals, once again, is to acquire Western knowledge in the hope of gaining quicker access to our markets. From Beijing's standpoint, Chinese computer and notebook producer Lenovo's acquisition of IBM's personal computer division was a great success. While the IBM label remains on the exterior of Lenovo's products, much of their inner workings are from Chinese production. Lenovo's strategy can be interpreted as either a clever chess move or gross deception, depending on one's point of view.

The same game is taking place in the entertainment electronics industry. Chinese manufacturer TCL has bought up an attractive collection of trademarks and shares in European and U.S. companies, thus allowing it to continue selling products—now Chinese made—to discerning customers under well-known Western names like Alcatel, Schneider, and Thomson. This strategy of tying low-wage production to established brand names has resulted in the world's largest producer of television sets. Li Dongsheng, the CEO of TCL, now heads a company that employs 20,000 people worldwide and does two-thirds of its business outside China.

The development of this new Chinese TV giant is intricately tied to the demise of French, German, and American entertainment electronics companies. RCA was once *the* American television manufacturer. The constantly recurring price offensives from the Far East, which would approach the United States like the shock waves of an earthquake, disappear for a short time, only to reappear with renewed strength, were a problem for RCA long ago. To avoid being buried under the rubble of its own high-wage production, RCA soon outsourced its production to Taiwan and Mexico.

But the rise of new competitors brought another surge of shock waves as the Asian Tiger economies followed in Japan's footsteps.

In the end, RCA's management offered itself to the Japanese, who had not yet acquired a name in the United States, as their willing helpers. That allowed Japanese manufacturer Hitachi to sell its video recorders in the United States under the RCA name. At a 1983 symposium at Harvard University, then RCA CEO Thornton Bradshaw boasted about the strength of the company's brand name, which, as he said, "is so strong that Hitachi products can be sold at higher prices under the RCA name."

Three years later, RCA ceased to exist as an independent company. The brand name lives on, but merely as window dressing for Chinese-dominated TCL. The quiet giant from China now controls the global market for television sets, its empire built on the ruins of Western television manufacturing.

China is already the world's largest market for more than 100 products, including mobile telephones and toolmaking machines. Whoever dominates this domestic market can feel confident enough to venture into the markets of the West. China's political leadership has already identified a number of candidates to lead its economic offensive.

China Mobile, China's largest mobile services supplier with its more than 230 million customers, plans to challenge U.S. and European companies like Vodafone for their dominant positions. Ningbo Bird, the country's top mobile phone manufacturer, has set its sights on Motorola, Nokia, and Samsung. Internet auction house Alibaba.com plans to give eBay a run for its money on the global market. The Chinese government is encouraging Baosteel to challenge the world's steel producing giants. Despite excess global capacity in the building market, the head of China's largest construction company, China State Construction Engineering, has declared: "We plan to become one of the world's 10 largest constructions companies."

Another Chinese success story is Haier, which, with its 50,000 employees in 13 countries, produces refrigerators and washing machines and sells them in 165 countries. The company structured its growth in the last two decades in such a way that it barely appeared on the radar screens on the Western public. Instead of making a grand entry into Western markets with its 90 product lines, Haier initially opted to introduce only a few products in the West. In the United States, for example, the Chinese company identified the miniature refrigerators used in hotel rooms as a profitable niche market that had been neglected by the competition. Haier entered the European market in the profitable air-conditioner business.

Today Haier is the fourth-largest U.S. seller of household devices across the board. The company controls 30 percent of the U.S. market for miniature refrigerators and half of the market for wine refrigerators, and in Europe it holds a 10 percent share of the air-conditioner market. The company has its U.S. headquarters in Manhattan and operates a design center in Los Angeles. It has gained a foothold in the productive core of the U.S. economy, from which it can now attack the few remaining giants still ahead of it in the household devices industry: Whirlpool, General Electric, and Electrolux. The declared goal of Haier CEO Zhang Ruimin, who is also a member of the Central Committee of the Chinese Communist Party, is market leadership. China, says Zhang, cannot be content to remain the world's factory. Instead it must "develop national strength."

The State as Protector: China's Controlled Market Economy

The state plays an important, perhaps even the deciding, role in the redistribution of wealth and power. In the West, it ensures that the productive core of the economy makes a portion of its wealth available to society as a whole. Companies retain their profits, but not entirely. Those who live outside the sphere of pure value creation also benefit from corporate success. The state serves as the relay station for the diversion of funds from the sphere of production into those sectors of the country devoted entirely to consumption. In this way, the prosperity generated in a country's productive core also reaches those who are not involved in the creation of value. Retirees were once part of the productive core, but they have since migrated to its crust. Current workers are partly responsible for generating the retirees' incomes.

Children are also part of this crust of the productive core, although they are moving in the opposite direction. As they grow older, they approach the economy's productive core, where they will later contribute to building prosperity. It is important, at this point, to fully grasp the role of the Western state: it ensures that the sphere of production is connected to the sphere of the unproductive members of society. Capitalism and the welfare state are thus interdependent.

The state serves a different function in China. It inserts itself, like a fireproof layer, between the core and the crust, ensuring that nothing can escape from the red-hot core to the perimeters. The departure of state-owned industry went hand in hand with an abandonment of the social welfare. Former Chinese premier Deng Xiaoping took China, which he insisted was already in an "advanced stage of socialism," a few steps backward. That allowed the government to claim, from then on, that the country was in fact in the first stage of socialism, as well as to terminate virtually all social contracts. Lifelong employment contracts, which had been the norm until then, were replaced by term contracts. Workers were forced to either buy the factory apartments they had been living in or move out. Social benefits were kept out of the private economy from its inception. The obligation to provide a social safety net went to the family—or to no one. Since then the government has been consistently prepared to use force to maintain its separation between the core and the crust of its economy. The labor market in China today is the world's most ruthless when it comes to employee welfare.

Even in India, the world's largest democracy, only a fraction of the population has benefited from the earnings of the country's economic machinery. One-quarter of the world's poor live in India, where they have been completely sidelined during the current economic boom. Perhaps that explains India's traditionally low voter turnout, with only half of the adult population participating in elections.

The Hindu caste system, which assigns the faithful to their place in society at birth, has proven to be an instrument of oppression that continues to thrive in a capitalist age. India's "Untouchables" still perform the most degrading tasks, which even include cleaning the toilets of other Indians with their bare hands. The modern age has yet to arrive in the countryside, where residents often get their drinking water from a nearby river or not at all. An estimated 350 million Indians continue to have no access to sanitary facilities. Hygienic conditions reminiscent of the Middle Ages prevail in rural areas, a glaring problem the government has taken few serious steps to correct. Modern India exists on islands of prosperity that are completely disconnected from the overwhelming poverty of the majority of its people.

That official callousness was the dominant political issue in the last elections, in which the governing party in power at the time used "Radiant India" as its campaign slogan. But despite this attention, India's government has yet to consider the establishment of a nationwide welfare state, mainly because its main competitor, China, has also failed to take any serious steps in this direction. "We will not take any steps that would hold up the rate of growth in any form," Indian Finance Minister Chidambaram said.

The Chinese Communist Party is also familiar with the needs and desires of its population, to which it even pays lip service. As part of its eleventh five-year plan, Beijing voices the stated intention of creating a "harmonious society" by 2010. In truth, however, the Communist Party has done nothing to change its ways. Beijing only recently introduced its biggest program ever to foster capitalist enterprise, a new system under which government support for private enterprise will no longer be behind the scenes and almost conspiratorial, as it was in the past. The Chinese communists have made their change of heart loud and clear, even amending the constitution to make it clear to all that this is not just another reform, but a revolution. Until March 2004, the state was responsible for the "instruction, supervision, and regulation" of the private sector. As Big Brother, the state had the power to discipline and harass, dispense or withhold its favor. Under the new constitution, private property is defined as truly private for the first time.

Private property is now considered "inviolable." Even inheritances will be protected in China in the future. Article 11 of the new constitution even calls upon the state to make itself useful to private enterprise, to provide "encouragement and support" to capitalists. The capitalists are the new master class. Entrepreneurs have never been courted in quite the same way by any other country in the world. In China, capital now has more rights than the people.

Even deaths are tacitly accepted in Chinese economic life. According to Western estimates, there were roughly 100,000 fatal industrial accidents in 2006, including about 10,000 in the mining industry. These are the biggest casualty figures that have ever been reported in the country. Also public health is heavily crippled. Pollution has made cancer China's leading cause of death, the Ministry of Health has announced.

The use of child labor plays an important role in export promotion, an essential component of the Asian economic miracle. About seven million children are sent to work in China, and about 130 million in all of Asia. They weave carpets, haul heavy loads, and assemble plastic parts to make plastic toys. But most of all, they pull down the cost of labor.

We have not seen this sort of raw capitalism, which places profit above everything else, even the rights of children to a proper childhood and the rights of the population to decent health care, since the wild days of the Industrial Revolution. It is as if Karl Marx had arrived at his conclusions about the unscrupulousness of capital in Chinese mines and Indian textile mills. "Capital," Marx wrote, "is terrified of the absence of profit or of a very small profit, just as nature is terrified of emptiness. But with the appropriate profit capital becomes bold. At 10 percent security capital can be used everywhere; it becomes lively at 20 percent, positively daring at 50 percent, and for a 100 percent return it crushes all human laws beneath its feet. At 300 percent, there is no crime it is not willing to risk, even at the prospect of the gallows."

By now the 70 million members of the Chinese Communist Party practically form an honor guard whenever major corporations register their demands. What began as an underground party of intellectuals in the Chinese imperial era now feels committed to what former president and party leader Jiang Zemin, at the beginning of this century, called "triple representation." Under this approach, the Communist Party seeks to simultaneously serve the workers and farmers, those who produce culture, and "the development requirements of the progressive productive forces." Corporate envoys, like Haier's CEO, have been accepted into the party's inner sanctum, the Central Committee.

China's communists are not the sorts of communists who were once in power in Moscow. They are nationalists who, after decades of wandering, now plan to guide their country into the upper echelon of affluent countries. China's private capital, which the authoritarian state protects as if it were its greatest treasure, plays the decisive role in this endeavor. As a result of this state-sponsored nurturing, the private economy has been growing at a record pace—by a phenomenal 40 percent in 2000, and at 20 percent per year since then. Two decades after the country launched its reform policies, the private sector already produces more than one-third of China's total economic output, a share that increases to more than 60 percent when semiprivate businesses are included. In return, the state-owned sector is declining in importance, a shift that also affects the labor market.

Today, large swathes of the country are special economic zones. Their sole purpose is to allow profit to develop, profit in its purest, virtually crystalline form. That is precisely the difference between the Chinese and Soviet systems. The Soviet communist state was a great drag on wealth, sucking it out of the innermost core of its already ailing economy. Nationalist China, however, is a protector of the productive core. The party has molded itself around the productive core and does its utmost to prevent any energy from escaping. In the Soviet Union, political circumstances led to a decades-long flow of energy out of the core, allowing it to cool off to such an extent that the state could no longer provide for its own population. Europe's breadbasket became a wheat importer. Its weapons systems deteriorated, its production machinery was dependent on Western spare parts, and, with declining oil prices, what was once a superpower soon lacked the economic energy to be able to continue defining itself as a superpower.

We observe the opposite taking place in China, where the government looks after, protects, and nurtures the economy's initially puny but now powerful productive core. To do so, it neglects all other obligations. Farmers are suffering, after being forced to accept significant declines in income in recent years. China's farmers earned an average of $60 a month in 2004—the same as in 1993. The miserable existence of the country's migrant workers is blatantly obvious. Nearly 500 million people lack access to safe drinking water, and even the military went through two decades of significant cutbacks before the leadership decided to begin a new arms buildup. With the brutality with which only an authoritarian regime can go about its business, the Chinese leadership forces everything out of its way that could possibly slow the country's ascent to economic dominance.

The productive cores in China and India are constantly being fueled with new energy derived from the economy's crust. It is the state that ensures that the unemployed and poor rural workers are gradually integrated into the process of production. That may appear to be a contradiction, but in fact it is not. The state provides the necessary fuel for growth by neglecting the needs of the population. The misfortunes of millions are in fact a boon to their leaders.

The contrast to the West could not be more obvious. While European economies steadily shed their workers in the direction of retirement, job creation schemes, welfare, and unemployment, Asia is taking the opposite approach. More and more new workers are being injected into the production process, but under the brutal conditions the process itself dictates. In other words, the nonexistent welfare state fulfills an additional function. Not only does it protect the innermost core of the economy, but it also adds additional productive workers to the core as a result of its nonexistence: workers who have no choice but to offer their services at whatever price they can get.

Corporate profits are the difference between the poverty wages of workers and the revenues of companies. Profit is the fuel that constantly raises the temperature in the innermost cores of the Chinese, Indian, and many other Asian economies. For the foreseeable future, the enormous supply of human labor will ensure that labor, as a commodity, will remain as cheap as it is today. Every year, millions of people in China alone abandon agriculture to work in the country's industrial operations. They live in cramped conditions, sleeping two and three to a bed, and they accept wages sometimes as low as a few cents an hour. Breathing down their necks are the unemployed, an estimated 175 million in China and 100 million in India, as well as the 375 million waiting in the wings in the two countries' agricultural sectors for their chance to live and work in the cities. This labor reserve is larger than the entire active workforce in the United States and Europe combined.

In addition to these existing reserves, China and India are both giant countries with burgeoning population growth. As long as their governments manage to keep these people in reserve and willing to work for next to nothing, they will continue to represent a vast industrial reserve and thus the Indians' and the Chinese' greatest boon in the global war for wealth. The people themselves suffer as a result, but the economy only becomes stronger.

It is important to understand the differences between an emerging economy and a society in decline. Even the word *unemployed* means two different things in the two systems. The unemployed in the West are yesterday's workers, while the unemployed in China are tomorrow's workers. The former are a burden on the economy, because they cost money. The latter are useful to the economy, because their mere presence alone is enough to depress the wages of others. They ensure that China's employed workers remain cheap and willing.

The approach taken by Asia's leaders is as brutal as it is ingenious. It is brutal because it excludes millions from the ability to participate in the fruits of economic growth, with many rural residents, especially in the country's north, witnessing a China on television that has nothing in common with their daily lives. It is ingenious because the state uses this strategy to protect its growth cores as fiercely as an eagle protects its young, anxious to prevent an export industry from escaping that would strike fear into the hearts of the rest of the world. Given China's limited capital resources, a redistribution policy oriented toward the West would slow the development process or perhaps even make it impossible altogether. Only the concentrated deployment of resources in the coastal regions, where the country's profitable new factories are being built, promises quick breakthroughs.

The Chinese and Indian ascents are not in fact the ascents of entire countries, but of only portions of the population and parts of the country. Both are coincident with the relative decline of millions of people. India's slums, where animals and people alike lead a miserable existence, are often a stone's throw from the country's sparkling new hospital complexes, pharmaceutical factories, and computer plants. It's been 60 years since the British left the country, and yet more than half of the Indian population remains illiterate. Only one in four children attends school.

The government in Beijing is pursuing a two-China policy. Shanghai, a city of 18 million people, is another New York, with a standard of living on par with that of Portugal. Barren western China, however, which makes up two-thirds of the country's total land mass, remains virtually untouched by the boom. Ethnic minorities living in China's border region are familiar with the Chinese economic miracle by hearsay alone. Their standard of living corresponds to that of the poorest of African countries. For them, the special economic zones, with their sparkling cities, are paradise on earth and the sum of all desires.

Additionally, the state extends its protection of its productive core beyond the domestic front, taking great pains to do so on the international stage. One of the first steps it takes is to use a currency that is not freely convertible. By fixing an artificially low exchange rate for the Renminbi, the Chinese government has constructed a protective barrier that has served the country well.

Foreign capital can enter the country with relative ease, but getting it back out is another story. The Chinese currency's value represents the biggest export promotion program a government has ever funded. In return, China's currency policy keeps the cost of imports, that is, orders in America and Europe, artificially high.

China's successes are impressive. Significantly more goods are shipped to the United States than China imports from the United States. For years the Chinese finance minister and the U.S. secretary of commerce have encouraged a significant currency appreciation, a policy even the U.S. president has supported. Meanwhile, the Chinese leadership is busy laughing its way to the bank. The country's productive core can depend on the state for protection.

Betrayed, Poisoned, and Sold Down the River: Why Exploiting the Environment Is Good for Growth

In addition to human labor, a second resource is available to the emerging nations to fuel their economic machinery at bargain-basement prices: the natural environment. They exploit the environment to their heart's content and with few if any misgivings. Mother Earth serves as a cesspool, the desert is used as a garbage dump, and the lungs of neighboring residents often double as the initial filter for factory exhausts. The pesticides used liberally in intensive factory farming end up in the food and water supply, turning the human body itself into a toxic waste dump of sorts. The light gray layer of smog that has developed in Shanghai probably contains most of the industrial hazardous particles and pollutants known to humans. Many local residents seek to protect themselves from this toxic cloud by wearing masks. Chinese industrial zones lead the world in the incidence of respiratory disease.

China is responsible for nothing short of monstrous growth in emissions of carbon dioxide (CO_2) gas, the main culprit in global warming—an increase of 100 percent since 1990. In a few years, perhaps as early as 2008, the People's Republic will have surpassed the United States as the world's largest emitter of greenhouse gases. The effects are already palpable in China. Last year was the warmest since 1951, and last winter brought new record highs. In Beijing, the normally frigid Chinese New Year was the warmest on record—a springlike 63 degrees Fahrenheit. Meteorologists point out that China has had 19 warm winters since 1987. The effects of these higher temperatures are already clearly reflected in the water balance of huge sections of the country. In addition to fast-paced urban and industrial expansion, erosion and silting have cost the country valuable farmland. As one of the consequences of this shrinkage, China has become a major buyer of basic foods on international markets.

If American standards for fine particulate matter, the quality of drinking water, and the pesticide content in foods were applied in Asia's cities, many of the continent's factories would have to be shut down and cars banished from the roads altogether.

For economic reasons alone, it seems high time to put an end to China's game. In addition to posing health hazards today, burning up environmental resources at this rate jeopardizes tomorrow's growth. In the cold light of day, this policy of overexploitation of natural resources is nothing but an especially cunning form of government debt. The banks see and feel nothing, the government can claim to be producing budget surpluses and not deficits, and international observers praise the country for the tremendous progress it has made in developing its economy. But what is really happening is a depletion of assets that will come at the cost of future generations.

China, the country with the most impressive growth rates in recent years, also tops the list of countries with little respect for their people and environment. Last spring, a World Bank study done with SEPA, the national environmental agency, concluded that outdoor air pollution was already causing nearly 400,000 premature deaths a year. Indoor pollution contributed to the death of an additional 300,000 people, many of them as the result of bladder problems, diarrhea, and stomach cancer.

China's deserts are growing at a rate of more than 965 square miles (2,500 square kilometers) per year. Two-thirds of urban wastewater flows untreated into rivers or seeps into the ground-water. Seventy percent of China's bodies of water are already highly polluted. Toxic chemicals such as arsenic, phosphates, and fluorine, as well as herbicides and pesticides, are disseminated from there, some into the human body. Sadly, the number of cases of liver cancer has reached record levels in many parts of China. In many places, local environmental laws are little more than a way of placating the West, and violations have become the rule rather than the exception.

China's dictatorship and India's democracy vie with each other when it comes to the unscrupulousness with which they exploit nature as a free source of raw materials and receptacle for waste. Overgrazing, excessive fertilizing, and salinization have laid 210 million acres of fertile land to waste since India's independence. Under a forest management plan devised in 1951, one-third of the country was to remain forested. Satellite images show that only 14 percent of India's forests remain standing today. As it happens, Asia's economic growth is not based solely on increasing the performance and efficiency of human beings and machinery, but also on the increased exploitation of natural resources. The Asian economies are energy intensive but not energy efficient. The Chinese economy consumes four times as many resources as American manufacturers to produce the same $10,000 worth of goods. While Wal-Mart may offer goods at discount prices, the true cost of these goods is much higher.

American companies play an unattractive role in China. They cooperate with the polluters of Chinese industry. Their internal environmental standards, drafted in the United States, are usually valid only on paper in China. An environmental scandal involving a Chinese company, Fuan Textiles, shines a glaring light on the Chinese connections of U.S. corporations.

Fuan, a company based in southern China and a supplier to dozens of American retailers, including Wal-Mart Stores, Land's End, and Nike, received a surprise inspection. Nearby residents had complained to authorities that the river flowing past the company's plant was colored bright red.

The authorities discovered a pipe buried underneath the factory floor that was dumping roughly 22,000 tons of water contaminated from its dyeing operations each day into the river. The multinationals noticed nothing. Why? Because they chose not to notice anything. Nike prides itself on its strict environmental compliance requirements, which include regular water quality inspections. But those regular inspections were in fact performed by a laboratory selected by Nike—on water samples taken by the Chinese joint venture partners. "It is possible," Nike admitted after the scandal broke, "to forge these samples."

In many cases, the sole purpose of government inspections is to allay the concerns of the population. The Chinese government literally encourages industry to continue its antisocial practices in the future, because it considers water, air, and ground pollution little more than a minor infraction, a necessary by-product of development. China has laws designed to protect the environment but very few to ensure compliance. The government shamefully looks the other way as industry steadily pollutes rivers, the soil, and the air.

At the first United Nations environmental conference in Stockholm, Sweden, a Chinese delegate readily admitted: "We will not give up eating for fear of suffocation, nor will we abandon our plans to develop our industry for fear of polluting the environment." This statement was made in 1972. The bad news is that the Chinese official's words are as true today as they were three and a half decades ago. A country fighting hunger cannot reduce its CO_2 emissions at the same time, officials in Beijing said before the last Group of Eight (G8) summit. "China is not getting its environmental problems under control," says Zhu Guangyao, deputy minister of SEPA, the country's environmental agency. "The situation does not give rise to optimism."

To mark World Environment Day, Zhu presented China's environmental report for 2006, the first significant assessment of its kind in a decade. The report's conclusions were shocking. The annual cost of damage to the environment, according to the report, already amounts to 10 percent of China's gross domestic product—which also happens to equal the country's economic growth rate.

Losers and Winners: An Interim Assessment of Globalization

Do cheap imports offer the West a tremendous price advantage, or are they an unmistakable sign of its demise? Who are the winners and losers in this game of poker for power and wealth? Is globalization a blessing or a curse for the West?

There are three possible answers to these questions, and they depend exclusively on the observer's point of view. Anyone can call a spade a spade, but each of us must answer individually the question of whether globalization is good or bad. A person's stance toward globalization depends to a large extent on how he or she fares under globalization. The fact that some welcome it, others mistrust it, and a third group wants nothing to do with it is a matter of their respective interests. It goes against human nature to support something that contradicts our interests, and no one should expect others to do so.

The powerful see the world through different eyes than the weak. Those who, like Wall Street's CEOs, stand resolutely before a map of the world, constantly scoping out new opportunities around the globe, clearly see globalization in a different light than those who are already on their knees. A phenomenon that promises untold opportunities to some represents the height of unfairness to others.

Most business executives take a more relaxed view today of the newly developing world than do workers and the unemployed. Businesses earn profits from a development that allows them to make their companies more competitive, and by increasing imports they may even be able to improve on their own exports. They have an easier time of dealing with unions than they did in the past, because they hold virtually all trump cards in their hand. It is no longer the high-wage workers at home who are setting wage levels, but low-wage workers abroad. The declines in real wages during the Bush years, as disappointing as they have been for the affected families, are a boon to businesses. Business owners are eager to embrace a new era that promises them the best of all worlds: millions of new customers and cheap labor.

While capitalism has extended its reach, the welfare state has been diminished. Both circumstances translate into handsome profits for the entrepreneur. Smart capitalists who know how to take advantage of imports produced by low-wage workers, if only as a means of applying pressure to their domestic employees, are clearly some of globalization's biggest winners. They can report growing revenues and generally rising profits to shareholders, which in turn do wonders for the prices of their companies' stocks. In addition to having the right to vote in their native countries, capitalists now have access to a convenient exit strategy. For entrepreneurs, investing at home remains a possibility but no longer a necessity. Armed with their capital, they can now travel far and wide. The free capital and labor market have made them free people. We can condemn, admire, or envy these entrepreneurs for their actions, but we should not overestimate them. They, too, are herd animals, eternally damned to continue trotting along behind trends. If they refuse to abide by the customs of the global economy, all they can expect is a speedy demise.

Blue-collar and low-wage, white-collar workers face the new age with growing skepticism. Who can blame them? Their experiences with it so far have been overwhelmingly negative. Because labor has become so cheap and abundant worldwide, workers have lost the clout they may have once had to defend their interests during wage negotiations. The wage pressure that invariably springs from globalization is far more beneficial to a company's shareholders than to those employees who are being forced to accept lower wages.

The decline in the real value of unskilled labor is especially evident in the United States. There is no social class that is permitted to live off of the handouts of others. To wit, there is the phenomenon known as the "welfare queen," but she has remained marginal, especially since the welfare state is unprepared to offer anything approaching a royal lifestyle to welfare recipients. To confront the new reality, yesterday's industrial workers seek alternate employment. But the new jobs are no longer as lucrative as the old ones. The former land of factory workers, in which one-time steelworkers, furniture makers, and computer assemblers must now toil as masseurs and masseuses, cleaning staff, and messengers, is not a promised land for those adversely affected by this shift. American wages in the new professions are lower than those in the old by about one-third. For this reason, the mountain of consumer debt is not the consequence of unbridled consumer spending, as some claim. Instead, it is emblematic of the attempt by workers to prolong their old lives with the help of credit cards and bank loans.

Those who have managed to keep their jobs have been living in a different, happier world. Most members of the middle-class workforce have been among the winners of globalization for many years. Many blue-collar and white-collar workers might have considered the new age with a healthy and, more recently, growing sense of mistrust. But they have not suffered any damage, at least not until now. Their incomes might have risen, stagnated, or declined, but their purchasing power has increased substantially. That has brought down the real cost to them of television sets and clothing. In some cases, a new car costs even less than its predecessor, a circumstance that has significantly helped preserve the buying power of declining incomes. Many employees have benefited as a result of the misfortunes of others, but their delight at getting the same products for less has outweighed any lingering sense of guilt. The decline in prices, including the price of labor, has suddenly given them access to inexpensive products. The standard of living, or what we believe to be the standard of living, has risen.

Those making a living in the export industry have been considered lucky beyond compare. The attackers from the Far East have been their most willing buyers. Earnings have blossomed everywhere, so much so that workers in exporting industries in fact have seen respectable wage increases. The engineers, lawyers, and marketing specialists in these companies have earned a good living. For a long time, it has even appeared that the winnings of the winners would more than offset the losses of the losers.

Many have now begun to realize that the cost of cheap imports is twofold, and that low store prices and declining wages are in fact two sides of the same coin. The net result for the worker is the ability to purchase more goods. But in many cases this ability has come at the cost of lower net earnings for the worker. The competitiveness of companies and the declining pay of workers are interdependent, not contradictory. Professor Jagdish Bhagwati, a declared proponent of and leading authority on globalization, says, "It's like being in a crowded lifeboat. Only if one of the passengers jumps into the water can the other nine survive."

Many Triumphs and One Death: The Tragic History of Trade Unions

A tragic death has taken place in American society, but it is one that has not yet been announced to the public. What makes it especially tragic is the fact that even close relatives are reluctant to talk about it. But whether we know about it or not, the fact remains that the trade unions, at least what we once defined as trade unions, have died. Today's unions no longer exist as a protective cloak for society's ordinary members, because they lack the power to provide protection to anyone. In fact, even the unions need protection. They once viewed themselves as a buffer against corporate capriciousness. They played a powerful role in achieving fair wages, and sometimes they even acted as a political counterweight within society. Nowadays these types of unions are part of history.

The development of a global labor market, the addition of 1.5 billion new workers, and the willingness of millions of other people to work at all costs have robbed the brokers of labor, as a commodity, of their once-powerful position. For decades they controlled an asset with no equal: the well-trained—and thus irreplaceable—industrial worker. Industrial robots were not yet sufficiently advanced and most of today's wage competitors lived in Eastern Europe behind high walls and barbed wire or were trapped in the quagmires of Asian slums. They were all people, but on the labor market they were not full-fledged individuals. They were barred from participating in the West's international division of labor, an impediment that kept the price of Western labor comfortably high.

Union leaders were powerful enough to continually force businesses to raise wages. Factory owners had no choice but to use the unions as middlemen, because all they had to choose from were their domestic markets, or at best the Western labor market, but not a global labor market with its unique and abundant supply of willing workers. Workers were scarce after the two world wars, and the unions in some industries practically held a monopoly on this scarce commodity. They took full advantage of their powerful position.

To prevent the demise of the unions from being too conspicuous, union leaders today continue to take part in wage negotiations. Like their predecessors, they still wear leather jackets and plaid shirts, and sometimes they even give the same rousing speeches. In recent years, the fickle public could even be forgiven for believing that the corpse is still alive. The employers sitting across the table are willing participants in this gruesome game, fearing that the news of the unions' death could frighten people and encourage them to demand a replacement. Employers never liked the unions, especially in their energetic and courageous days, when they were powerful enough to force companies to jump through hoops. Businesses are much fonder of unions in the form of corpses.

A closer look reveals all too clearly that the new union leaders lack the same power as their predecessors. They lack the energy and drive needed to cause trouble, present demands, and stage strikes. Unions have long abandoned their traditional task of improving the working and living conditions of ordinary workers. Their primary goal today is to prevent things from deteriorating even further. Union officials are no longer proud workers, but victims.

The new union leaders are even in the process of jettisoning the great union achievements of the past. The workweek is getting longer, laws protecting workers against unlawful termination are filling up with loopholes, real wages are declining, and the ratio of wages to national income is dropping as profit margins increase. Autoworkers are even being pressured to give up portions of the retirement pensions they were once guaranteed. The union, which now supports the dismantlement of social benefits, once fought bitterly to expand these same benefits.

At issue is not whether the unions have always acted correctly. Nobody's perfect. Of course, union officials have sinned, sometimes even acting against the interests of union members. And, of course, they occasionally have been prone to exaggeration, which has not done the workers any good.

But there was one thing the unions undeniably had: they were alive. Unions might have been a thorn in the side of capitalists, but they were a necessary one. In its unrefined state, the system of supply and demand was clearly not designed to benefit all. Millions of workers suffered brutal treatment at the dawn of capitalism. They were forced to work until they dropped, and even then there was no one there to catch them. There was no safety net for anyone. The elderly remained poor, the disabled were left to their own devices, and widows could consider themselves lucky if they received condolences from factory owners. The unemployed were even worse off than workers, often starving or freezing to death. Fewer than 80 years ago the global economic crisis was so severe in the United States and Europe that people there were dying of starvation. Work accidents were common in mines and chemical factories, partly because so little value was attached to human life. The worker was a production factor, not a full-fledged member of society.

For this reason, the birth of the Western trade union movement was not just another footnote in world history but instead a historical necessity. Workers and their representatives formed a community of interest, while reckless capitalism and an authoritarian state, two entities incapable of establishing common ground, were the glue that bonded them together. The unions soon began growing in many countries. In their heyday, Western Europe's unions boasted 50 million and American unions 22 million members. They staged strikes and demonstrations, partly as a show of strength.

Labor organizations took longer to become established in America, but when they did, they managed to bring about important changes. They achieved the eight-hour workday and a legal minimum wage, first changing the climate and later the commercial basis of the country's economic system. The predatory nature of American capitalism never quite disappeared, but it became less apparent. The Great Depression was a boon to the unions. In the wake of those dark years, their membership rolls doubled, and then grew to 15 million people between 1930 and the end of World War II. The Depression shattered the public's belief in the wisdom of business owners, while the call for a counterforce, in the form of unions, became louder and louder. For the first time in U.S. history, being a union member was considered modern. The country experienced a first under President Dwight D. Eisenhower: Martin P. Durkin, the former president of the American Federation of Labor (AFL) Plumbers' Union, was appointed secretary of labor, although his tenure lasted only eight months.

Working hours declined and wages rose. Companies agreed to pay their employees' contributions to retirement pensions. The unions were able to expand their power base even further, adding about 100,000 new members per year in the postwar era, until 17 million U.S. workers held a union card. At the unions' peak in 1953, close to 33 percent of the U.S. workforce was unionized—giving organized labor a key trump card in wage negotiations.

This game has ended. In fact, if the union success story were a movie, it would have been running backwards for some time now. The working week is getting longer, and wages are stagnating or even declining. The unions have been backed into a corner, and while there have been sparks here and there, the unions show few signs of fighting back. Like their Western European relatives, American unions bit the dust long ago. The disappearance of industry has robbed them of their strength. Only 8 percent of workers in the private sector are members of a union today. Since its zenith in the mid-1950s, organized labor has lost three-fourths of its membership.

The unions' ability to shape wage policy in the United States has never been immense, but today it is marginal. Eighty-five percent of all workers in the United States work without collective wage agreements. Those blue-collar and white-collar workers who are organized are represented by a wide range of individual unions, the smallest of which, the blacksmiths' union, has all of 85 members. About 100,000 individual wage agreements are currently in force—an average of one wage agreement for every 160 employees.

The story is similar in Europe, but the time of death varies from one country to the next. The demise of unions came earlier in Great Britain than in other European countries. Former prime minister Margaret Thatcher broke the backbone of Britain's unions in the 1980s, with the help of parliament and the police. Recalcitrant mineworkers, led by Arthur Scargill, offered the prime minister the opportunity to strike. In fact, it was in this dispute that Thatcher first acquired the nickname "Iron Lady." In 1984 she ordered the closure of unprofitable mines. Scargill, an avowed Marxist and experienced hothead, called for a nationwide strike. In the years leading up to the mine controversy, 2,000 strikes a year were not uncommon, but this time Scargill was calling upon British workers to stage a large-scale attack, leaving Thatcher with no other choice but to go into battle.

The country faced a mountain of debt, and the government's budget, like that of a third world country, was dependent on support from the IMF. British industry was in the doldrums when, in June 1984, striking mine workers and mounted police faced off in what became known as the "Battle of Orgreave." The ensuing year-long strike in the country's traditional coal-mining regions ended with such a crushing defeat for workers that it took them back decades.

During her time in office, Thatcher eliminated many of the key achievements of the labor movement, including the requirement that British companies hire only union members. Since then, secret votes must be held before strikes, sharply reducing the clout of union leaders. Nowadays standard wage scales exist only in public service. Since labor's most combative days, the country's unions have lost close to half their members, an exodus of six million people. Despite being a Social Democrat, former prime minister Tony Blair did not even attempt to revive the union movement.

The retreat of unions was not to remain a British phenomenon. Nowadays Italy's labor organizations are little more than clubs of retirees. More than 50 percent of the members of the moderate and the socialist union are retired. France's labor unions seem happiest when quarreling with one another. In a population of 60 million, the membership of all labor organizations combined amounts to only two million, predominantly in the public sector. Unions have all but disappeared from the French private sector, where 95 percent of employees are not members of any organized labor group.

The declining support of workers for organized labor in the United States led to a split in the umbrella organization of American unions in the fall of 2005. A few days after the organization's 50-year anniversary, two top unions representing four million members split off from the American Federation of Labor /Congress of Industrial Organizations (AFL/CIO). They accused the organization's leadership, especially its 72-year-old president, John Sweeney, of having failed to stem the decline of unions. The renegade unions formed a federation they called "Change to Win," but in reality the move, by dividing labor, has only weakened the trade union movement. A more apt motto would be "Change to Die."

But this death should be kept a secret for as long as possible. This is something on which, for once, union bosses and corporate leaders can agree. The unions are embarrassed by their own powerlessness, while employers fear that singing a requiem could spark a desire for the rebirth of strong unions.

The Emergence of a New Underclass

Members of today's underclass are poorer than their predecessors were at the beginning of the industrial age, despite the fact that they enjoy a higher standard of living. They are not starving, have a roof over their heads, are not afflicted by disease, and even have significantly more money in the bank. In every country of the West they are both citizens and customers of the welfare state, even when its benefits are no longer as abundant as they once were. In the early days, the poor slept in homeless shelters or male dormitories. They ate their meals in soup kitchens, sometimes in the open air. The fortunes of the elderly depended on the generosity of the young or religious charities.

Nevertheless, workers of days gone by had many things that today's poor lack: a uniform and generally valid concept of the enemy, class consciousness, true opponents, and, in many cases, even a well-developed cultural life. They sang songs, chanted slogans, established organizations, and worshiped the great theorists of the day, even if they never quite understood what they were talking about. They were often able to choose among political groups that vied for their approval. Looking back on the past, it is by no means an exaggeration to declare yesterday's poor the subjects of history. But poor people today are little more than victims of circumstance. Their predecessors stood on the perimeter of society, but today's poor have been excluded entirely.

We now know a great deal about the members of today's lower classes, even though they are a largely silent group. They choose to remain inconspicuous, burrowing ever more deeply into their ghettoes, hotly pursued by scores of sociologists. Their living habits have been researched like those of wild rabbits. We have developed a carefully mapped out typology that enables us to better identify these strangers in our own countries.

This is why we know that today's underclass people have more money than the workers of past generations. They also exhibit clear symptoms of intellectual decay. The new underclass members spend half of their day watching television, have a copious and high-fat diet, and often are heavy smokers and drinkers. They have many children but tend to lack a stable family life. They expect next to nothing from politics. Indeed, a modern-day Martin Luther King would be hard-pressed to recruit more than a handful of followers. The depoliticization of the working class is already well underway. Those who are cut off from the U.S. welfare machine become increasingly apathetic when it comes to taking part in the democratic process.

Today's poor people are no reincarnation of yesterday's poor people. Their lack of interest in education is one of their most defining characteristics. They have no education, and yet they make no effort to acquire one. Unlike the workers of the early industrial age, who joined workers' organizations, which often offered the additional benefit of providing vocational training, it appears that modern members of the underclass have already given up on themselves. They even make little effort to help their children find a better future. Their language education is as poor as their ability to concentrate. As illiteracy grows, the opportunities available to the working class to become more integrated into society shrink.

The new underclass class has only developed as a homogeneous class within the last decade. None of the industrialized nations that call themselves the world's leaders are immune. The modern economy apparently has nothing to offer people who have either no knowledge or scant knowledge that is often flawed.

It is no accident that the emergence of the new underclass coincides with the loss of jobs to emerging nations. The process of deindustrialization may very well be more significant to the United States than the fall of the Iron Curtain was for Europe. The processes of disintegration within society pose a greater threat to the United States as a whole today than international terrorism, despite politicians' propensity to focus on fighting the latter. Poverty is also color-blind. Indeed, the majority of the roughly 38 million Americans living below the poverty line at the end of 2007 are white, not black.

Bombs can shake democracy and the market economy but not eliminate them altogether. The economic erosion process we are discussing here is far more destructive. First, it eradicates a society's jobs, then it eats away at its financial underpinnings, and, in the end, it deprives society of its democratic legitimacy. How much is it worth to be citizen of a country in which other citizens are shut out of the working world? What good are civil liberties if the right to leading an independent life is lost? Is it acceptable that only the educated are able to effectively exercise their constitutional right to participate in society, by voting, for instance? And what happens if another 40 million white-collar jobs do in fact go offshore in our lifetime, as Princeton professor Alan Blinder has predicted?

Questions of fundamental importance are now coming to the fore. Can a democracy truly accept that some of its people are permanently excluded from the chance to acquire wealth? And if it does accept this state of affairs, will we witness the serious consequences of this decision in our lifetimes? Will we see wars erupt between nations because the underprivileged classes will need an outlet to vent all of their bottled-up rage, or will the poor ultimately challenge conditions in their own countries?

Both scenarios are possible. More unrealistic is the notion that nothing will happen. The "two Americas" that 2008 Democratic presidential contender John Edwards made a central theme of his campaign are a reality today. It would be pointless to question their existence. This raises another fundamental question: will the two Americas clash, or will society manage to come to terms with itself?

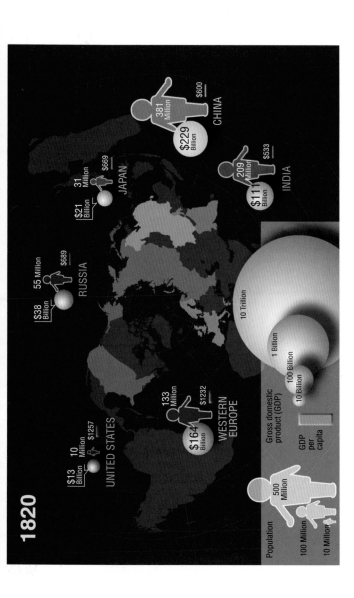

1820

The world in the preindustrial age: China lies ahead of the countries that will later form Western Europe. The United States is still an economic dwarf.

GDP in 1990 prices, PPP (purchasing power parity) adjusted; map based on current territorial borders

Source: Maddison

Population
500 Million
100 Million
10 Million

Gross domestic product (GDP)

GDP per capita

10 Trillion
1 Billion
100 Billion
10 Billion

UNITED STATES
$13 Billion
10 Million
$1257

WESTERN EUROPE
133 Million
$1232
$164 Billion

RUSSIA
$38 Billion
55 Million
$689

JAPAN
31 Million
$669
$21 Billion

CHINA
381 Million
$600
$229 Billion

INDIA
209 Million
$533
$111 Billion

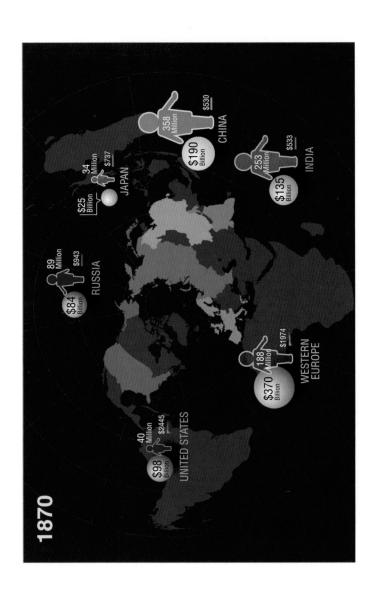

1870

The industrial age has begun. Europe becomes the world's leading producer of wealth. China falls behind and America awakens.

GDP in 1990 prices, PPP (purchasing power parity) adjusted

Source: Maddison

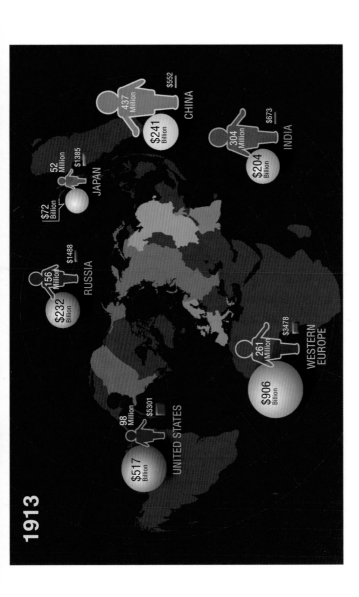

1913

The European age: Before the outbreak of World War I, Europe leads the industrialized world. China and India have stagnated, while America is booming. Tomorrow's world power is beginning to emerge.

GDP in 1990 prices, PPP (purchasing power parity) adjusted

Source: Maddison

1950

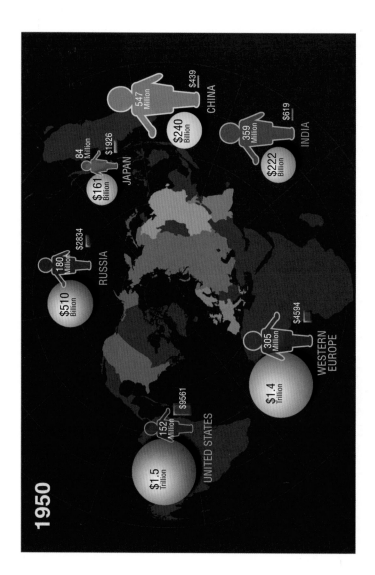

Two world wars have shifted the balance, as America rises to become the "Master of the Universe." Europe is preoccupied with reconstruction. China and India fall further behind.

GDP in 1990 prices, PPP (purchasing power parity) adjusted

Source: Maddison

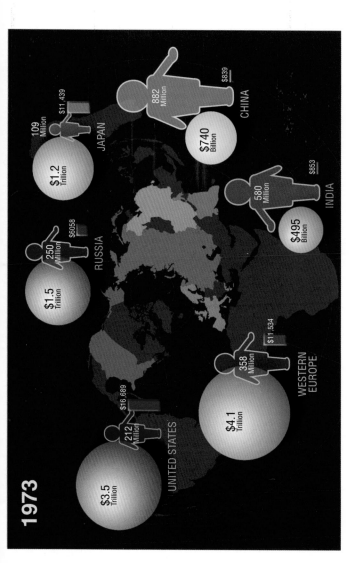

1973

Europe after the economic miracle. The old world is opening itself up to the new world once again. The Soviet Union cannot keep up in the competition for wealth. China and India remain marginal in terms of economic importance.

GDP in 1990 prices, PPP (purchasing power parity) adjusted

Source: Maddison

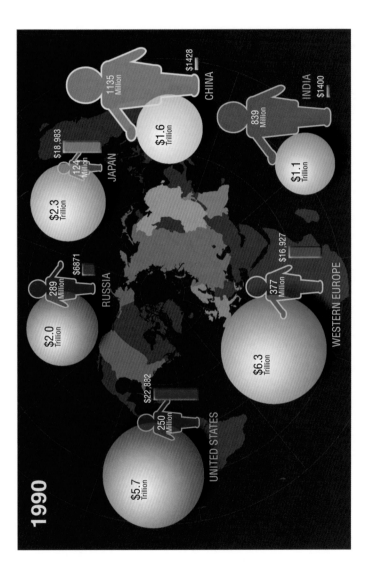

1990

The West dominates the rest of the world. But Japan has moved ahead of the Soviet Union, and the rest of Asia is also beginning to catch up. China, under Deng Xiaoping, launches into an impressive surge of growth.

GDP in 1990 prices, PPP (purchasing power parity) adjusted

Source: Maddison

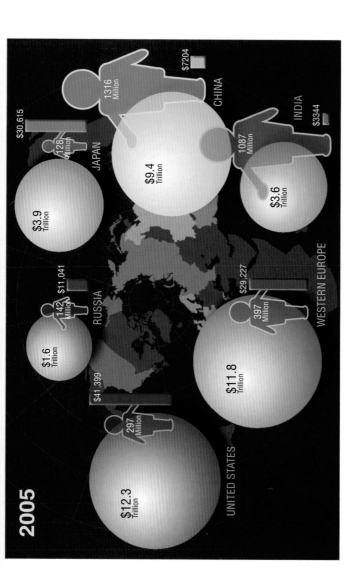

2005

China has entered the club of global economic powers and prepares to move ahead of other countries. Russia falls behind, while India develops, but only gradually at first.

GDP in 2005 prices, PPP (purchasing power parity) adjusted

Source: IMF

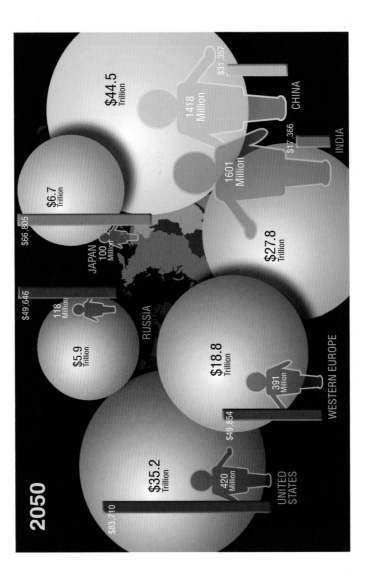

2050

A prognosis by investment bank Goldman Sachs projects the present into the future, placing China ahead of the United States. Europe, once the engine of industrialization, falls back significantly, even behind India. Russia, with its abundant natural resources, reappears on the global stage.

Prognosis: Goldman Sachs, Western Europe: Estimate based on the Goldman Sachs prognosis; GDP in 2003 prices

UNITED STATES — $35.2 Trillion — 420 Million — $83,710 — $49,854

RUSSIA — $5.9 Trillion — 118 Million — $49,646

JAPAN 100 Million — $6.7 Trillion — $66,805

WESTERN EUROPE — $18.8 Trillion — 391 Million

CHINA — $44.5 Trillion — 1418 Million — $31,357

INDIA — $27.8 Trillion — 1601 Million — $17,366

CHAPTER 6

AGGRESSIVE ASIA
A THREAT TO WORLD PEACE?

Rich and Rowdy

In private life we say: money makes you wealthy, not happy. Translated into the political life of nations, this means: wealth makes you powerful, but not necessarily peaceful.

The man I had a chance to observe during his visit to New York last September was living proof. His country is beautiful and wealthy. Its businesses have tightly woven relationships with trading partners the world over. Its economy has grown twice as fast as the U.S. economy for a number of years, and its young people are motivated and well educated. But the man who represents this beautiful and wealthy country is aggressive to the core.

He stood at the podium in front of the U.N. General Assembly in New York, the collar of his white shirt open, his black hair freshly parted. Heard at close distance, his voice sounded soft, almost silky.

But these external features were deceptive. Iranian President Mahmoud Ahmadinejad was there to provoke, especially to provoke the West. The sentences he was hurling at his audience were as fiery as they were calculated. He said the countries that claim to be the greatest champions of human rights are in fact the worst violator of those same rights. He told the delegates that he was pleased to see that many nations are resisting this aggressor. Of course, he was referring to the United States. The world's major powers, he said, are incapable of solving the problems of today. A day earlier, in an appearance at Columbia University, he questioned the mass murder of six million Jews during World War II. When asked about his government's harsh treatment of homosexuals, Ahmadinejad said: "In Iran, we don't have homosexuals like in your country."

The man wouldn't be worth our effort if he were a savage among civilized people. But he is in fact a crackpot among the naïve. Indeed, the most surprising thing about his speech was the resounding applause at the end. His gaze traveled across the main United Nations assembly hall until it had reached the visitors' section, where I was sitting. I couldn't believe my eyes and ears. Everyone around me was clapping: men in suits, women in business attire, young people and somewhat older men were celebrating the man who wants to wipe Israel off the map, as he had announced in one of his earlier hate-filled speeches.

I should note that no one in the visitors' section was wearing a headscarf, a turban, or a Palestinian scarf. My fellow human beings have rarely been as foreign to me as they were in that moment. The most generous interpretation is that many in the audience simply wanted to show their respect to the guest speaker. Or perhaps many simply lacked the imagination to realize that actions can follow words, and that the current era of relative peace could be nothing but an interlude on the road to the next war.

It is a common misconception that intensive trade and close economic cooperation make the world a more peaceful place. The captains of industry believe this, as do many politicians. And it is no less a misconception when great thinkers fall prey to it. John Stuart Mill, the famous economic theorist, once said, "The great extent and rapid increase of international trade are principal guarantees of the peace of the world." In 1910, Sir Norman Angell, who would later become the publisher of *Foreign Affairs*, even said that a war between the major powers had become unthinkable, because of the "complete economic senselessness of conquests." World War I began four years later. Within months, previously close trading partners became bitter enemies, trading nothing but cannonballs and bombs, and eventually dumping phosgene and mustard gas on one another's heads.

Did the nations of the world learn any lessons from the experience? There is good reason to believe that they did not. Economic relations had barely normalized after the war before the losing power, Germany, began instigating the next conflict. The Japanese, following Hitler's example, also reckoned that war was the best way to rake in a handsome profit. On the morning of December 7, 1941, they launched an aerial bombardment of the U.S. naval base at Pearl Harbor. Instead of the usual oil shipments, the United States returned the favor by dropping two atom bombs on Japan. If there was a lesson to be learned, then it would be this: when war approaches, merchants are forced into the passenger seat while politicians and military men take the wheel.

Today's globalization of our economies is also not a work of peace. It can produce wealth and well-mannered political interaction, but it can also achieve precisely the opposite effect—and with great force. The world is home to more than Ahmadinejad. And there is a relationship between wealth and the eagerness to go to war, one that many overlook.

For national governments, the world's economic interdependence is primarily an opportunity to increase power and wealth. Although peace creates trade, the reverse does not apply. Trade is no guarantee of peace among states, nor does globalization establish some pacifistic international order. As difficult as it is for economists the world over to accept, human beings are driven by motives both more exalted and lowly than engaging in trade. When interests change, so does the flow of goods. The prospect of a nation's trade being interrupted for a period of time has never stopped it from going to war with others.

Two seemingly contradictory sets of circumstances come to mind. The world's economies have never been as interdependent as they are today. The volume of world trade has grown twenty-five-fold in the last 100 years. Yet these surging flows of goods and wealth are making the world more dangerous, not more peaceful. In fact, in many ways accelerated globalization even increases tensions in the world because it heightens inequality, both within and between nations.

A threat to world peace is unlikely to come from Africa, Latin America, or Russia. African countries lack the economic strength to wage major wars, while the Russians and their military currently lack the self-confidence, even if their vast reserves of natural resources enable them to regain the status of a world power. Latin America's heads of state do not pose a threat to one another. In fact, they are united in their struggle to keep up with Asia. Even Islam is not at its most dangerous where most Muslims live. Indonesia's 200 million Muslims are poor and angry, and although they may frighten the West, they are not a threat.

In truth, the most threatening combination of risk factors for a continental war has developed in the countries that have had the most economic success in the past few decades. One of the reasons mullah-controlled Iran is such a threat is that its economy has been growing twice as fast as the United States' and Europe's for years. Instead of frittering away their oil billions, the Iranians are pumping the money back into their economy. That has enabled them to develop self-confidence and aggressiveness in equal measure. Without his country's overflowing war chest, Iranian President Mahmoud Ahmadinejad would be little more than a loudmouth.

Nor are success and cockiness far apart throughout Asia. The continent has experienced a virtually unheard-of expansion of its economic zones, fueling the ambitions of its leaders. Who would have believed it was possible that Japan, after emerging from World War II a shattered country, would recover so quickly; that hopelessly backward China would come as close to the West as it already has; that India would join the race to catch up with the West; and that a city that rivals New York would rise from Singapore's once malaria-infested swamps? The Asian era is no longer a prophecy today, but a reality. Asia's productive core has become larger within only a few decades. It is red-hot today where it once only smoldered. But although it provides growing prosperity, it also produces the explosive material that can turn into war.

When we think of Russia we think of oil. When we think of China we think of toys and Wal-Mart. But it would also be a good idea to think about tanks and missiles at the mention of these two neighbors. In the fall of 2007, China and Russia held a joint military exercise, "Peace Mission 2007," that involved the deployment of 6,000 troops along the Asian-European border. Chinese Premier Hu Jintao and Russian President Vladimir Putin watched the tank maneuvers through binoculars. The two men stood peacefully together on a temporary command post, overlooking abandoned houses that were being bombarded from the ground and by air. As smoke engulfed the battlefield, the red color of the Chinese flag on the tanks was the only bit of color in the otherwise grayish-green landscape of the battlefield.

The two Red leaders may distrust each other, but they share the common goal of curbing U.S. influence in the region. This is the political glue that holds the two powers together. Oil is the economic glue. Russia is the world's second-largest producer of oil, while China is its second-largest consumer. This creates a relationship not unlike that of the junkie with his dealer: one needs the other to survive.

Business between the two countries only became possible as a result of globalization. The currency that changes hands between the Chinese and the Russians is the U.S. dollar. Much of the cash in the registers at U.S. retailers like Home Depot, Wal-Mart, and Safeway goes to Beijing, and from there it travels to the coffers of the Russian military industry. In return, Putin's corporations supply the Chinese with submarines, tanks, fighter jets, and aircraft carriers. Seen in this light, "Peace Mission 2007" was also a shopping spree of sorts for the Chinese.

The exercise was no spontaneous idea, but is in fact part of a Sino-Russian cooperative effort that has become institutionalized, largely unnoticed by the Western public, in the form of the Shanghai Organization (SOZ). A few smaller countries are part of this regional alliance, while a number of larger countries like Iran, Pakistan, and India are associate members. Ahmadinejad, coming from a visit to Baghdad, attended the most recent meeting of the SOZ member states, in Kyrgyzstan. Ahmadinejad spoke a great deal about common interests, while Putin nodded his head, clearly liking what he was hearing. In its combined territory, the SOZ and its associate members can claim 45 percent of the world's population, 50 percent of its natural gas reserves, and 17.5 percent of its oil reserves. Experts consider the SOZ an "OPEC with bombs." Iran is interested in becoming a full-fledged member. The Russian military wants to see the alliance expanded into a counterforce to the North Atlantic Treaty Organization (NATO), and in fact has already presented the Chinese with plans to that effect. But Beijing has hesitated, reluctant to jeopardize the influence of the dollar, which has made this political game possible in the first place.

What this shows is an aggressive side of globalization that has gained little public attention until now. The steeper the growth rates and the greater the successes achieved in the economic world, the greater the risk of political failure. The tremendous acceleration of Asia's emerging economies affects their societies in two ways.

First, tensions are growing within Asian societies, because not everyone has benefited from this rapid modernization. Some have become affluent while others have not. The differences between up-and-coming residents of Bangalore and those of Indian slums are enormous, and the gap between Shanghai's nouveau riche and the farming communities in the Chinese hinterlands couldn't be wider. Tensions are building in populations that were once regulated by bureaucracy. The authorities, in China and elsewhere, tend to offer their less fortunate citizens an aggressive nationalism as a substitute for wealth.

Meanwhile, the people also flee into the arms of religion. Another of today's paradoxes is that the road to modernity takes many on a direct path to the spirituality of their ancestors. The Asian continent's four major religions—Islam, Hinduism, Buddhism, and Daoism—are all growing, which by no means lessens the tensions in social life. All nations may be subject to the same laws of economics, but their cultures have remained separated. Modernization in Asia doesn't mean Americanization or Europization, even if many in the West had hoped this would be the case. What it really boils down to is the development of a new group of people we might call Americasians. Later on we will see what this means and how this process of becoming an Americasian changes our everyday lives.

The second effect of rapid globalization on Asian societies is that, in the wake of great economic success, relations between countries have become more tense instead of less so. Fueled by gains in technology, foreign currency reserves, and political self-confidence, the leaders of the emerging economies are suddenly seeing the world map from a new perspective. Some believe that there will be a redistribution of power in the foreseeable future, and that they will soon assume a leading role in this changed world.

This new confidence has led to a new and threatening arms race, with Asian countries stocking up on submarines, midrange missiles, frigates, destroyers, cruise missiles, and—as a badge of special potency—nuclear weapons. Asia's leaders are taking Mao's motto to heart: "All political power comes from the barrel of a gun." Stalin had the same idea when he asked, cunningly: "How many divisions does the pope have?"

Before beginning their ascent, these nations were busy organizing their own affairs. But now, their ambitions have expanded onto the geopolitical map as they attempt to divide the world into spheres of interest, just as the Americans and the Russians did before them. Some Asian countries are already attempting to dominate their smaller neighbors, turning economic success into political rivalries.

We can see imbalances developing throughout Asia, though they may not always be readily apparent. This is what is so dangerous about the early phase of globalization. These imbalances lack the palpable drama, clarity, and directness of a military threat and are easily overlooked, and yet they contain the seed of war.

Where Is the New Sarajevo?

Asia's future could look like America's past: big, glowing, and completely untouched by the boots of foreign soldiers. But Asia's future could also look like Europe's past: dark and blood-stained, a poor and yet productive breeding ground for all sorts of violent acts. What began in Sarajevo in the spring of 1914 with the assassination of Crown Prince Ferdinand triggered a chain reaction of violence.

There are more indications today of a brewing Asian horror scenario than many believe. In fact, there are too many of these indications to be attributed to chance. Today's situation in Asia bears similarities to the Europe of the early twentieth century, similarities that have not been given the attention they deserve.

Up-and-comers have always tended to be cocky and likely to overestimate their strengths. World War I, which was essentially a European war, was triggered by political stupidity beyond compare, although stupidity alone, no matter how great, cannot ignite a war. Large doses of two things—stupidity and wealth—are in fact needed to produce a truly dangerous mix. In the last century, ambitious powers set a European civil war into motion that would soon expand into a world war. The two ingredients were political aggressiveness and economic wealth.

In Asia, rivals fluctuate between a feeling of superiority and a feeling of threat. And as in early twentieth-century Europe, today's Asian rulers have long been prepared for armed conflict, although no one seems determined to go to war at the moment. There are no realistic war objectives that would make fighting worthwhile. China unquestionably wants to get Taiwan back, but not immediately. Pakistan would like to be in charge in Kashmir, and so would India. But both countries have time.

And yet the situation was similar in early twentieth-century Europe. There was no objective important enough to be worth the risk of a world war. The powers that clashed in the summer of 1914 had nothing to show for themselves that could justify or even explain the massive war that ensued in the eyes of the rulers of the day. It was a war without an objective.

War can be an extension of politics by other means, but this is not a requirement. In many cases war is nothing more than an extension of human idiocy with military means. France wanted Lorraine, but not at the price of well over a million dead French people. Germany wanted to spar with Great Britain over European dominance, but did this goal justify the risk of total defeat?

Within a short time during the Industrial Revolution, Europe's nations had transformed themselves from agrarian to industrial, just as the Asian countries with large amounts of land are doing today. Their newly acquired economic strength gave the Europeans financial and political wings. It made them confident and increased their willingness to take risks. On top of that, hardly any European leader was answerable to his people. For the powerful of the day, being voted into office was the exception.

During this transformation, feelings of national superiority with a sense of feeling threatened and hemmed in began surfacing in Europe's states. At the time—just as in Asia today—there was no natural leading power accepted by all. This provoked a need for alliance, which in turn led to the shaping of counter-alliances.

Ultimately, it was two things that, because of their simultaneous occurrence, led to World War I: mutual mistrust and elation, fear and heroic courage. In the end, the rulers and generals could hardly wait to position their military machines opposite those of their neighbors. Sixty-five million soldiers were mobilized, more than ever before and more than would ever be mobilized again. "The warring industrialized states had transformed themselves into monstrous foundries and Vulcan-like forges," the writer and soldier Ernst Junger later wrote.

A new coarseness gradually became part of the way of thinking of an entire generation, one that had learned to live with the language of war: mobilization, war on two fronts, positional warfare, war of attrition. In the end, the concept of total war was on everyone's mind, because the war was no longer just a battle between military forces, but had also drawn in the civilian populations.

In Asia today we see a similarly robust urge to stick it to others before being done in by them. Mutual mistrust is deeply rooted in Asia's history. The dramatic interactions among Asian nations in the past few centuries are not unlike those the Europeans experienced in the nineteenth and twentieth centuries. One nation could hardly turn its back on another before being attacked and subjugated. The traditional animosity between the French and the Germans corresponds to the rivalry between the Japanese and the Chinese. The friction between the Indians and the Pakistanis is comparable to the aggressive suspicion between the English and the Germans in the second half of the nineteenth century.

The Japanese have attacked a number of their Asian neighbors on several occasions. They occupied Manchuria in 1931. In World War II, they drew a trail of blood through more than half a dozen countries. "Asia for the Asians," was their battle cry, but what they meant was: Asia for the Japanese. Their soldiers were stationed in Saigon, Hong Kong, Manila, and Singapore. They marched into Burma and New Guinea, and they also occupied China, a largely defenseless nation at the time. "Let their heads swing," students in Shanghai and Beijing say today when they are reminded of Japanese atrocities.

In Beijing, both the people and the government look to the island nation of Japan with revenge in their hearts. The Japanese, for their part, have yet to issue an apology for past atrocities—or at least one that would be considered suitable in China. The dispute between the nations over the correct form of apology is like a fight between quarreling spouses. In August 1995, reconciliation seemed imminent. Thanks to some diplomatic legwork, the Japanese prime minister expressed his "feelings of deep remorse" and his "heartfelt apology."

And yet there was a big "but" at the end of the story: Japan refused to issue this apology in writing, which was precisely what the Chinese had demanded.

Conversely, few in Tokyo have any warm feelings toward the Chinese, which is something the Japanese have in common with almost all of China's neighbors. The Chinese are not liked anywhere, perhaps because of their sheer numbers and the fact that they have been too proud and successful recently. Chinese living in Thailand are forcefully assimilated, and are required to assume Thai names to eliminate their Chinese identity. Malaysia, in an effort to prevent "infiltration" by Chinese, has introduced quotas in filling government jobs. Indonesia has seen repeated pogroms against ethnic Chinese, who are perceived as playing too powerful a role in economic life.

These aversions against the Chinese are not without justification. China's more recent history includes a series of recurring aggressions against neighboring countries that cannot simply be dismissed out of hand. In the early 1950s, China intervened in the Korean War and helped to install the Stalinist regime in North Korea. The Chinese military was involved in border wars with India in 1959 and 1962, and in the late 1960s Chinese and Russian troops clashed along the Ussuri River. There have also been repeated disputes in the South China Sea, whose islands and atolls are claimed by a number of countries. The Beijing leadership set its sights on Vietnam twice in the 1970s. Chinese Premier Deng Xiaoping called the second invasion an "educational campaign."

Distrust of the Chinese has lasted through the decades. Even Deng Xiaoping's announcement of a peacefully worded foreign policy doctrine was generally interpreted as a sign of treachery. To avoid jeopardizing the growing Chinese economy, Deng advised that his country take a cautious and reserved approach. China, he said, should "hide its light under a bushel." This seemed reasonable, but it also sounded unsettling to neighboring countries. The wolf, in full view of everyone, had donned sheep's clothing.

Since then Asia has lived with growing tensions but has lacked adequate safeguards. The overlapping interests and ideological alliances are to those of Europe before the first World War.

Today's Sarajevo could very well lie on the Korean peninsula. Since its division into a Stalinist north and a capitalist south, this territory jutting into the East China Sea has been home to a political powder keg that could explode in response to even just a few sparks. Since partition, the side-by-side existence of North and South Korea has been characterized by enduring and, over the years, growing aggressiveness.

One of the most pointless wars of the modern age erupted between the two halves of the Korean peninsula in 1950. Neither of the two nations gained territory as a result, but more than three million people died. Since then the North has kept the South in check with its constantly recurring threats and missile tests. The North owes it survival to the construction of nuclear warheads and midrange missiles, which, in order to obtain hard currency, it has even sold to enemies of the United States. The economy is in a sorry state, the population is starving, and the government is too poor to keep the lights on in the capital Pyongyang. And yet the elite remains politically in control.

China has remained loyal to the North Korean regime, helping it with components for its nuclear facilities and by providing rice imports, so that the elite is not threatened by starvation. North Korea's ability to build a nuclear bomb has proven to be an effective instrument of blackmail against the West, compelling even the United States to repeatedly accommodate Pyongyang. A few years ago former U.S. secretary of state Madeleine Albright attended a parade in Pyongyang to mark the fifty-fifth anniversary of the Korean Workers' Party, a move that can only be characterized as political prostration before the world's last remaining Stalinist state. The result of such expressions of submissiveness was hardly surprising: mounting tensions with South Korea.

Or perhaps the new Sarajevo could be a border town along the 435-mile line of demarcation between India and the Islamic Republic of Pakistan. Hindu-dominated India and the Islamic state accuse each other of disregarding each other's religious sentiments. There have been repeated skirmishes between the two countries, as well as religiously motivated massacres. Even before the two states became independent, Hindus and Muslims were sending each other trains filled with corpses. Indians killed a trainload of Muslim refugees and sent the corpse-filled cars back to Pakistan with the words "Gift to Pakistan" scrawled on the engine, and the Pakistanis responded in kind.

With the help of their Russian friends, the Indians launched a nuclear program that was mainly intended to impress their neighbor. India detonated its first atom bomb in 1974. Pakistan, aided by China, followed suit. "We will eat grass or leaves, perhaps even go hungry, but we will have our own atom bomb," said then Prime Minister Zulkifar Ali Bhutto. It would take another 24 years, but Pakistan eventually joined the nuclear club.

It was U.S. president Bill Clinton who reminded us that this sort of muscle-flexing has already led the world into disaster once before, namely in Europe. Clinton said that he couldn't believe that the Indian subcontinent is "entering the twenty-first century repeating the worst mistake of the twentieth." But Pakistan has been ignoring the warnings of the West for a long time. Today the mountainous region between Pakistan and Afghanistan is seen as a safe haven for terrorist leader Osama bin Laden and his fellow murderers.

India's security also depends on the mood of the Pakistani leadership. But even the word *leadership* is misleading. Who in the country is following, and who is leading? Fundamentalist forces already hold a larger share of power in Pakistan today than can possibly suit the West. Nevertheless, Pakistan is an indispensable ally of the United States, but it's an awkward partnership. The survival of U.S. ally Pervez Musharraf is no longer a matter of course. Radical Islamists are seeking to gain power in Pakistan. Indeed, they have already made inroads toward achieving that goal.

The Taiwanese capital Taipei could also be the new Sarajevo. Beijing insists on reintegrating what it calls its "renegade province," although it is in no hurry to do so. "We have a hundred years' time," Mao once said. America recognizes the position of the Chinese leadership, while at the same time supplying Taiwan with weapons and military equipment. Militarily, the small, obstinate state, founded by Mao's opponents during the course of the Chinese civil war, is under a U.S. protective shield.

If this shield were suddenly lifted, Taiwan's days would be numbered. So far, Taiwan's powerful friends in Washington have made sure that this will not happen. For many Americans, Taiwan is a thorn in the side of China's communists, which they would like to see pushed in even a little farther.

And yet all of the U.S. military commitments and promises to the Taiwanese are presumably not worth the paper on which they are printed. Washington cannot afford a military conflict in the region. America is currently too isolated in Asia, both politically and culturally, to pacify a rebellious Asian nation. Its military first-strike capability is undoubtedly enormous, but this is not enough to be able to successfully wage an entire military campaign. The Iraq invasion is a case in point, where the war after the war is the real problem facing the United States.

American experiences in this corner of the world are not encouraging. In the Korean War, many U.S. soldiers lost their lives, not to mention the enormous casualties the Vietnam War claimed. During the eight most intense years of that war, from 1965 to 1972, the U.S. Air Force dropped more than six million tons of bombs over Vietnam—three times as much explosive power as the country detonated in Europe, Africa, and Asia combined during World War II. But it was to no avail. The poorly equipped but highly motivated rebels in the Vietnamese civil war, the Viet Cong, eventually managed to expel the superpower. Absent a miracle, the United States could face a similarly humiliating defeat in Iraq and possibly in Afghanistan.

The United States is practically without friends in Asia today. The U.S. military maintains bases here and there, its aircraft carriers crisscross the South China Sea around the clock, and it has respectable allies in Japan and South Korea. But unlike the Europeans, no one in the region sees the Americans as friends and peacemakers. Japan relies on the United States, but the United States would be ill advised to rely on Japan.

The American leadership, regardless of who captures the White House, also has relatively little influence on the rulers in Beijing. The Western world power supported Mao's adversaries in the Chinese civil war. After that, the only time that the United States seriously sought closer relations with the Chinese was during the Nixon/Kissinger era. America distanced itself from Beijing after the Chinese authorities' bloody suppression of student protests on Tiananmen Square, and both the right and the left in Washington demanded an immediate cooling of relations. Deng defended his actions by claiming that he was combating chaos, not democracy. But it didn't do him much good.

Both Republicans and Democrats want to be standing on the right side of the barricades should the Chinese people act on their fundamental desire for freedom. Many Americans still hope that economic liberalization will eventually bring about change in the political system. Inequality in the country and corruption within the Communist Party could speed up this process, or so they believe. But it is precisely this hope that comes packaged with the worst of fears. The Chinese Communist Party will not give up power voluntarily. A civil war in a country with continental dimensions—China's population is almost twice as large as that of the United States and the European Union combined—would shake the entire world.

Just how high the pressure is in China today can only be conjectured, not measured. Even the Chinese leadership probably has no reliable assessment of when the patience of millions who are not benefiting from the economic miracle could be exhausted. But because the key to the success of China's economic policy consists precisely in focusing government investment on the export industry, thereby promoting inequality, some concessions may be expected in the foreseeable future, but no fundamental correction. According to Western estimates, the current situation is as follows: 3 percent of the Chinese are immensely wealthy, while 17 percent have modest retirement savings, and 80 percent have none. In no other country on earth has inequality between people progressed as rapidly as in China.

What the Communist Party is doing in China is nothing short of an outrageous human experiment. It appears to want to test the limits of how much inequality people can bear and determine when a downtrodden populace will strike back at its tormentors. There are already rumblings in the country. The global public is rarely, if ever, made aware of the demonstrations, strikes, and minor armed rebellions taking place in China today. For the Chinese, there is too much temptation to divert internal pressure outward, that is, against neighbors. In the course of world history, the powerful of many nations have already succumbed to this temptation.

A Continent of Bomb Makers: Asia Arms Itself

If the virus of a world war can even develop nowadays, it will find a favorable breeding ground in Asia's heated climate. No one can calculate this probability, because we can only make out parts of the equation. However, a look at military expenditures has always served as an indicator of what heads of state expect to see in their futures. If they are spending less on weapons, they are probably in a peaceful mood or simply weary of war. If they are beefing up their military might, they may not have written off peace altogether, but they want to be prepared should circumstances change.

The difference between these types of leaders and terrorists is obvious. Strapping on explosives can be done in secret, but ramping up military spending for large populations is a virtually public affair. Wars are prepared well in advance. They do not erupt as spontaneously as many may sometimes believe. In fact, it is even possible to observe generals and commanders-in-chief as they make their preparations, which go hand in hand with both significant increases in military spending and costly test runs involving human beings and materiel.

The first and second world wars were preceded by an arms buildup that went on for years. It began at a leisurely pace in the 1880s and accelerated throughout the next decade. From then until the outbreak of World War I, Britain's annual military expenditures doubled. Even the planned military strategy was reflected in the country's defense budget, so that anyone who was familiar with it could predict whether he would be attacked by land, air, or sea.

The British navy was growing at the fastest pace at the time. Its annual budget quadrupled between 1885 and 1914, the first year of the war. The message to the rest of Europe was that the British were preparing for a naval war.

Even the general population, which may not be as well-versed on military matters, cannot help but notice when its leadership begins sharpening the knives. Citizens, after all, pay for the arms buildup during the preparatory years with higher taxes. They also notice traditional weapons manufacturers rapidly turning into huge conglomerates within a very short period of time. In 1873, German arms manufacturer Krupp employed only 16,000 workers. That number increased to 45,000 by the turn of the century and 75,000 by 1912—a jump of more than 450 percent. Arms expenditures in Germany at the time far outpaced growth in the rest of the economy—an unmistakable sign of the government's hostile intentions.

The same, transparent preparations took place before World War II. Adolf Hitler had hardly come into power before he began diverting government revenues into weapons production. The size of his military ambitions was clearly reflected in the growth of his military budget. In 1937, two years before it went to war, Germany spent 23.5 percent of the national income on the armed forces. By comparison, military spending was only 1.5 percent of government revenues in United States, 5.7 percent in the British Empire, and 9.1 percent in France. The military budgets of the other belligerent countries were also noticeably high. Italy was spending 14.5 percent of its national income on arms, while Japan's military expenditures at the time were a whopping 28.2 percent. In all three countries, a deadly fruit was ripening that would devastate half the world a short time later.

And now to twenty-first-century Asia, where the situation is similar but by no means identical. New economic opportunities have prepared the way for an arms buildup unprecedented in the region. Japan's military expenditures are as high as those of the French and the British, and exceeded only by those of the United States. China, India, Pakistan, and the two Koreas are also investing heavily in their militaries. Experts estimate that total Asian expenditures for missiles, tanks, and aircraft carriers will exceed the European defense budget by 2010. Based on the dollar's real purchasing power in Asia, the countries in that part of the world are already not far behind the West when it comes to military spending.

A number of bilateral arms races are taking place in which the two respective sides seek to outdo each other when it comes to ordering deadly weapons: South Korea versus North Korea, China versus Taiwan, Pakistan versus India, China versus India, and Malaysia versus Singapore. Seen as a whole, these countries seem to be preparing for a naval conflict, because among all weapons manufacturers, the ones selling frigates, submarines, and sea-based guided missiles are reporting the greatest demand for their products.

America has already pricked up its ears. According to the most important planning document in American defense policy, the Pentagon's "Quadrennial Defense Review," the Pacific Ocean is the most likely theater of war in the near future.

Nuclear technology has gained great popularity in Asia. The nuclear age supposedly ended with the end of the cold war, and yet it appears to have just begun in Asia. Seventy percent of all new nuclear power plants are being constructed in Asia. The number of countries with nuclear weapons in their arsenals has doubled worldwide since 1960, and three-quarters of the new nuclear powers are on Asian soil. Both the Indians and the Taiwanese shocked the global public in July 2006 when they conducted missile tests that were nothing but thinly veiled threats.

While the Americans, Russians, and Europeans have reduced their armed forces in the past decade, Asian countries have continued to maintain large conventional ground forces. Taiwan currently has about 200,000 troops under arms, Pakistan commands an army of 550,000 soldiers, North Korea's armed forces number 950,000, while the Indian military, with 1.1 million soldiers, and Chinese military, with 1.6 million soldiers, are the largest of them all.

The new Chinese military doctrine expressly mentions the likelihood of regional instability and limited wars, conflicts for which the giant country clearly aims to be prepared. Nowadays, China is not just an important buyer of industrial equipment and oil. Within the last five-year period, China has been the world's largest importer of weapons. Politicians in Beijing are making a concerted effort to convince the European Union to lift the weapons embargo it imposed after the Tiananmen Square massacre. They seek to attract weapons manufacturers with an impressive military budget, which will have exceeded government social spending by close to 50 percent for 2006. A government could hardly document its priorities more clearly.

It is apparent that, once again, there are no international institutions capable of reducing the imbalances and alleviating the tensions in Asia. The organizations created after World War II are not suitable, because they do not reflect the new balance of power in Asia. The United Nations Security Council is a living World War II museum. As if preserved in time, the four Allies of the war, the Americans, French, British and Russians, sit opposite the Chinese in that body. Asia's other large regional powers—India, Pakistan, Indonesia, and Japan—are not even part of the club.

This United Nations is better than nothing, but it can provide no safeguards against an uncontrolled discharge of energy in such an overheated region. Unless we manage to transform the world's architecture of security, which also means developing it in many places where it has been nonexistent, the rivalries between the world's rising and falling empires could easily erupt into a new war. It has always been the case that political and economic conflict soon leads to gunfire, and that gunfire, technology permitting, soon leads to bombing.

That was why the Americans and Western Europeans developed a policy of détente against communism in the 1970s. They wanted to prevent the cold war from turning into a blazing inferno. The maxim of the day was simple: where there is talk there will be no gunfire.

A large number of treaties, conferences, and panels have developed among the hostile blocs in the West and East, all of which have served one overriding purpose: to recognize and diminish conflicts in their early stages. This was followed by various disarmament efforts, including the Nuclear Non-Proliferation Treaty and the Strategic Arms Reduction Treaty. The Conference on Security and Cooperation in Europe (CSCE) made its way through Europe like a traveling circus. A number of proxy wars erupted in Asia and Latin America at this time. It was an era of threats and negotiations, but major conflict was avoided. There was much talk between the Americans and the Russians, but little gunfire.

A comparable architecture of détente is absent today. The Asian house is everything but fireproof. There is no single alliance with responsibility for the entire continent. The new emerging nations live in a world that is marked by instability similar to that which prevailed in the days of the League of Nations. This precursor of the United Nations championed the principles of nonviolence and national sovereignty with verve, but without relevance. It was not created to be capable of issuing threats or putting offenders in their place, which is why Hitler, Mussolini, and Japan's war-hungry leaders felt not the least bit intimidated by the League of Nations. And why should they have?

The aggressors had an easier time of it, because although the years they had spent building up their militaries were noticed, they were not met with any appropriate political response. Politicians lived from one day to the next, a circumstance that British Prime Minister Ramsay MacDonald openly confessed to his successor: "We were so distracted by our day-to-day problems that we never had the opportunity to examine the overall situation and develop a suitable policy; instead, we lived from one excitement to the next."

Today's politicians bear an uncanny resemblance to their forerunners. They like to talk about the opportunities of globalization. But many fail to appreciate what is brewing above their heads. Like their forerunners, they live from one excitement to the next.

CHAPTER 7

THE UNITED STATES OF THE WEST

IT'S A JOURNEY, NOT A DESTINATION

What the Future Is Made Of

Human beings have already deciphered close to everything there is to decipher. Even our genetic code has been laid bare, like the circuit plan of some electronic device.

Only history remains inscrutable, refusing to let itself be boxed into predictable formulas. In the history of one country, high unemployment led to a New Deal—in another, to the rise of Adolf Hitler. History shows us that reason usually prevails in a democracy, as is the case in contemporary Europe. But historical events can also lead to the triumph of lunacy, as they did in Germany in the last century.

The past denies us absolute certainties, which is why we cannot treat the writing of history as a science in the classical sense. We would be more honest with ourselves to admit that history bears a closer resemblance to literature.

When we try to use the past to draw conclusions for the future, things become even more complicated. Another word for this activity is *speculation*. The best we can do is to take ourselves a few steps closer to the future. But even if the attempt is bound to be fraught with error, predicting the future is at least worth a try. We look into the past hoping that it will enable us to see into the future. We want to be able to look around the next corner and catch a glimpse of the future, as fleeting as it may be.

The future, of course, is more a variation of than a direct extension of the present. We even have the luxury of choosing among several versions of the future. Much depends on how ordinary people behave, whether they produce smart and effective leaders, and how much effort they are willing to undertake. A nation's citizenry must have enough confidence in itself to fight for its own future.

The Shock Scenario: A Design for Disaster

In overly simplified terms, we can imagine three future scenarios that globalization may bring. Let us begin with the shock scenario, the most horrific of them all. It's a classic worst-case scenario. It describes what happens if nothing happens, an impasse in which politicians are unable to find a way to reduce the current tensions in the global economy. In this instance, the leaders of the United States, Europe, and Asia simply go with the flow, hoping that the future will be much like the present. But they forget the most important tenet of history: if everything remains as it is, in the end nothing will be the same as it was.

The shock scenario is filled with doom and gloom. At its center are people who cannot live up to the enormity of their tasks, people who speak self-importantly of leadership while in reality doing nothing to lead. Those few politicians who even have a sense of the coming radical changes in history will anesthetize themselves with successes of the moment and devote themselves to the minutiae of political life, from fund-raising to nominations to party conventions. Their lives become a permanent political campaign. In the end, they lack the endurance and strength to build the consensus that can overcome the status quo. Finding consensus is as cumbersome in a democracy as it is in a dictatorship. The powers of stagnation are undeterred by boundaries between political systems.

The shock scenario is a lose-lose situation that would revolve around China and the United States. One of the two countries—and it doesn't matter which one comes first—would be unable to withstand the pressure of economic circumstances and would begin to falter, dragging the other one down with it. In China, a blatant disregard for the environment and a workforce denied political rights are the key ingredients in a powder keg that could explode easily. America's problem is that its high growth is based on a production system that is no longer rooted in high domestic performance. Instead, growth is increasingly fueled by foreign debt, a system of readily available consumer debt, and a gradual frittering away of assets.

All other differences between the two countries aside, there is one important similarity between growth in the United States and in China: it is not sustainable in either country. This lack of sustainability is so explosive because the two economies have unknowingly entered into a diabolic pact with each other. The one borrows against its own environmental capital. The other lives on borrowed capital being pumped into it by an environmental polluter. The lunacy of the current situation is that each of these two giant nations depends on the madness of the other. China needs America's greedy consumption, while America needs China's obsessive growth. Greed and obsession are the two motors of today's global economy. If one of them fails abruptly, one of the longest periods of prosperity in human history will come to an end.

If this were to happen, Beijing's once-impressive growth rates would snap as quickly as trees in a hurricane. The standard of living of millions of people on all continents would plunge. While some people would seek to compare this process with the world economic crisis in the late 1920s, the difference is that this time the crisis would affect the entire world, not just the Western Hemisphere.

As a result of economic collapse, the political system in authoritarian China would face serious challenges. No one knows if, and in what condition, the leadership would weather the storm. Nowadays, Chinese leadership is made up primarily of technocrats with no experience in crisis management, a deficiency that makes them the flower children of the country's economic wonder.

In China's system, an economic disturbance would quickly and adversely affect a society that is now being held together only by the hope of further growth. Political demands, which are still trumped by the desire to succeed economically, would come to the fore. The word that so terrifies the Chinese elites today could spread like wildfire in the streets of Beijing, Shanghai, and Hong Kong: *democracy*! Away with the one-party state! This, in turn, would set the country's military and security machine into motion, which would quickly respond with tanks and machine guns.

The dictatorship would hold up its ugly face to the cameras of CNN. Many people in the West would be horrified. But those in the know would have no trouble seeing traces of Mao in the faces of China's leaders. In the worst case, China would go from being the commercial state it is today to a warrior state.

America would not come away unharmed in this scenario. The country would have nothing to fear militarily, but its global influence would suffer and it would be facing a new problem: domestic strife. Current U.S. society, which consists essentially of three classes—an affluent upper class, a middle class that is fighting decline, and a growing underclass—could be shaken to its very foundations by a severe economic crisis. The inequality that has grown in recent years and is already a hot topic of conversation today would suddenly be visible to all. Poverty would turn into squalor and frustration into fury, with grave consequences for the cohesiveness of American society.

The superpower would face a painful process of self-assurance, in which business, academic, and political leaders would be forced to account for their actions in the early years of the new age of globalization. Wasn't what Hillary Clinton called the "happy talk" and former Federal Reserve chairman Alan Greenspan the "rosy assumptions" of the Bush years nothing but self-deception? A new generation would be asking old questions, but this time the tone would be angry and perhaps even irreconcilable:

Did you really believe that you could live, in the long term, on borrowed money?

Who actually claimed that such a large nation doesn't need an industrial base?

Where are the men and women who made us believe that a negative balance of trade is a sign of strength?

Why did no one on Wall Street sound the alarm bell when the U.S. dollar became eroded and lost intrinsic value for such a prolonged period of time?

Is it possible that no one could have noticed a country that was once the world's biggest lender selling off its assets to others?

How could the entrenchment of economic inequality in a democratic nation have been tolerated for so long?

What happened to the upward mobility that was once this country's trademark?

And, last but not least: why did democracy, which is supposed to react more quickly to malfunctions than other forms of government, fail so miserably?

From the standpoint of power politics, this scenario comes with one saving grace. Neither of the two rivals could triumph over the other. The old superpower and the rising superpower would both be weakened. The world in which they exist would emerge from the turbulences relatively unharmed. America and China would become partners in disaster.

The Asia-Above-All Scenario: When the American Dream Turns to Dust

In the Asia-above-all scenario, America would continue its relative decline while Asia would continue its ascent. Americans still do not perceive this ascent as the central challenge of the twenty-first century. Since 9/11, the country has been otherwise occupied. The so-called War on Terror, which is being waged as a major ideological, military, and political conflict, consumes much of the public's attention span. The superpower is not, as historian Paul Kennedy once feared, "imperially overstretched." It is simply distracted.

Contemporary Asia no longer fits into any of the tried-and-true valuation models. India is still seen as a developing nation, because its ascent is accompanied by poverty and suffering. Many contemporaries take a mild view of China's brand of communism, in which the leaders utilize the methods of capitalism to preserve their power and increase wealth. The idea that this combination of communism and capitalism is so dangerous precisely because it makes China more powerful, more stable, and more expansive has somehow been left out of the political debate.

In this scenario, Asia would manage to keep its people content even while denying them involvement in the political process. In a time of rapid growth, this is no great feat. Most Asians are more interested in cars than election ballots, preferring freedom of consumption over freedom of speech.

Society would continue its current imbalances as long as the economic miracle continues. A 7.5 percent growth rate translates into a doubling of the national income within 10 years. But China has been even more successful than that, growing at rates of about 12 percent a year for some time—and generating tremendous material wealth to satisfy material interests.

The political leadership in China, which has already shown an interest in the social systems of the West, would have many options. It could take advantage of its unbroken stranglehold on the economy and its unquestioned authority to embark on a policy of reforms. In other words, China's national and party leadership would manage to take the rudimentary capitalism of modern-day China to the next stage of development. Production would become more environmentally compatible and the fruits of prosperity distributed more equitably. From the standpoint of China's leaders, the trick would be to structure the transformation process in such a way that neither the export machine nor the party would falter.

Under these circumstances, the United States would continue to fall behind in the international race. Its share of the gross world product would decline, its balance of trade would remain deeply in the red, purchasing power would shrink, and its rate of innovation would not keep up with that of its Asian competitors. There also would be a noticeable decline in the Americans' tendency to keep their old lifestyle afloat with more and more debt. In an effort to keep attracting fresh capital to a weakening economy, the Federal Reserve System would be forced to raise interest rates and the government to raise the yields of Treasury bonds. Everyone would begin to realize what has been concealed for years: when the supply of outside blood comes to an end, this once-proud country will collapse. America will be exhausted.

Simultaneously, China would begin to make itself independent of the United States. China's economy, once fixated on exports, would use its handsome profits to develop itself into an impressive domestic economy. The demand coming from 1.3 billion people, whose purchasing power has grown considerably, would be China's guarantee of growing independence. Instead of having solely an export economy, the Chinese have been becoming consumers.

On the foreign stage, this even more powerful China would become a role model for much of Asia. Beijing likely would assume a leadership role in both international and new Asian organizations. The government would continue to strengthen ties with Russia and India—ties based on a shared skepticism toward the United States as a superpower. If neither of these two competing powers beats the Chinese to it, the People's Republic of China will become a giant within the next two decades. For the first time since the demise of the Soviet Union, the United States would find itself facing off against a world-class rival.

This powerful China would encounter an American society that, beneath a veneer of national pride and joie de vivre, is in fact deeply insecure. The internal difficulties of the United States would be further aggravated by the baby boomers reaching retirement age and by continued immigration pressures from Latin America.

What we see today is only the beginning of this tremendous shift. The working segment of society is shrinking relative to the number of retirees. Only 17 million Americans were 65 or older in 1960. This number had almost doubled, to 31 million, by 1990 and, according to the most recent estimates, will increase to about 70 million by 2020. That means that the number of producers of wealth is declining relative to the number of consumers of wealth.

As the baby boomers retire, both risk averseness and the desire to preserve the status quo grow as well. Politicians are tempted to pander to the wishes of millions of new retirees, and the willingness to change suffers. America will bear a closer resemblance to the Europe of the 1990s than can possibly be good for the country.

Additionally, according to recent surveys, for the first time more people take a negative (35 percent) than a positive (30 percent) view of the country's future prospects. The rest are undecided. Although these surveys say nothing about the probability of these expectations, they do testify to a change in the general mood. Aging societies that come under pressure have a tendency to become pessimistic and sentimental.

Despite all this, there is no natural expiration date for major powers. If the United States can somehow come up with the political will and each individual citizen can again become involved in the nation's direction, a great deal is possible—even another triumph over a formidable adversary.

The American Renaissance Scenario: How to Remake History

In the best-case scenario, America reacts—energetically, intelligently, and with great resolve—to changes in the age of globalization. The new generation of political leaders will go about its work with a refreshing absence of ideology, even if the election process tempts many to descend into the usual politics of mudslinging. But in truth this generation will have left political parti-sanship behind and will feel bound to pursue a new objectiveness. For these men and women, serving their country will come before serving their party. They want to convince people instead of cajol-ing them, and their approach to politics would be to work with and not against others. They will not pursue a "progressive" or a "conservative" agenda, and they see themselves as the leaders of their nation, not as the warriors of their respective parties.

That would allow the country to continue its tremendous achievements of the last 250 years, a period in which giant steel mills and automobile plants were built, literally out of nothing, followed by banks and software corporations. The greatest super-power in world history grew on this economic foundation, and both political parties had their share of the success. The conser-vatives were not obsessed with the preservation of tradition, while the progressives were not insistent on attacking traditions.

This balance between renewal and preservation was lost. Nowa-days, the country's relevant political and social forces are attempt-ing to restore the U.S. economic foundation and repair the damage that has been done abroad. They know that economic growth and international recognition will best serve America's security.

The unproductive, vicious circles that characterized the polit-ical discussion for years finally will have been broken. After real-izing its fundamental pointlessness, the ritualized, never-ending debate between good and evil, liberals and conservatives, the East Coast and the West Coast, nationalists and multinationalists, Wall Street politicians and Main Street politicians, supporters of small versus big government will have ended. After a decades-long struggle, one of the country's most important and symbolic debates has been decided—in favor of a pragmatic, third way.

Neither the die-hard free traders nor the protectionists can pre-vail. Millions of people finally will recognize the growing trade deficit, the country's shrinking industrial base, and the continu-ing rise in inequality. But the most important thing they will see is the connection between these phenomena. Americans will understand that what is touted as free trade is not free at all. In fact, it costs a lot of money. Of course, Americans will also remain unconvinced that closing off the borders is a good idea. A return to economic autonomy was never an option.

In this best-case scenario, a pragmatic trade policy would gain the upper hand. Trade policy once again would be based on interests, not dogma. Its objective would be to politically influence the terms of trade, which have deteriorated almost continuously for the United States in the last two decades. The United States will have started defending itself in the war for wealth.

A new economic policy would aim for a shift back to traditional industry, which, as it turns out, isn't so traditional after all. Auto manufacturing, machine building, consumer goods production, the aviation industry, the food industry, as well as the media industry, banking, insurance, and software manufacturing form, at a constantly changing technological level, the foundation of the American economy. This is where innovations are created that are more than just another franchising concept.

What used to be called "old industry" will have transformed itself—and the new government will help out where it can. It will eliminate the tax benefits of offshoring. It will support companies with an ambitious technology policy, although its ambitions are not necessarily expressed in dollars. Strict antipollution regulations for U.S. automakers would work wonders, because they would force an entire industry to rely on its technological creativity to innovate instead of devoting its inventive spirit to the work of lobbyists. The individual states' would establish ambitious energy conservation goals to promote the rise of an independent efficiency industry, which changes virtually all production processes, and by extension, the entire economy.

The new America and the other industrialized western nations would engage in a multilateral trade policy. The goal would be to integrate rising nations into the existing global economy instead of allowing them to integrate us into their system.

In this integration process, America would depend on international bodies such as the World Trade Organization—but not exclusively. Immediately after coming into office, the new government would seek to establish closer ties with the European Union. The Americans and the Europeans would develop a strategic partnership to address their shrinking shares of world population, global industrial potential, and gross world product. In the war for wealth, the nations of democratic capitalism would join forces to form a confederation that would address the challenges and opportunities of the new age.

The blessings of the new policy would soon be reflected in the country's balance of trade. The import quota would decline as America suddenly has products and services to offer its citizens and those of other countries. The new America could finally benefit again from the worldwide prosperity boom. The news spreads like wildfire: the United States, a proud industrial and trading nation, has two important commodities in stock once again: the hardware and the software.

America's resurgence is the result of a change in awareness, which in turn becomes the trigger for new policies. The country's triumphant comeback is based on a six-point plan, as outlined below.

Step 1: Rethinking Globalization

We can thank Nobel laureate Ivan Petrovich Pavlov for his sensational discoveries on the behavior of dogs. At the beginning of the twentieth century, Pavlov, a biologist, conducted experiments with puppies in his Physiological Laboratory for Experimental Medicine in St. Petersburg, Russia. He discovered that the animals have an innate reflex, which is triggered when food is placed in front of them—almost as if at the press of a button, saliva begins to flow in dogs' mouths at the sight of food.

Pavlov began to manipulate this natural reflex. When he rang a bell, the dogs showed no reaction at first, except perhaps a certain curiosity. Then Pavlov combined the two stimuli, food and the sound of the bell, until the dogs understood. The sound of the bell meant food, and food automatically meant the flow of saliva. As soon as the dogs had reliably learned the reflex chain bell sound = food = salivation, Pavlov modified the experiment again.

He shortened the reflex chain by removing the food. The dogs continued to salivate, even when feeding no longer followed the bell tone. In other words, the reflex chain bell sound = food = salivation could also be shortened to bell sound = salivation. Thus, it had lost its original meaning. The dogs were frustrated and hungry, but they were salivating nonetheless.

What Pavlov showed is that reflexes can be manipulated. An experience, once stored in memory, becomes stronger than reality. The past dominates the present in a way that incorporates physical reflexes.

Fortunately, we also have Pavlov to thank for the discovery that false reflex chains can be repaired. If the test animal is exposed to the sound of a bell for an extended period of time without being fed, the reflexive salivation gradually disappears. The animals learn to recognize the new reality. History fades away and so does the false reflex. Pavlov called this process "deletion."

It is precisely this "deletion" that we are about to face in the West. It is the first, mental step toward the politics of renewal. Our political reflexes behave in a similar manner to the physical reflexes of dogs. Most of all, they can be manipulated and abbreviated in a very similar way. In the age of globalization, many of the reflex chains that were once learned throughout the history of Western societies are proving to be false or only true under certain circumstances. What made sense yesterday no longer makes sense today.

The key questions for the dog are: Does food follow the bell tone? Is it worthwhile for the body to activate salivation, or is this a waste of time that could be put to much better use in other ways? The key questions for human beings are: Do the things that worked yesterday still work today? Have we reacted sufficiently to a change in reality by modifying our behavior?

The collective memory of voters today is filled with abbreviated forms of conditioning. For decades, free trade meant growing prosperity. As a result, free trade was like a button that could be pushed to generate political approval. Because the relationship between free trade and prosperity was so clear, both parties incorporated free trade into their canons of fundamental beliefs. The old world of the West was in order. When someone rang the bell, food would appear on the table.

But this automatic behavior no longer works. Reality has abbreviated the reflex chain, so that now, in people's minds, free trade is no longer immediately followed by the thought of rising wealth for everyone. As the rules of engagement have changed, free trade, for many members of the workforce, has come to signify the devaluation of their labor—and thus the loss of their standard of living.

If we want to change this situation, we must change our behavior, which means that we must first change our perspective. For example, we should stop expecting to see our wealth increase, because this is no longer an option, at least not in the way to which we are accustomed. As we have seen, nowadays trade can also lead to a decline in wealth. For millions of Americans today, the bell may be ringing but there is no food on the table.

We are also dealing with abbreviated reflex chains in financial policy. For decades, the standard equation went like this: tax cuts = economic growth = prosperity for all. Thanks to the trickle-down effect, a tax cut would even benefit those who were not directly affected by the tax cut. The money that was returned to citizens would essentially flow downward, ultimately reaching the poorer segments of society. The beneficiaries of tax cuts spend their additional cash on shoes, furniture, and cars. They may even feel sufficiently stimulated by the windfall to launch a new business.

In the days of a networked global economy, this equation is no longer automatically correct. In fact, we are increasingly witnessing a trickle-out rather than a trickle-down effect. The money the government returns to citizens trickles out sideways, flowing into the economic cycles of other countries. Investment and consumption are worldwide activities today. A tax cut no longer automatically benefits the domestic economy. Because the government generally spends its money within the country—on road construction, teachers, and defense—government spending stimulates economic growth. But nowadays the return of government funds to private households can also trigger domestic economic decline. This is still no reason to be opposed to tax cuts. But it is certainly a reason to reexamine our old thought patterns. A tax reform meant to stimulate the domestic economy must be structured differently today than it would have been 20 years ago.

The political candidates in both parties find it exceedingly difficult to delete their reflexes. It seems that politicians across the political spectrum have decided to deceive the public over the true extent of global shifts in power. They aren't doing this out of maliciousness, but probably out of fear that voters could be offended by too much openness. As many politicians have learned, honesty doesn't always pay off in the voting booth. In gauging the public's mood, modern politicians assume that voters don't want to be provided with solutions to problems, but are in fact satisfied with politicians who are adept at suppressing problems—hence the advent of the now-fashionable obligatory lie.

Anyone who hopes to end America's relative decline must first recognize the dangers. Truth is a powerful force, and to be able to judge a situation correctly we must remain true to the facts. Perhaps we should proceed the way the early environmentalists did. They made sure that, in addition to financial accounts, balance sheets were prepared for pollutants, energy, and waste. That practice exposed the previously invisible consumption of resources, making this information accessible to the political leadership and exposing reality. A tangible value was assigned to the environment. The word *sustainability* celebrated its global premier.

Dying rivers, fruit soaked in pesticides, and polluted air were still the generally accepted by-products of industrial society until, almost overnight, the public suddenly perceived them as scandalous. The malodorous chemicals that were once accepted as a necessary evil were now unacceptable. The pressure to bring about change affected both the political sphere and ordinary people, who began reforming their habits. Recycling came into fashion, automatic thermostats were installed in heating systems, and the first shimmering, bluish solar panels began appearing on roofs—only to be ogled by an awe-struck public as if they were landing pads for extraterrestrial spacecraft.

Laws to protect the environment began popping up in every state. Waste and energy management programs were introduced, and solar, wind, and biomass came to represent the world's new energy reserves. Previously unknown words like *recycling* entered the language.

The United States must understand that the country's gradual deindustrialization, so clearly reflected in the trio of deficits in the balance of trade, current account, and government budget, is a process as momentous as the environmental outrages of earlier years. Depletion is just as much a catchword today as it was then, but this time we are depleting ourselves. We are playing fast and loose with the future once again, even though the current wave of destruction doesn't taste like anything or give off an unpleasant odor. Once again, we are enjoying the present at the expense of the future, this time, with our economic standing, not just the environment.

The decline of the American production is such a grave threat that it should be a burning issue for a new generation of politicians. They know that balance-of-trade deficits are never an expression of strength. They also know that shrinking production potential always means declining wealth. Finally, they know that there can be no free trade with state-controlled economies.

They should insist that the obligatory lie be exposed. To some extent, all that is necessary is to reactivate the original reflexes.

Step 2: It's the Rules and Regulations, Stupid

What do you need to play a game of football? Most people would say: all it takes is two teams, a playing field, and a ball.

But they overlook the two other things needed to get a game going: a common set of rules for both teams and mutual trust in the validity of these rules. If trust is lacking, perhaps because one team is known for pulling out knives after a game, that game will not materialize.

It's the same thing in the economic world. It needs rules and the confidence that the rules will be observed. "When truth is lost," says Alan Greenspan, "a nation's ability to transact business is palpably undermined." Even Milton Friedman admitted, shortly before his death, that he had been mistaken when he recommended one thing above all else to the countries of the former Soviet bloc to overcome socialism: "Privatize, privatize, privatize."

"I was wrong," he said in an interview published in 2002. "It has become clear that the rule of law is probably more important than privatization."

Today's globalization is by no means a lawless environment. But many of the laws being made today are little more than laws of the jungle—the law of the cheapest, the dirtiest, and the fastest, or, in many cases, simply the law of the most unscrupulous.

The global economy has produced a new sphere, a huge, non-governmental space in which markets are solely responsible for setting prices and developing standards. It is filled with financial investors, lobbyists, lawyers, and corporate strategists and, in the case of the major Asian corporations, the governments that are all-too-apparently behind them. This sphere is not only largely unregulated and lacking tradition, but devoid of trust and commitment as well. The rules that apply in it have no firm consistency. In fact, they are volatile and subject to constant change. Most of all, they are unreliable, and not everyone plays by them.

For example, look at the food industry. Between 1990 and today—a period that parallels the boom in imports—the number of food-borne illnesses reported by the U.S. Food and Drug Administration (FDA) almost tripled. Importers held a 50-percent market share in the late 1990s; now it is 83 percent. Today, a staggering 13,916 foreign seafood processors deliver their products to roughly 400 U.S. ports. Understaffed and lacking adequate authority, seafood inspectors are poorly positioned to control this sensitive segment of the food industry. A proposal to have U.S. inspectors travel to source countries to inspect products there failed in the face of overwhelming political opposition in those nations.

Experts agree that the food market has become global while food inspection has remained local, leading to a decline in food safety in the United States. In a story on October 15, 2006, the *Wall Street Journal* writes: "Now the industry is looking to strengthen regulation, including broadening the use of preventive controls. Apparently realizing that a weak FDA affects consumer confidence—and their bottom line—several trade groups, such as GMA and National Fisheries Institute, are lobbying for more funding and authority for the agency to oversee food safety."

Even those who have always lobbied for less government intervention find the volatility in this newly created sphere unsettling. Many industrialists clearly sense that they have lost the power to set standards. In the course of a global price war, others are increasingly making decisions over the quality of products sold in the United States. But who exactly are these elusive "others"? One thing we do know is that these nebulous entities take no responsibility for their decisions. The U.S. food industry is blamed for contaminated food products, not its suppliers from the Far East. Hazardous toys are made in China, but they harm Mattel. Chinese corporate executives are responsible for environmental degradation in the Yangtze Delta, but Land's End and other U.S. clothing retailers are the ones whose images suffer.

After a summer of scandal, U.S. industry seems to be rethinking the way it does business. In a front-page story on September 16, 2007, the *New York Times* reported on what it called a "broad tactical shift" in American industry: "After years of favoring the hands-off doctrine of the Bush administration, some of the nation's biggest industries are pushing for something they have long resisted: new federal regulations. The tactical shift is motivated by a confluence of self-interest: growing competition from inexpensive imports that do not meet voluntary standards."

Industry demand for worldwide standards should be a wakeup call for politicians. The message is loud and clear: the government is in demand once again. It's not about big versus small government, the issue that Republicans and Democrats have been debating for decades. What companies want is a modern government—smart, streamlined, and strong—a government whose role is to modify rules and regulations to conform to new realities. International financial markets are calling for international standards to protect investors. An international value creation chain in the food industry requires international rules and regulations, as well as a system for monitoring compliance. Antitrust laws designed to fight cartels and monopolies must also be globalized. The increase in state-owned investment funds in Asia and the Middle East, where countries are buying companies, creates the need for new rules to regulate the transparency of such investments.

When Western democracies enter the new sphere in the space between nations, they tend to do so with hesitation and, more often than not, temporarily: at G-8 summits or global economic summits, for example. They arrive with their large entourages, only to abandon the playing field the minute the meeting ends. Political leaders get together for meetings in this newly created nongovernmental sphere, in places like Gleneagles or Heiligendamm, but these are places where no one lives.

The real decisions about our wealth are being made today in that supranational space devoid of foreign ministers and presidents. Statespeople specialize in questions of war and peace, and diplomacy is their métier. But they avoid the broad field where American and European economic interests reside.

But globalization has tremendously expanded the need for regulation, standardization, and agreements between nations. The world of business has become a borderless world. Those who wish to influence the social and economic conditions under which people work and live (and vote!) must adjust their range of action to accommodate new possibilities. Politicians must do the same thing major corporations have already done: they must become global players.

Democratic capitalism also has trouble accepting the fact that markets set the rules, because this devalues the term "democratic." Virtually all standards that play a role in guaranteeing the well being and advancement of citizens are currently being pushed aside by a seemingly invisible hand.

But there is no reason to feel despondent. It is not the most populous nations—countries like China, India, Pakistan, and Brazil—that have the greatest power to regulate, but the representatives of the largest consumer markets, that is, Europe and the United States. The power of consumers in private life translates into the power of consumer nations in political life. These nations have many rights, especially the right to say no at their international borders. The customer is king, even when it comes to international trade relations.

Step 3: Let's Level the Playing Field

The modern state is not a market vendor selling his or her wares directly, but it is a strict custodian of markets. Goods may come from all over the world, but the airports in Paris, London, and New York, and the seaports in Rotterdam, Amsterdam, and Boston are the points of entry and control for these goods.

It is important to distinguish between *trade* and *trade policy*. Merchants look at the world and see the flow of goods pushing its way through the continents like some primeval river. This current should remain untouched by human hands, they believe, because that interference would only impede the rate of flow.

Trade politicians see the same current, but they sense the political need to give it structure. They want to increase the wealth of their nation, not the assets of importers. They know that the common good is greater than the sum of individual interests.

Protectionism is not the fundamental idea behind trade policy. Those who isolate themselves end up losing their wealth. Instead, the fundamental idea of trade policy is a worldwide, peaceful balancing of interests designed to smooth out an uneven world and create a level playing field for workers and their bosses, consumers, and producers, a field in which global competition can take place in a free and fair manner.

The state should keep its fingers out of the flow of trade. It can only cause trouble by intervening. That has been the position in Brussels and Washington until now. Anyone with even a rudimentary understanding of the politics of our day must admit that this concern is not entirely unwarranted. The state has often proved that it could not live up to high expectations. The state as manager of international trade is not an entirely pleasant concept.

And yet it is a necessary concept. Although the state does not, for the most part, intervene in trade in the United States, it certainly does so in India, Singapore, Japan, Korea, Malaysia, and especially in China. The state has a strong presence—as the biggest promoter and protector of exporting industries—everywhere in the world where the most spectacular successes are being celebrated today.

As a result, the West today faces a phalanx of controlled market economies for which it was not prepared. They may look like our economies, but they are not the same. Indeed, to this day this economic phenomenon, this mixture of state-controlled and market economies, lacks a name, a theory, a textbook, a symbol, or an interest group. It doesn't even have any prominent proponents who could be invited to interviews in television studios.

The Chinese economy is irrigated by a banking system that does not operate under the criteria of profitability. Tariffs surround entire industries like protective walls. As a shoe exporter, China has no interest in importing shoes. To preserve the status quo, the domestic market is sealed off against countries that produce even cheaper shoes with a 27 percent price markup.

What is most obvious about China is the resoluteness with which it defends its interests. In the summer of 2006, the World Trade Organization (WTO) was confronted with a new Chinese customs law that pressures the Western auto industry to outsource all of its production to China. Under the law, manufacturers who assemble more than 60 percent of a vehicle outside China are slapped with a 25 percent punitive tariff on parts they import to China. The Chinese leadership hopes to use this strategy to force foreign automakers to shift their entire production to China or purchase their parts from local suppliers. This sort of punitive tariff is strictly prohibited under the rules of the World Trade

Organization, as is any regulation stipulating that a certain percentage of value be produced domestically.

China is aware of this, but it also knows that Western democracies are slow to make decisions. It can take a number of years before this sort of violation of the rules turns into an official complaint proceeding before the committees of the WTO.

The West seems spellbound as it observes the goings-on in Southeast Asia. When it comes to economic policy, today's America is a pacifist, uneasy at even the thought of having to put up a fight. Those members of the business and economic policy worlds who consider themselves so rational are in fact our biggest dreamers today.

The question today is not: should we put an end to global free trade? The real question is: when will the West acknowledge that there is no such thing as flawless free trade? For China and most other Asian nations, the conditions of trade are a question of usefulness, not faith. America and Europe would be well advised to adopt this way of thinking.

The liberal economic order is only liberal within a regulatory framework. The market is not automatically free. Indeed, its freedom depends on authorities having the power to both monitor and penalize.

The state must be allowed to show an interest in what happens in its markets. Who is delivering a given product? Under what conditions? How did the price of the product materialize? And what reasons to benefit domestic production exist other than the price list?

It was disputed for 50 years, but today every child knows that without NATO there would be no free West. If the Western defense alliance had not, repeatedly and with great resolve, paraded, modernized, and periodically beefed up its bomber squadrons and tank divisions, Soviet communism would not have imploded but would have expanded toward the West. By the end of the cold war, even the last skeptics had grasped the bottom line of history: the noblest achievements were defended by a willingness to accept the greatest of atrocities. The dove of peace survived because the hawk was perched on the ramparts.

The global war for wealth demands a no-less-contradictory response. Those who want to secure free and fair trade must be willing to defend it. The integration of the Asian economies into the global economy will not happen automatically. It will be a process involving arguments, threats, incentives, and negotiations. And it will ultimately revolve around the following questions: Who is integrating whom into his economic and value system? Will we permit our social and environmental agreements to be invalidated? Will we look on as government funds are used to establish new monopolies elsewhere that will later be in a position to dictate prices and terms of delivery? Are we willing to achieve economic growth at the cost of humanity? Will we all become Americasians?

Throughout Asia, we encounter a similar indifference to Western values, even though no one would be willing to put it quite as directly. It is precisely the unspoken that divides our worlds. Free trade unions are not ridiculed, but they also happen to be prohibited. The environment is held up as an asset worth protecting, and yet it is being systematically dismantled like a totaled car. Child labor is condemned in theory yet tolerated in practice. There are many laws to protect Western inventions, but most of them are not applied. What we consider to be fundamental is often nothing but window dressing in their eyes. They see the state (India) or the party (China) as playing the decisive role in setting prices, promoting technology, obtaining natural resources, and protecting and encouraging all sorts of economic and political activities. They perceive the triumphant success of their export industries as a judgment of history—and one that doesn't merit an appeal.

Americans and Europeans could regard these attitudes toward human beings and the role of the state—attitudes that are so foreign to us—with the requisite liberalism, if it weren't for the enormous reaction this would produce in the current world of international commerce. Where there are no mechanisms in place to enforce compliance with the same rules and regulations, the controlled economies are forcing the West to play by its own less-than-savory rules. The West, unless it wants to come away as the clear loser on every trading day, must also domesticate its workers, loosen its environmental laws, and trim its system of social safeguards.

The West believes it is selling machinery, automobiles, and airplanes. But it also happens to be selling a piece of itself.

Step 4: It's Time to Think about Job Protection

Nowadays the state is interested in all kinds of things. It makes sure that no dirty money crosses its borders. It uses every possible method in the sophisticated arsenal of modern criminology to track down the millions of dollars earned through drug smuggling, human trafficking, and illegal weapons deals. It sniffs around and it confiscates, putting stress on money launderers. And while all this effort doesn't automatically translate into victory for the state, at least it isn't avoiding the issue. Its message to criminals is clear: be alert, because so are we. There is no hinterland where the rule of law does not apply.

When it comes to the importation of technical devices, at least the government takes a second look. Vietnamese regulatory laws for toasters, refrigerators, and nuclear power plants apply in Vietnam. They don't have to be of any further interest to us. But import regulations determine what devices can be connected to the power grid in American households and cities. Their purpose is to protect citizens at home, because there is a consensus that life has a value and not just a price. Customers can put their minds to rest when they see toasters made in the United States, Canada, and Korea on the shelves at their local retailers. All are subject to the same laws.

Access to virtually every sensitive market is regulated in this manner. The sale of pharmaceuticals is not left up to the discretion of Indian pharmaceutical companies. A nuclear power plant made by the Russian company that built Chernobyl wouldn't stand a chance of receiving approval anywhere in the West. We do not permit cars without modern catalytic converter technol-

ogy to drive on our roads. For good reason, the environmental
and safety standards applicable to a given product are written by
the country in which that product is sold. No one would think of
lowering our safety standards for pills, power plants, and cars to
support Asia's young economies and improve the lot of its
poverty-stricken rural populations.

This is how America protects its citizens and educates its suppliers. The customers decide. But whenever customers are somehow unable to make that decision, the nation protects them, and
without making much of a fuss about it.

There is only one exception: labor. Labor, as a commodity, is
subject to virtually no regulation. In international commerce,
labor is at the whim of capitalism in its most rudimentary form.
The labor component of every product can be as cheap as the
market wants it to be, and it can be provided under inhumane conditions and with complete disregard for all domestic standards—
from occupational hygiene to equal rights for women to
prohibitions on child labor—and yet no one at the customs office
is evenly remotely interested.

Of all goods that can be traded, labor is the most liberated. It
enters our countries freely, and we are only too willing to suspend
our ideas about value and price to allow it unimpeded entry.

A customer eyeing two mobile phones on a store shelf isn't
interested in the fact that they were produced under different
social conditions. The first phone contains all of the social obligations of a developed, industrialized nation, from regulated
working hours to maternity protection. The second phone was
produced under the conditions of a primitive capitalist society, in
which workers have no more rights than a farm dog.

It should also be the responsibility of modern global economic
policy to develop minimum standards for labor as a commodity,
the goal being to initiate a convergence on the global labor markets and reduce the widening gap in the cost of labor around the
world. The level playing field that major banks seek for themselves
and their investments should also be the objective in the labor
markets. Only a gradual harmonization of working conditions and

wages can put an end to competition based on undercutting competitors on the basis of wages.

For this reason, allowing free trade unions is not a purely political demand, as it was in the days of Poland's Solidarity Union. Nowadays it is an economic condition for the harmonization of a widely disparate global labor market. Without free trade unions there can be no free formation of prices. Without free pricing, the wage drift will only continue on the most important of all markets, the labor market.

So far, the WTO's rules and regulations have excluded basic labor norms like free unions, minimum hygiene standards, and acceptable ranges for a global minimum wage. The WTO refuses to even discuss a contractual framework for a global labor market. This refusal destroys the validity of all national minimum standards, on the one hand. On the other hand, it uses precisely the mechanism that was once intended to protect domestic workers against those very same workers. That's because the American minimum wage is by no means applicable to all American companies, only to those that actually produce in the United States.

Former U.S. president Bill Clinton was the first to at least attempt to establish minimum standards for working conditions within the WTO. His efforts failed, partly as a result of European opposition. Brussels, at the time, sought to justify its noncooperation by arguing: "Economics takes place in the economy." A new approach is now long overdue.

Step 5: The Social Welfare State Is Dead; Long Live the Social Welfare State!

No one should be shedding any crocodile tears over the demise of the social welfare state. But this is also no reason to feel discouraged. The minimalist state as a response to globalization is not an inevitability. Globalization doesn't prevent the West from maintaining a social welfare state of its own design. It can be more substantial or more streamlined, more generous or on the parsimonious side. No one can prevent the Europeans from expanding their social welfare state into every conceivable aspect of life. The health-care system can be costly or cheap, privately managed or government-run, and even if the U.S. government decided tomorrow to make drinking herbal tea, applying leg compresses, and attending yoga classes mandatory for everyone, there would be plenty of reasons to object, but globalization would not be one of them.

The globalized world does not act universally as a standardization body with the goal of prescribing uniformity for everyone on earth. Societies can consume large amounts of gasoline, as the Americans do, or they can conserve gasoline, as the Germans do. Like the British, they can invest 7 percent of their national income in their health-care system, or they can take the American approach and invest significantly more in health care. The products on which they spend their money are not important. For an economy, it is completely irrelevant whether the majority of a population travels by train or by air, whether it builds nice houses or prefers to invest the same amount of money in an impressive system of masseurs and nurses for the elderly. The difference lies in the fact that money is being spent, not what it's being spent on. This is where the globalized world is strict and practically dictatorial in its methods. In this world, nations that persist in employing their old financing methods are penalized in the form of declining wealth.

For example, in the United States, big corporations are still largely responsible for keeping the social welfare state afloat. This approach stems from the days when Western economies were competing among equals. After World War II, both work and workers were abundant. There was almost no unemployment when these company-based social systems were conceived and developed. At the time, it made abundant sense to divert a relatively small percentage of workers' earnings into funds to support retirees, war widows, and the disabled. The social welfare state was as national as the labor market when President Franklin Roosevelt and the corporate executives of the day created the social welfare state we know today.

Nowadays politicians and unions battle over the continued existence of these social contracts of the past, and yet the conditions under which they were introduced no longer exist. That is why the social welfare state funded by corporations does not make labor more costly, as is so often claimed. It only increases the cost of American labor. When it comes to mobile phones from Korea, refrigerators from Taiwan, and computers from China, these added costs of labor are nonexistent, which is why the U.S. company-financed social welfare state is in a crisis.

For importers, labor is unaffected by the U.S. social welfare state system. In fact, it even makes their products cheaper in relative terms. The American model of the social welfare state is actually a huge import promotion program. It attracts foreigners and their goods to the country and it even provides them with special treatment. Meanwhile, it remains unrelenting in requiring local manufacturers to pay a steep surcharge on the cost of their labor.

It would be easy to destroy the importers' advantage and at least achieve parity. There are two ways it could be done, both significantly more effective than the current system. The first is to finance the social welfare state through a consumer tax, that is, a national sales tax. This method of raising money for the state would not differentiate in the least between domestic and foreign entities—both would pay the same sales tax. A sales tax would affect the price of a Korean-made car in exactly the same way as it would a Chrysler or a Ford. Consumers would be the ones paying for the social welfare state, not American workers.

The second approach would be for the government to regulate the social welfare state by requiring, for example, mandatory health insurance and retirement insurance for every American. But insurance companies are private enterprises and, as such, are only subject to the requirement that they may not refuse to insure anyone. In cases in which children and their parents could not afford their own insurance, the government would become their insurer. Under this model, companies would also be relieved of their social burdens.

But, some might ask, why should the state be so accommodating to corporations? The answer is that the government would be motivated not by any charitable sentiments toward big business but by the realization that a company-based social insurance system is causing serious damage to the domestic economy under current conditions. This system may seem to be socially minded, but under the current conditions of competition it is in fact inhumane.

Step 6: The Grand Design: A Journey to the United States of the West

The days of a unipolar world are numbered. Different powers will shape the face of the twenty-first century, and the United States will become one of several superpowers.

America has nothing to fear from Europe in this respect. The ghosts of the last century are not about to return. The real threat to the U.S. sphere of influence stems from the rise of Asia and the Middle East. America's economic strength is declining relative to that of these emerging economies, just as its share of the world's population is also slightly shrinking.

Let us take a closer look. In East Asia, we are seeing the coming of age of new powers armed with extraordinary economic performance and a burning determination to succeed. The sheer force with which India and China are surging ahead is unprecedented in world history. The shift in the international balance of power is quietly creeping up on us because the new powers are not claiming any power for themselves at the present time. Our political radar system, developed during the cold war and later revised to address the threat of Islamic terror, is programmed to deal with leaders like Stalin, Khrushchev, and the current Iranian president, Mahmoud Ahmadinejad. But the small, quiet blips appearing on that outdated political radar screen are going unnoticed or are being registered with considerable delay. This lack of awareness is all the more troubling because China's development into a major power, when it occurs, will eclipse any comparable phenomenon of the last 500 years.

Cooperation between the Americans and the Europeans could act as a counterforce to the new, rising economies. A closing of ranks among Western democracies could also serve as a peaceful and yet unmistakable response to China's cultural and political expansion. The West would expand its effectiveness, as Europe and America developed a significant political counterweight to Asia's increasingly wealthy nations.

History in its embryonic state is often little more than an idea. If it matures and gains stature it can change many things, including the lives of people. There is no great power that does not owe its prominence to a great idea. Power follows ideas, not the other way around. It makes sense to pursue the idea of a transatlantic alliance, as implausible as it may sound. The idea is unreal—as unreal as the idea of a European Union after the end of World War II. The concept is eccentric—as eccentric as the thought of British, Irish, German, and French settler families establishing the cornerstone for a new global power.

Today's commonalities between the two continents are more than an accident of history. If the Atlantic and its algae, fish, and endless volume of water weren't there to separate the two continents, Europe and America could very well have become an alliance of nations, though perhaps not a single nation, long ago.

Let us indulge, for a moment, in a thought experiment. Imagine that the Atlantic Ocean disappeared overnight and continental drift occurred. Instead of being on the ocean, Lisbon would border on Boston, it would be a short drive from the town of Plymouth in Great Britain to Maine or Massachusetts, and the fishing ports of Alesund in Norway and Halifax in Canada would become neighbors. The West would no longer be a primarily cultural and political place, but also a geographic entity. Its people would quickly come together, first physically and then constitutionally.

There are many conceivable scenarios. Perhaps the majority of today's 25 EU member states would want to become new states in the United States of America. Or perhaps it would be abundantly obvious that the United States be counted as one of the founding nations of a *new* European Union. The country's wealth of experience in forming consensus could certainly have benefited the original signatories of the 1957 Treaties of Rome that established the European Economic Community.

The ocean remains where it is, but the distance between the two continents has diminished in recent decades. Contrary to what essayist Robert Kagan once wrote, Americans and Europeans do not live on Mars and Venus. Instead, they reside on the two sides of a single moon. They breathe the same air, stand on the same geological subsoil, and look out at other galaxies from the same distance.

All the differences that are held up to characterize Americans and Europeans are in fact the result of differences in the way the sun shines on these two parts of the world. Before the shadow of two world wars darkened everything, Europe was on the sunny side. The Europeans were obsessed with their archaic visions of power. From their vantage points in Paris, London, and Berlin, they firmly believed in their own, natural superiority and were unable to imagine the rest of the world as anything but a zone dominated by Europeans. More than just conscious of their power, European governments were obsessed with it and unafraid of enforcing it militarily. Mars, the Roman god of war, might as well have been their original ancestor. The Americans, for their part, were peaceable—a trait many would now consider to be a part of the genetic makeup of Europeans. Some European governments were obsessesd with collecting colonies, while others were happy to be left alone. Venus, it seems, is of American descent.

With the failure of the European nations' power-hungry policies, the sun moved on and since then has been shining on the country located on the other side of the moon. Europe's cockiness disappeared, and the use of violence has been proscribed ever since. Contemporary Europeans favor the methods of diplomacy.

But America blossomed. Under the warming sun of history, the nation became self-confident, resolute, and pugnacious—but also arrogant. What we see in America today is the same quest for dominance that once characterized the other side of the moon, almost as if the gods had traded allegiances.

The angle of the sun changed again a few decades after the war ended. The darkness of the postwar era eventually disappeared from everyday life on the old continent, as Europe reemerged from the shadow of history. A new normalcy is developing that is now bringing the two sides of the moon closer together. Although the "strategic divide" between the old and the new world that Kagan mentioned has not been closed, it is becoming smaller. The trauma of Europe's battles among nations is finally subsiding. With its involvement in the military campaigns in the Balkans, Africa, and Afghanistan, Europe has found its way back to the path of realpolitik.

Europe and America have probably never been as close as they are today; for example:

1. *Americans and Europeans share many of the same ancestors.* More than one in two Americans is a descendant of a generation of settlers that came from Europe. Americans and Europeans have the same genetic code. They are basically the same species.

2. *Americans and Europeans are also kin in spirit.* They share all essential political, cultural, economic, and philosophical values. The differences are minute when we compare the United States and Europe with societies in the Arab, Latin American, and Asian regions. The human rights declarations of the late eighteenth century were the result of transatlantic cooperation, and together the two regions established the basis for the political project of the West. They were brought together for the first time, in a legally binding manner, in the U.S. Bill of Rights, which became law in 1791. In the Declaration of Independence of July 4, 1776, written in large part by Thomas Jefferson of Virginia, human rights are summarized in a single, brilliant sentence: "We hold these truths to be self-evident, that all men are created equal, that they are endowed by their Creator with certain inalienable rights, that among these are life, liberty and the pursuit of happiness."

3. The historian Heinrich August Winkler, author of the standard work *Long Road to the West*, concludes: "There are no European values as such, only Western values." The same thing can be said for the United States. There are no American values that are not based on European antecedents. The early Americans wanted to be better Europeans.

    Europeans and Americans have traveled down the same political roads since the end of World War II, close to one another on both good and bad days. They defied Soviet communism together. If a European and an American were to host a slide show today, the images they would project onto the screen would be the same: the Berlin airlift; the building of the Berlin Wall; the Cuban missile crisis; Kennedy, Brandt, Nixon, and, eventually, Reagan, Kohl, and George Bush. The final image would be of people dancing on top of a wall. The lights would hardly have been switched on in the room before people on both sides of the Atlantic would be looking, with collective concern, to Tehran, Kabul, Baghdad, Darfur, and with one eye trained on Beijing.

4. *Since the establishment of NATO, Americans and Europeans have also been comrades-in-arms.* In the Balkans, in Afghanistan, on the Horn of Africa, and in Iraq, American troops have joined forces with the militaries of virtually every European country, although the distribution of labor to date has demanded far more of the United States. Writing in the *New York Times*, Roger Cohen wants to see the Germans serve up a mixture of the old Wehrmacht and today's Bundeswehr: "A touch of Bundesmacht would be welcome." And yet it is precisely this European and American military cooperation that is so remarkable. Far from standing between the United States and Great Britain, the American War of Independence against the British colonial power actually serves as the basis for the special relationship between the two countries today. The bloody

crimes of the Germans under Hitler no longer engender
suspicions in America against modern-day Germany. And a
large majority of Germans perceive the former occupiers as
liberators and friends today.

5. *The American and European economies are tightly interwoven.*
    Democratic capitalism serves as their shared basis for doing
    business. Since the Social Security Act of 1935, the states on
    both sides of the Atlantic have been social welfare states
    worthy of the name. The West is a flat world, economically
    speaking. In contrast to Asia and the species of authoritarian
    capitalism unique to it, employees in America and Europe
    are also citizens, and not subjects, in their working lives. As a
    result of a multitude of mergers and joint ventures, as well as
    a dense network of branches and subsidiaries, the identity of
    most corporations is essentially transatlantic. After acquiring
    Bankers Trust, Deutsche Bank is also an American bank.
    And when General Motors bought German carmaker Adam
    Opel AG, it also became a German company.

6. *Americans and Europeans have formed a shared popular culture
    on a level that has never existed between two continents before.*
    We discuss the same issues, listen to the same music, and
    watch the same films, from the East German Stasi drama
    The Lives of Others to the latest Hollywood blockbuster.
    There is also a great deal of cross-fertilization when it
    comes to high culture. Writers like Philip Roth, Jonathan
    Franzen, and Susan Sontag are part of our joint cultural
    heritage. Briton Sir Simon Rattle directs the Berlin
    Philharmonic, and German Kurt Masur was with the New
    York Philharmonic. Intellectuals like Ralf Dahrendorf,
    André Glucksmann, Herbert Marcuse, and Samuel
    Huntington are part of a Western intellectual culture that
    cannot possibly be divided along national boundaries. We
    still have uniquely American, Italian, French, and Polish
    cultures, but a common Western culture is developing
    alongside them. Indeed, it seems that it is this part of the
    culture that is growing in leaps and bounds.

7. *Americans and Europeans are approaching the same future.* This is the most important commonality. They will either succeed together in dealing with new challenges—from climate change to terrorism—or not at all. There is no threat confronting America today that does not confront Europe at the same time. Conversely, there is no European challenge that is not an American challenge as well. Neither of the two would be well advised to seek its fortune at the expense of the other. Europeans and Americans will either march together or be defeated separately.

Henry Kissinger's fear that the new Europe could be yearning for an "identity through confrontation with America" has proven to be unfounded. Nowadays (almost) everyone in Europe knows that a future worth fighting for can only be achieved together with America. Today more than ever, Europe and America form a community of destiny, even if the threat no longer emanates from Russian tanks.

The United States of the West would have to be a confederation of independent nations, an alliance based on common values and interests. Anyone who looks hard enough can already recognize this new, supranational entity taking shape on the horizon. And if we look even more closely, we can even see it approaching. We would be wise to start taking a few steps in its direction.

The values of this confederation are those of the Enlightenment—notwithstanding the many differences among the partner nations. The system of government in the United States and Germany is more federal than that of the French and the British. Individualism is more pronounced in America than in Scandinavia. The Americans believe in God, and the Europeans in the social welfare state. But these differences become trivial in the face of an outside world that considers virtually everything that is important to us to be unimportant or even harmless; a world that ignores, ridicules, or fights our values.

The separation of church and state is by no means a matter of course in Asia and in the Arab world. In many parts of the world, democracy is ostracized, while those who support it populate the prisons and not the parliaments. Free trade unions are almost nonexistent, and the freedom of speech is only valued as long as it doesn't get in the way of the business dealings of the powerful. They perceive as offensive our Western system of checks and balances, power and countervailing power, speech and contradiction, as well as our system of government, which only grants authority for a limited period of time and in which those granting the authority are not kings, generals, rebels, or religious leaders, but the masses of ordinary people, regardless of education, gender, religion, or race. Indeed, it is probably as sinister in their eyes as the one-party state or the caliphate is in ours.

This brings us to the second pillar of an American-European identity: interests. There is a massive, and increasingly urgent, common Western interest to colonize this intermediate space into which the global economy is expanding its radius of activity, the goal being to establish Western values in this still largely apolitical sphere because others establish theirs.

The West's advance would be worth the effort. Globalization needs a regulatory framework, just as an apartment building needs tenant rules and the roads need traffic rules. We can only rid the global economy of the archaic, raw, and even brutal elements of its current character by establishing universally valid rules and regulations.

In the global competition with Russia, the Arab world, and Asia, common Western interests form a highly complex system that includes interests in security, natural resources and the environment, protections against child labor and product piracy, as well as the enforcement of common standards on the future markets for biotechnology and nanotechnology. Millions of people look forward to the day when the prevalence of justice, the social obligations of wealth, and the protection of natural resources become firmly ensconced principles in this new economic world.

This United States of the West would be open to all nations that share its goals. Values and interests would form the basis of this confederation, not language, religion, ethnic origin, or sovereign territory. Anyone who shares its values and interests would be welcome. Those who expressed an interest in becoming a part of it would receive every conceivable form of support. This is the new and revolutionary aspect that allows us to refer to this concept as the foundation of a new form of state. The United States of the West would be cosmopolitan in the truest sense of the word. Its guiding principle would be inclusion, not exclusion.

Establishing this entity would be the challenge of the century, comparable only with the founding of the United States or the development of a united Europe. We would need politicians who are prepared to look beyond their national horizons without betraying their national identities. There would be no lack of opportunities for a new generation of pragmatic visionaries. Its first task would be to inspire enthusiasm, preferably among millions and millions of people. A speech to promote this new, common future of Americans and Europeans could sound something like this:

> *As this effort for independence, inspired by the American Declaration of Independence, now approaches a successful close, a great new effort for interdependence is transforming the world about us. And the spirit of that new effort is the same spirit which gave birth to the American Constitution.*
>
> *That spirit is today most clearly seen across the Atlantic Ocean. The nations of Western Europe, long divided by feuds far more bitter than any which existed among the 13 colonies, are today joining together, seeking, as our forefathers sought, to find freedom in diversity and in unity, strength.*
>
> *The United States looks on this vast new enterprise with hope and admiration. We do not regard a strong and united Europe as a rival but as a partner. To aid its progress has been the basic object of our foreign policy for years. We believe that a united Europe will be capable of playing a greater role in the common defense, of responding more generously to the needs of poorer nations, of joining with the United States and others in lowering trade barriers, resolving problems of commerce, commodities, and currency, and*

developing coordinated policies in all economic, political, and diplomatic areas. We see in such a Europe a partner with whom we can deal on a basis of full equality in all the great and burdensome tasks of building and defending a community of free nations.

It would be premature at this time to do more than indicate the high regard with which we view the formation of this partnership. The first order of business is for our European friends to go forward in forming the more perfect union which will someday make this partnership possible.

A great new edifice is not built overnight. It was 11 years from the Declaration of Independence to the writing of the Constitution. The construction of workable federal institutions required still another generation. The greatest works of our Nation's founders lay not in documents and in declarations, but in creative, determined action. The building of the new house of Europe has followed the same practical, purposeful course. Building the Atlantic partnership now will not be easily or cheaply finished.

But I will say here and now, on this Day of Independence, that the United States will be ready for a Declaration of Interdependence, that we will be prepared to discuss with a united Europe the ways and means of forming a concrete Atlantic partnership, a mutually beneficial partnership between the new union now emerging in Europe and the old American Union founded here 175 years ago. All this will not be completed in a year, but let the world know it is our goal.

In urging the adoption of the United States Constitution, Alexander Hamilton told his fellow New Yorkers "to think continentally." Today Americans must learn to think intercontinentally.

Acting on our own, by ourselves, we cannot establish justice throughout the world; we cannot insure its domestic tranquility, or provide for its common defense, or promote its general welfare, or secure the blessings of liberty to ourselves and our posterity. But joined with other free nations, we can do all this and more. We can assist the developing nations to throw off the yoke of poverty.

We can balance our worldwide trade and payments at the highest possible level of growth. We can mount a deterrent powerful enough to deter any aggression. And ultimately we can help to achieve a world of law and free choice, banishing the world of war and coercion.

For the Atlantic partnership of which I speak would not look inward only, preoccupied with its own welfare and advancement. It must look outward to cooperate with all nations in meeting their common concern. It would serve as a nucleus for the eventual union of all free men—those who are now free and those who are vowing that some day they will be free.

John F. Kennedy delivered this address on July 4, 1962, America's Independence Day, in Philadelphia. It was his great vision to expand the transatlantic partnership beyond cooperation within NATO, to give it a political, an economic, and a cultural dimension, and to shape it into the nucleus of a new and better world of free nations. It was preceded by Winston Churchill's idea of a "United States of Europe." Kennedy borrowed from Churchill's vision without mentioning him by name. He referred to his concept of an interdependent West as a "Grand Design."

Forty-five years after this exceptional speech by an exceptional man, it seems that the time has come to revive his legacy. The European Union is now a reality, and one can only hope that the same will one day apply to Kennedy's "Grand Design."

The West is unfinished. But it doesn't have to stay that way. Those who seek to forge a new political alliance with both sides of the moon have much to gain. The crucial questions to the potential members of this alliance and their leaders are deceptively simple: Do they want it in the first place? Will America and Europe allow themselves to continue to fall or will they intervene once again, with great determination, in the course of their own history? Is the political class strong enough to abandon its intentional ignorance? Are the nations and their people willing to set aside their national egos for the greater good?

Complete freedom of choice is part of the West's fundamental view of life. This freedom also includes the freedom to fail.

INTERVIEW WITH NOBEL PRIZE WINNER PAUL A. SAMUELSON

"THE MARKET HAS NO BRAIN"

An interview with Economics Nobel Prize Laureate Paul A. Samuelson, 93, on rising unemployment, shrinking wealth, and his life in the age of globalization.

Samuelson, the son of Polish immigrants, was born in 1915 in the steel city of Gary, Indiana. He was educated at the University of Chicago and Harvard University, served under President Franklin Roosevelt on the National Resource Planning Board in World War II, and was economic adviser to President John F. Kennedy in the 1960s. Samuelson won the Nobel Prize for Economics in 1970. An emeritus professor at the Massachusetts Institute of Technology (MIT), he still tackles current political issues in his numerous publications. Samuelson has called for a basic reassessment of the impact of globalization.

r

Professor Samuelson, do you remember the America of your early childhood?

SAMUELSON: Yes, my childhood memories go back very far. For most people, memory starts when they are about four years old, but I remember some things from even before that. I should explain that I was born on the frontier, because Gary, Indiana, was a brand-new town created by the largest steel company in the world, US Steel, at the very bottom of Lake Michigan where Appalachian soft coal met Minnesota iron ore. People were living in tents when my family arrived there along with many other settlers.

Where did your parents come from, and what brought them to this remote area?

SAMUELSON: My father was a registered pharmacist, and it proved a lucky coincidence that my parents, who had emigrated as youngsters, both came from the part of Poland that borders on East Prussia. As a registered pharmacist, my father was predestined to benefit tremendously from World War I even before America entered the war. By that time, being in America was certainly better than life in troubled Europe. The workers in the steel company in Gary—most of them from Slavic countries—didn't know any doctors, and so my father, who could speak Slavic languages in some basic way, would be their doctor.

Did you or your father ever see the interior of the steel company?

SAMUELSON: That was impossible. It was like a military camp, with a guard. I never visited. No schoolchild in Gary, Indiana, ever visited the steel company. But we had a good idea of the working conditions.

By seeing the injuries and illnesses of the workers?

SAMUELSON: As I said, my father was a pharmacist and in some way their doctor. If a steelworker's leg got caught in the hot molten steel, they couldn't afford to stop the shift and you would lose your leg. From the age of 17 months, really a baby, until I was 5 years old, I spent half my time in twentieth-century rural

Indiana. So you may think I am 90, but I am really 140. No indoor plumbing, no indoor electricity. And in the steel company nearby, we are talking about 100 percent capitalism.

You began your studies at the University of Chicago. While you rose through the academic ranks, did you follow the development of Gary, Indiana?

SAMUELSON: Oh, yes. A few years ago, I got an honorary degree from a nearby Lutheran university, Valparaiso University. It wasn't given to me for any merit, but just because I came from that region. So, I thought it would be a good opportunity to look for my roots, but there weren't any left. The house I had lived in was now a parking lot. The wonderful library, Carnegie Library, was gone. Gary, I think, has become the murder capital in America. It was like Rotterdam, like bombed-out Rotterdam.

You lived the American dream. A son of immigrants, you became part of the academic and political establishment. What drove you?

SAMUELSON: I had my intellectual awakening in my father's library. Adam Smith's *Wealth of Nations*—I hadn't known it was there, so it had never occurred to me to open it up, and when I finally did, it was a whole new world to me. And I started economics at a perfect period to study—in the 1930s, at the Depression's bottom. On January 2, 1932, at 8 a.m. in the morning, I walked into my first University of Chicago classroom. That was almost the low point of the Great Depression, when in Germany at least one-third of the working population was unemployed. And tied with Germany were the United States. We had almost the same number of unemployed. This meant that every middle-class family felt it. It wasn't like recent recessions where the Harvard graduates, the graduates of the Stanford Business School, hardly know that there is a recession. This affected everything. All the banks in my part of the country substantially failed, and when the banks failed, the amount of money that the depositors recovered, with any luck at all, would be 10 cents out of the dollar.

In this period, many Americans died from hunger. Personally, did you experience the suffering of the working class?

SAMUELSON: No. But I do remember how in an urban section of Chicago a big truck that had just left the slaughterhouse would go down the street, and suddenly out from behind the fences 50 people would come and turn the truck over on its side, and 10 minutes later there was not a single person to be seen in the street and none of the hams and pork shoulders were left.

That was during the presidency of Herbert Hoover.

SAMUELSON: Hoover was certainly a man with a high IQ. But he was a man of principles, wrong principles for the times—orthodox. And so he would be shocked if a government program designed to produce grain for mules—part of agriculture—was abused to fill the stomachs of human beings instead. They would actually prosecute people for that. He believed in principles that I also learned in the classroom—that the presence of unemployed people would bring down the wages of all people and then the market would stabilize. However, I could not quite rationalize this with what I saw was happening on my way to the university each morning and on my way back from the university each evening.

You think the crisis turned into the Great Depression because politicians ignored the symptoms and failed to tackle the causes?

SAMUELSON: The fiction is that there was a big stock market crash on October 29, 1929, and this was the Great Depression. The truth, however, is that this was what started it, and by 1930 it just looked like a more serious recession. But then it became a major depression because nothing was done about it and because of the way things looked like internationally.

How did your family cope with the situation?

SAMUELSON: By this time, my family was prosperous but not rich. How do you think I spent my four summer vacations at the university? At the beach. Now, did I feel guilty? Not at all, because I had classmates who were poorer than me and who would apply at 400 different firms and report that there were no jobs. So, I knew it was pointless for me to learn the hard way that there were no jobs, and that is why I went to the beach instead.

Today, many governments adhere to the ideas of British economist John Maynard Keynes. One of the side effects is enormous— even irresponsible—federal debt. Would you consider massive public spending still an appropriate macroeconomic tool to fight off a recession?

SAMUELSON: Politicians need to react to concrete challenges or they will miss their goals. Back then, the Western economies got caught in the liquidity trap because the economy had contracted. Millions of workers were fired, which made the contraction even worse. The situation in contemporary Europe and America is a completely different one.

In your seminal economic textbooks, the problem of a "liquidity trap" is explained in great detail.

SAMUELSON: Yeah, we've put it back in. I always included it in my textbook, but the publisher revised the book on a regular basis, and the last time they cut out the paragraph 5 on liquidity traps. They said: "A textbook is like a cancer. It will grow to be more than 1,000 pages if you let it. So if there are a lot of new things to be taught, you have to go ahead and cut out old things." The publisher then said: "Get rid of the liquidity trap and get rid of the Keynesian notion that the desire to save, by the paradox of thrift, instead of leading to more investment may actually kill off purchasing power and leave it less." And I said: "In economics, what goes around comes back around. Please, to please me, let's put back the liquidity trap and so forth. Because the example of Japan has taught the world what a liquidity trap is."

As a young economist, did Keynes's ideas fascinate you?

SAMUELSON: First, I was against Keynes because he was contradicting what all my wonderful professors believed. But finally I decided, am I going to let reality take over or am I going to let ideological reverence prevail? My teacher at Harvard University was Joseph Schumpeter, the famous Austrian economist who had come to Harvard from Weimar Bonn University. Schumpeter was erroneous on the Great Depression. He saw it as a healthy thing. His diagnosis was that the Great Depression was a good thing because it was going to improve productivity. Well, of course it didn't. Of the 40 most gifted graduates in the physical sciences and the 40 most gifted graduates in the biological sciences, in my first year none had a job for the next year. What good was that going to do for the productivity of the subsequent U.S. economy?

Did you ever discuss your doubts with Schumpeter?

SAMUELSON: Of course. But it wasn't of much use. It used to be said that Schumpeter's nose was out of joint, that he was kind of jealous of Keynes. He said to me: "You are in favor of Keynes because you are a socialist." I said: "Professor Schumpeter, I come from the University of Chicago—the citadel of capitalism! When was I ever a socialist? You don't have to be a socialist to be in favor of Keynes." And he said: "Well, you are a socialist in the sense that you don't revere the capitalist system." Well, that was true. I spent my first 15 years under the rule of pure capitalism, and it had lots of advantages and lots of disadvantages.

The pure capitalism has been transformed into a welfare-state economy, even in the United States. Why did your scepticism persist?

SAMUELSON: Yes, yes. But notice that since 1980 Reagan and Bush policies seek to weaken the welfare state. And notice that, when we talk about globalization we are going through the same problems that I just outlined. Globalization also has lots of advantages and lots of disadvantages, as I pointed out in a much-cited article for the *Journal of Economic Perspectives*.

The reactions were mixed . . .

SAMUELSON: The article was met with great excitement—both great admiration and great opposition. The former chairman of the Council of Economic Advisers, Gregory Mankiw, wrote a 48-page rebuttal. He said that "Samuelson gives comfort to the enemy." He said: "I am not saying that what he says is not true. But I believe you shouldn't really say it." Well, I think it is better to tell people what is really going on in the world.

Among economists, the mainstream opinion is that globalization is a win-win situation for every nation participating in it. Your point is that that is a big misperception!

SAMUELSON: The globalization leads to a win-win situation for people in China. That's true for the poor people in China *and* for the wealthier people in China. In the United States, the development appears to be very different. Highly specialized and professional members of the workforce will profit, while the run-of-the-mill working-class people will be the losers. It's a win and lose situation.

But globalization allows poorer citizens to shop for less. Cars, toys, clothes, computers, and vacations are cheaper than ever before.

SAMUELSON: Go to a Wal-Mart store in America and you can see the contradictions of globalization with your own eyes. In the stores, you see poor Americans buying these cheap products, and this means a tremendous boost to their living standard. At the same time, they are afraid of losing their job or having to change from one job to a lower-paying one. It is not true that everything that enhances globalization is automatically good for everyone.

So, globalization is a zero-sum game? One side wins, the other one loses?

SAMUELSON: No. Only in warfare is it a zero-sum game. Just think about the German-French war of 1870–71 for example: if Bismarck goes up, Louis Napoleon goes down. In postwar times, it's different on both sides of the Atlantic. Your generation has lived better than your parents' generation, and your parents have lived better than theirs. We couldn't have such a strong economic increase around the world without the dynamic force of globalization. But at the same time, not everybody benefits from it—

large groups in each society will lose and can't offset their losses. The big question facing any developed nation will be this: is there a fair balance of wins and losses? And even more importantly: how do we offset one with the other?

And your answer?

SAMUELSON: The reason why I wrote this article was that I had come up with a new way of measuring just how much the winners will win when the prices at which they can buy are lower and how much the losers will lose. Today, we find ourselves in a win-lose situation when we compete with Asian nations. Some of our workers win, others lose.

What are the drivers of this development?

SAMUELSON: The expansion of knowledge worldwide made the West lose its comparative advantage. We lose market shares when China fosters its productivity by its own creativity or by copying our products. Where we lose a trade advantage and China wins one, that will affect both labor markets—it's as if plenty of cheap and well-educated workers came into our country.

So, developed nations are starting to feel the downsides of globalization?

SAMUELSON: Well, the process of globalization has always tipped the scales in economic history. It's stupid to think every country will profit from changes. Economically, Great Britain has never recovered from losing its hegemonic position in World War I. Actually, the United States had even surpassed them in terms of production earlier, in 1900. In 1946, however, we reached our climax. Five percent of the world population were Americans, and they produced half of the world's output. Of course, that wasn't sustainable. It was only possible because Europe was devastated, Japan was devastated.

While China slept . . .

SAMUELSON: Now, just look at what happened 10 years later— the Marshall Plan. Europe then was our present-day China. The dollar became overvalued, and we used to joke that it pays to be defeated because the countries that were doing best in, say 1950–1965, were Germany, Italy, and Japan. Ford, Chrysler, General Motors had been absolute kings. Well, then Mercedes, BMW, Volvo caught up and surpassed the American companies. Toyota and Nissan followed. So that what is happening now is only a repetition of what you could have seen if you had the right glasses to see through. I see a Wagnerian leitmotiv in world history, catching up toward still-growing U.S. influence.

You see world history as a story of permanent rise and demise?

SAMUELSON: Winners and losers alternate; nobody can stay on top forever. In the year 1000, China was probably the wealthiest country in the world. Then the Netherlands, in terms of per capita real GDP. Some time later the British predominated—until their kids that had immigrated into the United States later took over.

What's your assessment of the rise of China, economically and politically?

SAMUELSON: We are probably at the beginning rather than the end of the Chinese story. They have more than a billion people. Only a fraction of them are competitive right now. But I don't think the others have dumber DNA. They will also come into this. So, China can thumb its nose at us 100 times, and if you come back in 25 years China will not necessarily be equal to the United States in a per capita degree of affluence, but it will be way bigger than the United States in the total. And that is of course what counts in geopolitics. China is like an 800-pound gorilla already standing in the living room.

But even if it takes a long time, the rise of China should be a real turning point in world history. What will be its biggest impact for the West?

SAMUELSON: The changes on our labor markets. Unions are about to disappear from our lives. They started to dissipate a long time ago. Strikes have become a U.S. rarity—and every victory that a union won against one of the big companies was a pyrrhic defeat. It speeded up the rate at which Japanese suppliers would get the business. Nowadays, unions can't make the companies fulfill their pension obligations. Every time I open my newspaper I learn of a new company which has reneged on its retirement benefits. All this is happening according to the new law. The early success of the union movement is beginning to be reversed.

Are you expecting the coming century to be the Chinese century?

SAMUELSON: That is hard to predict. Human nature is so imperfect. China could have three generations of political chaos. That's what happened in Latin America. In 1945, if somebody like you had come to me and said: "What part of the world is probably going to grow most of all? Fastest?" Do you know what I would have said? Argentina and Chile. Do you know why? Because they killed off all the native Indians, they had a temperate climate, and so forth. They were ripe to do it. But populist antibusiness leaders killed that hope.

One and a half billion new workers are entering the global labor market. People from China, India, Eastern Europe. How will that expansion of the global workforce affect life in the West?

SAMUELSON: In the globalized society, we will see a deeper split within the developed nations. I think the lower half of the income distribution will be the losers. Globalization means two things: in all probability it means an increase in inequality, and in all probability it also means a loss of serenity. Globalization brings us more prosperity, but it also leads to more uncertainty, tension, and enhanced inequality. In America, it has already led to a cowed workforce. Even for an MIT graduate, things have changed.

Please describe these changes.

SAMUELSON: It used to be like this: you graduated from your college, you got a job, if you kept your nose clean, you could count on getting promoted, you would earn even more when you were 50 than when you were 40, you would earn more when you were 60, and at 65 they would give you a watch and you would retire with a safe pension. That is completely different today. My six kids, for instance, can't lean back and relax. Nobody knows what is going to happen next to his or her career. It is a tenser world, a more "anxious" world. After all, what is the actual value now of large corporations like General Motors or Ford? Maybe they are completely worthless unless management manages to cheat the workers of their pension funds. Many economists are still trying to downplay the contradictions of globalization.

Should governments try to fight the trend? Or should they give up? And how can they continue to intervene at all?

SAMUELSON: They have to focus on research and development to stay ahead in the game. What a government can do is help the people who suffer from the consequences. We could use the power of the fiscal system to transfer from the very wealthy to the less wealthy people and it would not slow down our rate of growth in a noticeable way. My hope is that in America as much of Franklin D. Roosevelt's and John F. Kennedy's New Deal as possible may be preserved in order to alleviate, but not wipe out, the inequalities. The current Bush administration is doing the exact opposite with their tax cuts for the superrich—that only exacerbates the negative aspects of globalization. These tax cuts will sharpen the tensions, the inequality, and the "anxiousness" in our society. Whenever Germans, Italians, or French ask me what to do, I tell them: don't follow all the American examples—that will fire up only one thing for sure: people's anger.

But Americans consume more than ever. Their shopping sprees have become a pillar of the global economy. How does that go together with your diagnosis of growing fear and anxiety?

SAMUELSON: American losers from globalization perforce work longer hours, more weeks per annum, and more years before retirement at the only low-wage jobs they can find. Our society has an extremely self-centered attitude: always me, me, me, and now. The workers should have been saving like the devil, but all they do is spend. We are actually using the savings of countries much poorer than ourselves who recycle their trade surpluses into very low-yield U.S. government bonds. Currently, the Chinese are happy to give unlimited credit to the United States for now. But this could change. So, the road ahead of us is bumpy. We Americans no longer serve as role models. We should rather look at European countries with low unemployment rates.

The Scandinavian countries?

SAMUELSON: Look at Denmark. Now, that is strange, because Denmark has a pretty good welfare state. But when I inquired, what happens is that in Denmark you can fire people, even with union consent, and for about a year you can get unemployment insurance. However, after that you have to attend reeducation. Even more important, you have to accept the jobs that are offered you, and these jobs can be a lot worse than the jobs that you had previously.

Critics say that that is nothing but a race to the bottom.

SAMUELSON: No, it is a race toward the reality of what is going to happen to you in a globalized economy. The labor market remains functional and the Scandinavian welfare state—much more generous than the American one—remains affordable. That's what they need to survive and grow.

But why is America better off than Europe in nearly all economic statistics?

SAMUELSON: Because these statistics focus on income and money. Countries like Germany or France have lost ground in statistics because they choose to take it out in leisure. You know what I am talking about—five to six weeks of vacations a year, a 35-hour workweek. Germans need to reconsider their work ethic. It's pointless to preserve outdated structures. It will simply lead to stagnation while the world around you keeps growing. Many Germans should get used to the idea of having to accept jobs that pay 30 percent less than their old ones.

For decades, economic growth and democracy went hand in hand in the West. What do you think of slowing down globalization instead of pushing for even more free trade in new political initiatives?

SAMUELSON: Maybe we should slow down the process of globalization a bit, but you can't stop it and you shouldn't. You ought to use the fiscal system more ethically. What you can't do is go outside of the market and by legislation equalize. You can't make the poor rich, or you will kill the goose that lays the golden eggs. But you can try to alleviate the consequences of the process.

What advice would famous late economists give current administrations? Karl Marx, for instance?

SAMUELSON: I don't consider him a good economist. I know his picture hangs on the wall in my institute here, but that's only because we are fair-minded people at MIT. He shunned pragmatic advice. He was full of unearned self-confidence.

And Joseph Schumpeter?

SAMUELSON: I was actually the last economist to talk to him 10 days before he died, at the 1949 American Economics Association. I knew his mind pretty well. He would have said that the recent burst of energy released essentially by the computer is fully consistent with his 1912 book *The Theory of Economic Development*. He would have liked it all the way. He wasn't going to waste a lot of time, as I might, brooding about the fate of the poor—and he never appreciated the productivity of economic systems with a strong private sector and a strong public sector.

What about Keynes?

SAMUELSON: The reason Keynes would be okay is that he changed his mind all the time. It is better, by the way, to change your mind all the time than to stand still—like a stopped watch.

If you could give advice to those currently in power, what would it be?

SAMUELSON: My first piece of advice would be: choose the middle way. There is no substitute for the market mechanism—but the market mechanism has no brain, it has no heart. Without political programs it will inevitably breed inequality. My second piece of advice would be: globalization in its current shape and speed makes the world a more insecure and nervous place. We should try to slow down, and, in our own long-run interest, try to be less aggressive.

ACKNOWLEDGMENTS

Wherever the imperfections of this book may lie, the author claims full responsibility. It has not been for any lack of assistance and encouragement from others. In return, I would like to express my appreciation to all those who have been involved.

I am grateful, most of all, to my wife, Andrea, and our two daughters, Timea and Malina, who have often had to make do without their husband and father. To them it must seem that the first victim in *The War for Wealth* was the author himself.

Without the support of my three research assistants from the documentation center at *Der Spiegel*, the work that went into this book would have been an impossible task. I extend my appreciation to Bernd Musa, Rainer Lübbert, and Holger Wilkop for painstakingly compiling and analyzing statistics from sources around the world. Their academic expertise is responsible in large part for the quality of this book.

I extend my thanks to all those who spoke with me and thus contributed to a better understanding of the global economy. I thank the current treasury secretary of the United States, Hank Paulson, for giving me such an extensive interview. I deeply appreciate the contributions of Henry Kissinger, the former secretary of state of the United States, and I owe a debt of gratitude to our shared acquaintance, my esteemed colleague Josef Joffe, who brought us together. I was honored to be the beneficiary of the life experiences of two great men, former German chancellor

Helmut Schmidt and Paul Samuelson, a winner of the Nobel Prize in Economics. I also extend my deepest appreciation to Sandy Weill, the founder of Citigroup; Josef Ackermann, the chairman of Deutsche Bank; the author Naomi Klein; and, not to be forgotten, New York Senator Hillary Rodham Clinton. I thank Harvard professors Dani Rodrik and Guido Goldmann for their support and, last but not least, Harvard graduate Gregor Peter Schmitz, who brought us together. Gregor and I conducted the interview with Professor Samuelson. I am convinced that it was the beginning of a great career in journalism.

A book of this kind is also based on one's own observations and research, as well as on the academic efforts of generations of historians and economists. I am grateful to Paul Kennedy, David Landes, Samuel Huntington, Robert Reich, Niall Ferguson, and Eric J. Hobsbawm. Without their groundbreaking work this book would not have been possible.

It would be impossible to write such a book without the well-intentioned and selfless advice of friends. I am deeply indebted to Wolfgang Nowak of the Alfred Herrhausen Society for his stimulating conversation, his wealth of ideas, and his willingness to wade through hundreds of pages of the manuscript in search of faulty reasoning. I thank Hans Halter, my former fellow journalist, who devoted a sizeable portion of his retirement to promoting the conception of this book. His linguistic critiques were invaluable, while his optimism in all situations was contagious.

I thank Christopher Sultan, who was more than a translator. Chris, with his sensitivity to language and attention to detail, helped give this book its character. I am deeply grateful to Knox Huston for his editorial efforts. He was both my first reader and critic, and I consistently valued his advice, his ability to motivate and encourage me. I am indebted to Herb Schaffner of McGraw-Hill for having shown an interest in *The War for Wealth* when it was little more than a collection of ideas. I thank him for his ongoing encouragement and support.

Finally, I wish to thank my agents, Bettina Keil, who has handled the international aspects of marketing this book, and David

McCormick, who lives in New York and deals with the American market, for their impressive efforts. Anyone who believes that a book is simply written by its author and then published is oblivious to everything else that happens along the way. An author owes it to his agents that he can remain an author and is not called upon to perform the tasks of salesperson, lawyer, marketing guru, or financial expert. Bettina and David, your work has been invaluable.

Washington, D.C., March 2008

SOURCES

Abele, Eberhard, Ulrich Näher, and Gernot Strube. *Handbook of Global Production: A Handbook for Strategy and Implementation*. Berlin: Axel Springer Verlag, 2007.

Ali, Tariq. *The Nehrus and the Gandhis: An Indian Dynasty*. London: Macmillan Publishers Ltd., 2005.

Ambrose, Stephen E., and Douglas G. Brinkley. *Rise to Globalism: American Foreign Policy Since 1938*. London: Penguin Books, 1998.

Anderson, Brian C. *Democratic Capitalism and Its Discontents*. Wilmington, DE: ISI Books, 2007.

Anderson, Sarah, John Cavanagh, Thea Lee, and the Institute for Policy Studies. *Field Guide to the Global Economy*. New York: The New Press, 2005.

Anonymous. *Primary Colors: A Novel of Politics*. New York: Random House, 1996.

Babbin, Jed. *In the Words of Our Enemies*. Washington, DC: Regnery Publishing, 2007.

Beck, Ulrich. *What Is Globalization?* Malden, MA: Polity Press, 2000.

Beck, Ulrich, Natan Sznaider, and Rainer Winter. *Global America? The Cultural Consequences of Globalization*. Liverpool: Liverpool University Press, 2003.

Beck, Ulrich, and Nathan Sznaider. *Empire America: Perspectives of a New World Order*. Munich: Deutsche Verlagsanstalt, 2003.

Bergsten, Fred C., Bates Gill, Nicholas R. Lardy, and Derek Mitchell. *China: The Balance Sheet. What the World Needs to Know Now about the Emerging Superpower.* New York: Public Affairs, 2006.

Birnbaum, Norman. *After Progress: American Social Reform and European Socialism in the Twentieth Century.* New York: Oxford University Press, 2002.

———. *The Crisis of Industrial Society.* London: Oxford University Press, 1969.

Blanchard, Olivier. *Macroeconomics.* London: Prentice Hall International, 2003.

Blumenthal, Sidney. *The Clinton Wars: An Insider's Account of the White House Years.* London: Penguin Books, 2003.

Bonner, William, and Addison Wiggin. *Empire of Debt: The Rise of an Epic Financial Crisis.* Hoboken, NJ: John Wiley & Sons, 2006.

Brown, Sherrod. *Myths of Free Trade: Why American Trade Policy Has Failed.* New York: The New Press, 2004.

Bush, Richard C., and Michael E. O'Hanlon. *A War Like No Other: The Truth about China's Challenge to America.* Hoboken, NJ: John Wiley & Sons, 2007.

Center for Strategic and International Studies, and the Institute for International Economics. *China: What the World Needs to Know about the Emerging Superpower.* New York: Public Affairs, 2006.

Chandler, Alfred D., Jr.: *Scale and Scope: The Dynamics of Industrial Capitalism.* Cambridge, MA: Harvard University Press, 1994.

Clinton, Bill. *Giving: How Each of Us Can Change the World.* New York: Alfred A. Knopf, 2007.

Davis, Mike. *Late Victorian Holocausts: El Niño Famines and the Making of the Third World.* London and New York: Verso, 2002.

Diamond, Jared. *Guns, Germs, and Steel: The Fates of Human Societies.* New York: W. W. Norton, 2005.

Dobbs, Lou. *Exporting America: Why Corporate Greed Is Shipping American Jobs Overseas.* New York: Warner Business Books, 2004.

Dorgan, Byron L. *Take This Job and Ship It: How Corporate Greed and Brain-Dead Politics Are Selling Out America.* New York: Thomas Dunne Books, 2006.

Draper, Robert. *Dead Certain: The Presidency of George W. Bush.* New York: Simon & Schuster, 2007.

Drezner, Daniel W. *All Politics Is Global: Explaining International Regulatory Regimes.* Princeton, NJ, and Woodstock, Oxford-shire, UK: Princeton University Press, 2007.

Edwards, John. *Ending Poverty in America: How to Restore the American Dream.* New York: The New Press, 2007.

Ehrenberg, John. *Servants of Wealth: The Right's Assault on Economic Justice.* Lanham, MD: Rowman & Littlefield, 2006

Ehrenreich, Barbara. *Nickel and Dimed: Working Poor in the Service Society.* New York: Saint Martin's Press, 2002.

Emmott, Bill. 20:21 *Vision: The Lessons of the Twentieth Century for the Twenty-First.* New York: Farrar, Straus and Giroux, 2003.

Faux, Jeff. *The Global Class War: How America's Bipartisan Elite Lost Our Future—And What It Will Take to Win It Back.* Hoboken, NJ: John Wiley & Sons, 2006.

Ferguson, Niall. *Colossus: The Rise and Fall of the American Empire.* London: Penguin Press, 2005.

———. *Economics, Religion and the Decline of Europe.* Oxford: Blackwell Publishing, 2004.

———. *Empire: The Rise and Demise of the British World Order and the Lessons for Global Power.* New York: Basic Books, 2004.

———. Sinking Globalization. 2005. *Foreign Affairs* 84 (2).

———. *The Cash Nexus: Money and Power in the Modern World, 1700–2000; Economics and Politics from the Age of Warfare to the Age of Welfare, 1700–2000.* London: Basic Books, 2002.

Fischer, Joschka. *Die Rückkehr der Geschichte [The Return of History].* Munich: Droemer/Knaur Verlag, 2006.

Frieden, Jeffry A. *Global Capitalism: Its Fall and Rise in the Twentieth Century.* New York: W. W. Norton, 2007.

Friedman, Thomas. *The World Is Flat: A Brief History of the Globalized World in the Twenty-First Century.* London: Penguin Books, 2005.

Fukuyama, Francis. *America at the Crossroads: Democracy, Power, and the Neoconservative Legacy.* New Haven, CT, and London: Yale University Press, 2007.

———. *State-Building: Governance and World Order in the 21st Century.* New York: Cornell University Press, 2004.

Garten, Jeffrey E. *A Cold Peace: America, Japan, Germany, and the Struggle for Supremacy.* New York: Times Books, 1993.

Garton Ash, Timothy. *Free World: America, Europe, and the Surprising Future of the West.* New York: Random House, 2004.

Gersemann, Olaf. *Cowboy Capitalism: European Myths about the American Reality.* Washington, DC: The Cato Institute, 2004.

Gerth, Jeff, and Don Van Natta Jr. *Her Way: The Hopes and Ambitions of Hillary Rodham Clinton.* New York: Little, Brown and Company, 2007.

Giddens, Anthony. *The Third Way: The Renewal of Social Democracy.* Cambridge, UK: Polity Press, 1998.

Gore, Al. *The Assault on Reason.* New York: Penguin Press, 2007.

Greenspan, Alan. *The Age of Turbulence: Adventures in a New World.* New York: Penguin Press, 2007.

Greider, William. *The Soul of Capitalism: Opening Paths to a Moral Economy.* New York: Simon & Schuster Paperbacks, 2004.

Habermas, Jürgen: *Der gespaltene Westen [The Divided West].* Frankfurt am Main: Suhrkamp Verlag, 2004.

———. *Zeitdiagnosen: Zwölf Essays, 1980–2001 [Diagnoses of Time: Twelve Essays, 1980–2001].* Frankfurt am Main: Suhrkamp Verlag, 2003.

Hacker, Jacob S. *The Great Risk Shift: The Assault on American Jobs, Families, Health Care, and Retirement and How You Can*

Fight Back. Oxford, UK, and New York: Oxford University Press, 2006.

Haffner, Sebastian. *Churchill*. London: Haus Publishing, 2003.

———. *Die sieben Todsünden des Deutschen Reiches im Ersten Weltkrieg [The Seven Deadly Sins of the German Reich in the First World War]*. Bergisch Gladbach: Gustav Lübbe Verlag, 2001.

———. *Im Schatten der Geschichte: Historisch-politische Variationen aus zwanzig Jahren [In the Shadow of History: Historical-Political Variations over Twenty Years]*. Munich: Deutscher Taschenbuch Verlag, 1987.

Harrison, Selig S., Paul H. Kreisberg, and Dennis Kux. *India and Pakistan: The First Fifty Years*. Cambridge, UK: Cambridge University Press, 1999.

Held, David, and Anthony McGrew. *Globalization/Anti-Globalization*. Cambridge, UK: Polity Press, 2003.

Hobsbawm, Eric J. *The Age of Empire*, 1875–1914. London: Weidenfeld and Nicolson, 1987, updated 2004.

Huntington, Samuel P. *The Clash of Civilizations and the Remaking of World Order*. New York: Simon & Schuster, 1998.

———. *Who Are We? America's Great Debate*. Charlotte, NC: Baker & Taylor, 2005.

Hutton, Will, and Anthony Giddens, Anthony. *Global Capitalism*. New York: The New Press, 2000.

Ikenberry, G. John. 2004. Illusions of empire: Defining the new American order. *Foreign Affairs* 83(2).

Ingraham, Laura. *Shut Up and Sing: How Elites from Hollywood, Politics, and the Media Are Subverting America*. Washington, DC: Regnery Publishing, 2003.

International Forum on Globalization. *Alternatives to Economic Globalization: A Better World Is Possible*. New York: McGraw-Hill Professional, 2004.

Irwin, Douglas A. *Free Trade under Fire*. Princeton, NJ: Princeton University Press, 2005.

Joffe, Josef: *Überpower: The Imperial Temptation of America*. New York: W.W. Norton, 2006.

Kagan, Robert. *Dangerous Nation: America's Place in the World from Its Earliest Days to the Dawn of the Twentieth Century.* New York: Alfred A. Knopf, 2006.

———. *Of paradise and power: America and Europe in the New World Order.* Charlotte, NC: Baker & Taylor, 2004.

Kahn-Strauss, Dominique. *Building a Political Europe: 50 Proposals for the Europe of Tomorrow.* Summary and Synthesis, 2004.

Keegan, John. *The First World War.* Atlanta: Vintage Books USA, 2000.

Kennedy, Paul. *Preparing for the Twenty-First Century.* New York: Random House, 1993.

———. *The Rise and Fall of the Great Powers: Economic Change and Military Conflict from 1500 to 2000.* London: Fontana, 2001.

Kenwood, A. G., and A. L. Lougheed. *The Growth of the International Economy, 1820–2000: An Introductury Text.* London: Routledge, 1999.

Kissinger, Henry. *Does America Need a Foreign Policy? Toward a Diplomacy for the Twenty-First Century.* New York: Simon & Schuster, 2002.

Klein, Joe. *Politics Lost: How American Democracy Was Trivialized by People Who Think You Are Stupid.* New York: Doubleday, 2006.

———. *The Natural: The Misunderstood Presidency of Bill Clinton.* New York: Doubleday, 2003.

Kletzer, Lori G. *Job Loss from Imports: Measuring the Costs.* Washington, DC: Institute for International Economics, 2001.

Kohut, Andrew, and Bruce Stokes. *America Against the World: How We Are Different and Why We Are Disliked.* New York: Henry Holt & Company, 2006.

Krugman, Paul. *Pop Internationalism.* Cambridge, MA: MIT Press, 1997.

———. *The Great Untravelling: From Boom to Bust in Three Scandalous Years.* London: Penguin Books, 2004.

Kulke, Hermann, and Dietmar Rothermund. *A History of India*. London: Taylor & Francis, 1997.

Kupchan, Charles. *The End of the American Era: U.S. Foreign Policy and the Geopolitics of the Twenty-First Century*. New York: Vintage Books, 2003.

Kurlantzick, Joshua. *Charm Offensive: How China's Soft Power Is Transforming the World*. New Haven, CT: Yale University Press, 2007.

Lafontaine, Oskar, and Christa Müller-Lafontaine. *No Fear of Globalization: Welfare and Work for All*. New York: Verso Books, 2001.

Lakoff George. *Whose Freedom? The Battle over America's Most Important Idea*. New York: Picador, 2006.

———. *Don't Think of an Elephant! Know Your Values and Frame the Debate*. White River Junction, VT: Chelsea Green Publishing, 2004.

Landes, David. *The Wealth and Poverty of Nations: Why Some Are So Rich and Some Are So Poor*. Charlotte, NC: Baker & Taylor, 1999.

Larsson Tomas. *The Race to the Top: The Real Story of Globalization*. Washington, DC: The Cato Institute, 2001.

Luttwak, Edward N. *The Endangered American Dream: How to Stop the United States from Becoming a Third-World Country and How to Win the Geo-Economic Struggle for Industrial Supremacy*. New York: Touchstone/Simon & Schuster, 1994.

Magaziner, Ira C., and Mark Patinkin. *The Silent War: Inside the Global Business Battles Shaping America's Future*. New York: Vintage Books, 1990.

Mander, Jerry, and Edward Goldsmith. *The Case Against the Global Economy*. London: Kogan Page, 2001.

Mazower, Mark. *Dark Continent: Europe's Twentieth Century*. New York: Vintage Books, 2000.

McArthur, Brian. *Historic Speeches*. London: Penguin Books, 1996.

McAuliffe, Terry, and Steve Kettmann. *What a Party! My Life among Democrats: Presidents, Candidates, Donors, Activists,*

Alligators, and Other Wild Animals. New York: Thomas Dunne Books/St. Martin's Press, 2007.

Menges, Constantine C. *China: The Gathering Threat.* Nashville, TN: Thomas Nelson, 2005.

Moynahan, Brian. *The British Century.* New York: Random House, 1999.

Narasimha Rao, P. V. *A Long Way: Selected Speeches.* Kottayam, Kerala, India: D C Books, 2002.

National Research Council. *Monitoring Intenational Labor Standards: Techniques and Sources of Information.* Washington, DC: The National Academies Press, 2004.

Nye, Joseph S., Jr. *Soft Power: The Means to Success in World Politics.* New York: PublicAffairs, 2004.

Obama, Barack. *The Audacity of Hope: Thoughts on Reclaiming the American Dream.* New York: Crown Publishers, 2006.

Olson, Mancur. *Power and Prosperity: Outgrowing Communist and Capitalist Dictatorships.* Cambridge/London/ New York: Perseus Books, 2001.

Olson, Mancur. *The Rise and Decline of Nations: Economic Growth, Stagflation and Social Rigidities.* New Haven, CT: Yale University Press, 1984.

Pilger, John. *The New Rulers of the World.* London: Verso, 2003.

Pilny, Karl. *The Asian Century: China and Japan on Their Way to Becoming New World Powers.* Frankfurt am Main: Campus Verlag, 2005.

Polanyi, Karl. *The Great Transformation: The Political and Economic Origins of Our Time.* Boston: Beacon Press, 2001,

Popper, Karl. *The Open Society and Its Enemies; Volume II: The High Tide of Prophecy: Hegel, Marx, and the Aftermat*h. London and Tübingen: Routledge & Kegan Paul, 1945, updated 2003.

Prestowitz, Clyde. *Three Billion New Capitalists: The Great Shift of Wealth and Power to the East.* Charlotte, NC: Baker & Taylor, 2006.

———. *Trading Places: How We Are Giving Our Future to Japan and How to Reclaim It.* New York: Basic Books, 1993.

Reich, Robert B. *Supercapitalism: The Transformation of Business, Democracy, and Everyday Life.* New York: Alfred A. Knopf, 2007.

———. *The Work of Nations: Preparing Ourselves for 21st Century Capitalism.* New York: Vintage Books, 1992.

Reid, T. R. *The United States of Europe: The New Superpower and the End of American Supremacy.* New York: Penguin Books, 2004.

Ricardo, David. *Principles of Political Economy and Taxation.* Charlotte, NC: Baker & Taylor, 1996,

Rivlin, Paul, *The Russian Economy and Arms Exports to the Middle East.* Tel Aviv: Jaffee Center for Strategic Studies, Tel Aviv University, 2005.

Rivoli, Pietra. *The Travels of a T-Shirt in the Global Economy: An Economist Examines the Markets, Power, and Politics of World Trade.* Hoboken, NJ: John Wiley & Sons, 2005.

Sachs, Jeffrey D. *The End of Poverty: Economic Possibilities for Our Time.* London: Penguin Press, 2006.

Safranski, Rüdiger. *How Much Globalization Can We Bear?* Cambridge, UK: Polity Press, 2006.

Schaaf, Jürgen. Outsourcing nach Indien: der Tiger auf dem Sprung [Outsourcing to India: The Leaping Tiger] in *Deutsche Bank Research*, Aktuelle Themen 335, 2005.

Schmidt, Helmut. *Die Mächte der Zukunft: Gewinner und Verlierer in der Welt von morge [Powers of the Future: Winners and Losers in the World of Tomorrow].* Munich: Siedler Verlag, 2004.

Scholte, Jan Aart. *Globalization: A Critical Introduction.* Charlotte, NC: Baker & Taylor, 2005.

Schrecker, Ellen. *Cold War Triumphalism: The Misuse of History after the Fall of Communism.* New York: The New Press, 2004.

Schulze, Hagen. *States, Nations and Nationalism: From the Middle Ages to the Present.* Oxford, MA: Blackwell Publishers, 2004.

Schumpeter, Joseph A. *Capitalism, Socialism and Democracy.* New York: Harper Colophon, 1978, new edition 2005.

Sennett, Richard. *The Culture of the New Capitalism*. New Haven, CT: Yale University Press, 2006.

Sieren, Frank. *The China Code: What's Left for Us*. New York: Palgrave Macmillan, 2006.

Stern, Herbert. *Presidential Economics: The Making of Economic Policy from Roosevelt to Reagan and Beyond*. New York: Touchstone, Simon & Schuster, 1985.

Stevenson, David. *1914–1918: The History of the First World War*. London: Penguin Allen Lane, 2004.

Stiglitz, Joseph. *The Roaring Nineties: A New History of the World's Most Prosperous Decade*. New York: W. W. Norton, 2004.

Strauss-Kahn, Dominique. *Building a Political Europe: 50 Proposals for the Europe of Tomorrow*. Report to the European Commission, April 2004.

Thurow, Lester. *Fortune Favors the Bold*. Charlotte, NC: Baker & Taylor, 2004.

U.S. Trade Deficit Review Commission. *The U.S. Trade Deficit: Causes, Consequences and Recommendations for Action*. Washington, DC, 2000.

Went, Robert. *Globalization: Neoliberal Challenge, Radical Responses*. London: Pluto Press, 2000.

Willke, Gerhard. *John Maynard Keynes*. Frankfurt am Main: Campus Verlag, 2002.

Winkler, Heinrich August. *The Long Road West*. New York: Oxford University Press, 2007.

Woodward, Bob. *The Commanders: The Pentagon and the First Gulf War, 1989–1991*. New York: Simon & Schuster, 2005.

Yergin, Daniel, and Joseph Stanislaw. *The Commanding Heights: The Battle for the World Economy*. New York: Free Press, 2002.

Yew, Lee Kuan. *The Singapore Story*. Singapore: Financial Times: 1999.

Zakaria, Fareed. *The Future of Freedom: Illiberal Democracy at Home and Abroad*. New York: W.W. Norton, 2003.

Shelton State Libraries
Shelton State Community College

INDEX

ABOUT THE AUTHOR

Gabor Steingart, 45, is an international bestselling author and an award-winning journalist. He is the senior correspondent for *Der Spiegel* in Washington D.C. and was the former head of *Der Spiegel*'s Berlin office. Similar to *The War for Wealth*, his previous two books, *Germany: The Decline of a Superstar* and *The Fall of Germany* were all top-10-bestsellers in his country. In 2004, leading German media magazine, *Medium Magazine*, named Steingart the Economic Writer of the Year. In 2007 he won the Helmut Schmidt Award for Advanced Journalism. His books have been published in numerous countries, including China, Sweden, South Korea, and the United Arab Emirates. His op-ed pieces are published in the *Wall Street Journal* and *European Affairs*. Steingart's weekly column, "West Wing—The Battle for the White House," appears on Spiegel Online (www.spiegel.de/westwing) and on RealClearPolitics.com. Steingart lives with his family in Washington D.C. To reach the author and join the discussion, visit www.gaborsteingart.com.